STRANGE HARP,
STRANGE SYMPHONY

Francis Thompson in 1898.

STRANGE HARP, STRANGE SYMPHONY

The Life of Francis Thompson

by John Walsh

Hawthorn Books, Inc.   Publishers   New York

First Edition: 1967

Design: Gene Gordon

8957

This book is dedicated to my mother

ANN WALSH

who long ago listened to
my talk of Francis Thompson

. . . sweeping from some strange harp
Strange symphony . . .
                              Shelley: *Alastor*

PREFACE

No poet ever put more of himself into his verse than did Francis Thompson. Indeed it has been said, with only slight exaggeration, that his three published volumes are the index to the forty-eight years of his life. Yet it is a remarkable fact that sixty years after his death, despite a half dozen biographies, some dozen volumes of critical discussion, and nearly two hundred articles, his life is still not known in anything like completeness. He has come down to the present as the property of the Meynell family, and their portrait of a shy, ineffectual personality, "clinging Heaven by the hems," with its casual approach to detail and chronology, has thrown a haze over the events of his life and obscured the man himself. Later writers have done little but copy and expand that model, even when they have disagreed as to its interior significance. As a result Thompson today remains a captive to some degree of distorted perspective, religious sentimentality, and Victorian reticence.

His entire career was passed under the Meynells' superintending influence, which in the beginning was almost a daily thing, but became more haphazard in the later years. Most of his surviving letters were written to one or another of them, and his notebooks and manuscripts were inherited by them, remaining largely in their possession for forty years. The first biography—still the fundamental text—was produced by them. Inevitably, the intimate (and for the living Thompson, fortunate) part they played in both his physical and his artistic life has given them in the eyes of subsequent writers an authority almost absolute. But the truth is, quite simply, that the Meynells were too close to Thompson for too long. It is not surprising that they lacked the objectivity, freshness and patience necessary to the ordered gathering and evaluation of facts.

The assumption that the Meynell view of Thompson is the fullest and most accurate one possible is false. To accept the picture of Thompson's continued great unhappiness at Ushaw, for instance, is to allow the poet's own artistic hyperbole to color the truth. To speak of his poetic period as virtually coming to a close in 1897, for another example, is to ignore the demonstrable fact that he wrote perhaps forty poems in the subsequent decade, though few of them were published. And to discuss

The Hound of Heaven with only desultory reference to the biographical background, as if it sprang to life full-blown in a moment's dream, is to overlook the fascinating genesis of one of the greatest of modern poems. (I reject the spurious critical attitude which insists that *The Hound of Heaven*, though it is Thompson's most popular poem, is not his greatest. A certain class of critics finds popularity insufferable, by no means permitting it to accompany greatness, and this attitude, unfortunately, has begun to seep into Thompson criticism.)

But my present aim is not a critical one, or is critical to only a very limited extent. My main purpose is to recover as much as possible of the factual truth—and in the absence of hard fact, the probable truth—of Thompson's life and artistic progress, and to supply interpretation only as it arises insistently from the facts. As an integral part of this main concern, however, I have treated *The Hound of Heaven* at some length in an attempt to show how it grew out of his own experience and his unparalleled immersion in literature. His other work, both prose and poetry, I have noticed as it assumes more than usual importance in his personal story.

I have not indulged overmuch in what Leon Edel has called the biographer's "as yet uneasy flirtation with psychology." Thompson's intriguing life is a compelling subject for such inquiry, but it must also be admitted that it lends itself too readily to the cheap variety—as witness Ella Sharpe's still quoted 1925 opinion that the poet exhibited an infantile breast fixation at the oral level, a conclusion she was able to reach only by ignoring the fact that the breast symbolism in Thompson's later work derived almost wholly from the *Song of Solomon* through Coventry Patmore. Believing with Edel that the proper use of "the psychoanalytic tool" requires specialized skills, I am content for the most part to provide a fuller and, I trust, more reliable narrative for future investigators.

A glance at the notes and bibliography will reveal how little dependent, comparatively, this book is on the usual printed sources. Among previous biographies only one is of primary value, the 1913 volume by Everard Meynell, but I have relied on it only where it was the sole source for information. Generally I have been able to work with the original documents used by Meynell, reaching my own conclusions. These included Thompson notebooks, letters and manuscripts, as well as letters and notes of others, scattered now to three principal sources: the Sowerby family at Greatham (Mrs. Sowerby is the former Olivia Meynell, daughter of Wilfrid and Alice), the Thompson Collection at Boston College, and the Harriss family at Chichester (Mrs. Harriss is the former Joan Meynell, daughter of Everard). The first two are by far the largest and most important and the collection at Greatham presented the most difficult task. Here, the extensive group of papers is still more or less unsorted and the present members of the family have only a general idea of what it contains. In addition to the obviously valuable items, there are minute but significant facts buried in the vast number of letters and other documents, accumulated in the course of the elder Meynells' sixty years or so of literary activity, stored now in many dozens of bulging envelopes. At Boston College the well-catalogued collection provides a biographer with a rich mine of material not accessible even so short a time as a decade ago. The Harriss collection, the smallest of the three but still of much interest, was not open to research until after the death of Everard Meynell's wife, Grazia, in 1965.

From the sources mentioned and others it has been possible, for the first time, to bring together (in photostat) a group of nearly two hundred Thompson letters, comparative study of which has afforded new and firmer ground for dating the material therein, as well as for the bare chronology of his life. On my two visits to England, in 1964 and 1966, my search was also extended to many of the places connected with Thompson, enabling me to add a stroke here and there to some of the more obscure parts of the picture.

I should perhaps also record my disappointed attempt to trace a monastery diary connected with Thompson's year at Storrington, particularly by visiting the monastery's mother house at Frigolet, near Avignon, where it was thought it might have been sent. This diary, whose existence is more than probable, could do much to further illumine Thompson's effort, at the quiet Premonstratensien Priory in the Sussex countryside, to lift himself out of the hopeless, drugged decay of his London derelict days. Despite some earnest searching, however, it has not yet come to light, and I must admit a hope that mention of it here may some day lead to its discovery.

Since I am presenting a connected account of Thompson the man as well as the poet, I have thought it best, in the interest of a more readable narrative, to confine much discussion and additional information to the notes and an appendix.

My gratitude for various kinds of assistance is offered to the following:

Mr. W. Clement Stone of Chicago, whose financial backing and understanding of the large amount of time and effort involved in a work of this nature made both the research and the writing possible.

Mr. and Mrs. T. Murray Sowerby, who gave me access to the papers at Greatham as well as hospitality. Their daughter, Mrs. Elizabeth Hawkins, did much to facilitate my work there.

Mr. and Mrs. Kendall Harriss, who afforded me the opportunity to study their Thompson papers in the convenience of their home in Chichester, and who permitted me to photograph the Thompson life-mask as well as to copy the unpublished picture of Thompson at the age of eleven. Alice Meynell, another daughter of Everard, kindly made available to me in London a large number of Thompson letters from the Harriss holdings.

Mrs. Percival Lucas (Madeline Meynell) of Greatham, who allowed me to make excerpts from a previously unquoted Thompson notebook and who patiently answered my many questions.

Sir Francis Meynell, who discussed his memories of Thompson with me in London, and supplied a number of Thompson letters for copying.

Fr. Brenden Connolly, Director of Libraries, Boston College, who gave me unhampered access to the Terence L. Connolly, S.J., Francis Thompson Collection in Bapst Library and permitted me to take photostats of many important items. Miss Martha Dubay and Mr. Bill Gallup, both former assistants at Bapst Library, gave me unfailing cooperation.

Fr. J. G. Neill, Prior of St. Mary's Priory, Storrington, who allowed me to search the monastery's archives, and whose kind welcome and hospitality made my work easier.

Mr. Norbert Thompson, half-brother of the poet, who answered my questions in correspondence and supplied a photograph of the medal won by Thompson at Ushaw.

Mother Clare and Sister Hilary, both of the hospital of St. John and St. Elizabeth, London, who responded with patience and interest to my unannounced appearances on their doorstep, and my requests for additional information. Also, in the same connection, Miss Lucy Ware and Sister Cecelia.

The Committee for Aerial Photography, University of Cambridge, for permission to use the picture of Wales reproduced on page 127.

For valuable discussion, information and sundry help along the way I must mention: Lady Winifred Tryon, of Newbuildings, Sussex; Mr. Fred Kenworthy of Ashton-under-Lyne; Miss Mary Gertrude Richardson of Manchester; Mrs. E. M. Clark of Chester; Father Malachy, Father Declan and Mr. W. Barrett, all of Pantasaph; Mrs. Agnes McIvor of London; Sister St. Felicien of Manitoba; Miss Filumena Burr of Cheltenham; Father Bernard Payne of Ushaw; Mr. Ted Gravely, Mr. Alfred Thompsett, and Mrs. H. Carman, all of Crawley; Mr. Thomas Burns and Mr. Jonathan Eden, both of London; and my wife, Dorothy, who supplied helpful discussion and moral support, as did John, Timothy, Ann and Matthew. I am also indebted to the office staff of Owens College, Manchester, and to the staffs of Lilly Library, Indiana University, Harris Library, Preston, the Guildhall Library, and the British Museum Reading Room.

J. W.

New York
March 1967

CONTENTS

ILLUSTRATIONS

One person told me that my own life
was a beautiful romance. 'Beautiful' is not
my standpoint.

Francis Thompson
in a letter of
August 1906

                                    fame
Comes to the man who means to have it
And cares about nothing else.

Beowulf

STRANGE HARP,
STRANGE SYMPHONY

PROLOGUE: ALASTOR

WHEN SEVENTEEN-YEAR-OLD FRANCIS THOMPSON STEPPED FROM THE
train in Ashton-under-Lyne, on a July day in 1877, he had already
started to live an imaginative life of rare intensity. In time the tendency
would deepen, would lead him into drug addiction, and would make
him, at last, the type of all wrapped and solitary artists. But as he walked
the half mile from the station to his home on busy Stamford Street he
was not aware of the role that awaited him; he only knew that he had
just come through his first real crisis. Shortly before, he had been at the
seminary, studying for the priesthood. Now he was home to stay, judged
lacking in a vocation because of "strong nervous timidity" and "natural
indolence"—reasons that must have been sufficiently puzzling to his
parents, who were not used to thinking of their son as neglectful in
things that mattered to him. But it was neither indolence nor nerves that
had come between Thompson and the altar. It was poetry. What no

one at home or at the seminary quite realized was that the frail, slope-shouldered young man with the slightly mournful eyes—the color "one sees in a mountain lake"[1]—had already become the living counterpart of the melancholy Poet pictured by Shelley in *Alastor*. In a life so full of curious events, this perhaps is among the most remarkable: *Alastor*, written more than a half century before Thompson's birth, by the man who was to become Thompson's poetic ideal, foreshadows with marvelous precision not only his personal life, but his character and his literary career. To be familiar with the theme and spirit of *Alastor* is to know Thompson in the flesh.

Shelley's description of his imaginary Poet, in the Preface to the poem, could have been written with Thompson in mind: "A youth of uncorrupted feelings and adventurous genius led forth by an imagination inflamed and purified through familiarity with all that is excellent and majestic, to the contemplation of the universe. He drinks deep of the fountains of knowledge and is still insatiate." Shelley's Poet in youth is nurtured by visions of a luminous future and he gradually acquires all the hoarded wisdom and knowledge and beauty "which the sacred past in truth or fable consecrates." Just so with Thompson, who became one of the most widely learned literary critics of his time, and in whose poetry there continuously sound reverberations of the great English poets. In young manhood, Shelley's Poet is led to forsake "his cold fire-side and alienated home," as Thompson fled from his father's house to destitution in the lower depths of the London streets. The Poet wanders far, gathering knowledge and inspiration, and while pausing on "the lone Chorasmian shore" he contemplates suicide, as Thompson contemplated, and attempted, suicide during the blackest days of his outcast existence. Two loves enter the life of Shelley's hero, as two loves entered Thompson's life. The first brought the Poet his food,

> Her daily portion, from her father's tent,
> And spread her matting for his couch, and stole
> From duties and repose to tend his steps

as Maggie Brien of the Welsh hills attended to Thompson while he was a lodger in her father's house. The second woman appears to the Poet in a vision or a dream, and "his strong heart sunk and sickened with excess of love," as Thompson's did after he met Katie King. But love was not for the Poet, as "night involved and swallowed up the vision," nor was it for Thompson who fell back into seclusion and drug addiction after losing Katie.

Shelley's Poet drifts on, finding no permanent home, and becoming strange of aspect and far removed from ordinary life. Anyone who ever knew the later Thompson would glimpse him again in Shelley's description:

> Now his limbs were lean; his scattered hair
> Sered by the autumn of strange suffering
> Sung dirges in the wind; his listless hand
> Hung like dead bone within his withered skin;
> Life, and the lustre that consumed it, shone
> As in a furnace burning secretly
> From his dark eyes alone . . .

And in that phrase, "the lustre that consumed it," did Shelley mean to imply the wasting of tuberculosis, the disease that weighed down Thompson's last years? Finally, the Poet enters a mountainous land, all barren and unlovely, though in the distance he can see a far-flung landscape of variegated beauty—just as Thompson's last years were spent in the dreary atmosphere of boardinghouses in the least inspiring part of London, often in pain and always dependent on drugs, but inhabiting the lovely precincts of his own imagination, and steadily producing some of the finest journalistic prose of the day.

The coincidence with *Alastor* becomes even more striking when it is remembered that Thompson was familiar with the poem from his boyhood, and that he felt for it a particular affinity. Did he see himself as Shelley's solitary wanderer? Was there, perhaps, a continuing subconscious drift toward emulation of the spirit of *Alastor*? Some answer to the question can be found only in the remarkable fact that *Alastor* is not an isolated example of convergence between Thompson's life and literature; some arresting parallels also occur with De Quincey, Coleridge, Blake, Chatterton, Rossetti, and Shelley himself—all men who exerted varying degrees of influence on him. The truth is that psychologically, Thompson was almost unique as an artist. He was a "literary intelligence," for whom the ideal conceptions of the great creative imaginations were more alive, were ultimately far more real, than the most vibrant life of every day. Certain among them—notably those who sounded a note of elevated grandeur—found readier welcome in the dim heights and obscure depths of his imagination, and their lives as well as their works seeped into his blood, his heart, and his brain, eventually to be echoed, nearly always unconsciously, in his own life and his own poetry. Ultimately, this was both his strength and his weakness, for it gave him a

poetic tone exceedingly rare, but it often marred his originality by streak-
ing his work with borrowed and ill-mixed colors. More important, in the
tensions set up between mind and heart by such a potentially dangerous
withdrawal and distortion, it laid his spirit open to the false enthrallment
of drug addiction.

The parallel with *Alastor* does break down at one point, and the fact
has special import. Shelley's Poet dies in obscurity, his tomb "a pyramid
of mouldering leaves," his life a failure. Thompson's death, for all its
poignance, was not entirely lonely—friends were beside his hospital bed
until almost the end. It was not unnoted—the press made due recognition of his passing and his grave in Kensal Green Cemetery, London, is
marked by a stone sarcophagus ("Look for me in the nurseries of
Heaven," aptly reads the inscription). Above all, his life, so tragic in its
outward circumstances, was not a failure. It was what he deliberately
and ruthlessly made it—a vehicle for poetic achievement. William
Butler Yeats, who met Thompson only once but knew his work well,
long ago placed a casual finger on the secret of Thompson's life when he
suggested that there was "some strange power in the forms of excess that
dissolves, as it were, the external will, to make the character malleable to
the internal will."[2] The excess he meant was that of the lyrical imagination, and it was in Yeats's sense of "will" that the man who knew
Thompson most intimately later described him, almost paradoxically, as
having "the strongest will he had ever encountered."[3] Quite early in life,
Thompson made the choice between fame and comfort, and it was no
more than the literal truth about himself that he uttered after some of
the bitterest experiences in the annals of literary struggle:

> A double life the Poet lived,
> And with a double burthen grieved;
> The life of flesh and life of song
> The pangs to both lives that belong . . .
> If one life worked the other wrong,
> What expiating agony
> May for him, damned to poesy,
> Shut in that little sentence be—
> What deep austerities of strife—
>   'He lived his life.' He lived *his* life![4]

By solemn vision and bright silver dream
His infancy was nurtured. Every sight
And sound from the vast earth and ambient air,
Sent to him its choicest impulses.

Alastor

1

THE BRIGHT SILVER DREAM

BORN A WEEK BEFORE CHRISTMAS,[1] 1859, IN A QUIET BACKSTREET OF the seacoast town of Preston, in Lancashire, Thompson inherited both a literary and a religious strain, the two elements he was to combine in producing his most memorable work. His father, Charles Thompson, a doctor of homeopathy, belonged to a family in which five of the eight children, and both parents, were converts to Catholicism. His mother, Mary Morton, was also a convert, having made the move in defiance of a stern Anglican father, and earning temporary expulsion from home as a result.[2] The literary inclination, of a modest sort, it is true, can be seen in two of his uncles—his father's brothers—who published volumes of poetry long before he was born. One of them had even achieved some reputation in Catholic circles for comfortably pious biographies of saints and mystics.[3]

*Thompson's birthplace, No. 7 Winck-
ley Street, Preston.*

In mid-nineteenth century England Catholics were a restricted minor-
ity and both laymen and priests as a consequence tended to draw
together. After Charles Thompson married Mary Morton in 1857, their
home in Preston quickly evolved into one of the gathering places of the
neighborhood clergy, and the custom was continued when the family, in
1864, joined the growing bustle in the market town of Ashton-under-
Lyne, just outside Manchester. Dr. Thompson set up both practice and
living quarters in a rented, two-story, attached brick house on Stamford
Street, Ashton's main artery, and it is here that young Francis comes into
focus, a sensitive, mildly abstracted little boy, for whom the sight of
black-clad priests coming in the front door was as familiar as the string of
patients, many of them the town's poor, that climbed the stone steps to
his father's offices at the back.[4] Though both of his parents appear to
have been more than ordinarily kind, even indulgent, neither had any
interest in literature, and their son's entrance into the realm of the
imagination came only from the obscure promptings of his own preco-
cious spirit.

At the age of seven or eight he was already rummaging in the pages of
Scott, Macaulay, Shakespeare, and even the Bible, often perched on top
of a ladder in the book cupboard or sprawled on the stairs. Though he
understood little of the real import of what he read, a certain awareness
of the beauty of language early began to stir; in *A Midsummer Night's
Dream*, especially, he felt the "sense of trance, of dreamlike dimness, the
moonlight glimmer and sleepwalking enchantment."[5] As he grew older,
Shakespeare's diction overwhelmed him and for the benefit of his sisters
and the servants he read some of the plays aloud—though his audience

"kicked against *Julius Caesar* as dry"—and on the tiny stage of a cardboard theater, in which the figures were worked by wire and hair, he even tried to bring the plays to life. His powerful assimilative tendency was already at work as the language of the plays crept unnoticed into the hidden recesses of his consciousness:

> When I was a child of seven, standing in my nightgown before the fire, and chattering to my mother, I remember her pulling me up for using a certain word. "That is not used nowadays," she said; "that is one of Shakespeare's words." "Is it, Mamma," I said, staring at her doubtfully. "But I didn't know it was one of Shakespeare's words!" "That is just it," she answered, "you have read Shakespeare so much that you are beginning to talk Shakespeare without knowing it. You must take care or people will think you odd." She was a prophetess.[6]

The quick response to the vitality he divined in language was elicited as much by the Bible as by Shakespeare, especially by the *Apocalypse,* which he also read first as a young boy. Its meanings, of course, were uncomprehended but its mysterious imagery and cloudy grandeurs sank deep into his spirit as "the pageantry of an appalling dream." Later, he vividly described what he remembered of the early effects of the *Apocalypse:* "Insurgent darkness, with wild lights flashing through it; terrible phantasms insupportably revealed against profound light, and in a moment no more . . . unknown voices uttering out of darkness darkened and disastrous speech." Though this is the studied expression of a mature man looking back on his youth, something akin to this disturbing beauty must have shadowed the random thoughts of the impressionable boy, crowding his imagination with chillingly Gothic murmurings as he walked, lonely and unsuspected, among his parents and sisters in the house on Stamford Street. The intellectual introversion soon took on an emotional undercurrent, making its grasp doubly potent: in comparing pictures of Medieval women, he explained later, with "the crinolined and chignoned girls of my own day, I embraced the fatal but undoubting conviction that beauty had expired somewhere about the time of Henry VIII . . . there being no beautiful girls left . . . I never dreamed of love as a modern sentiment at all."[7]

But such sensitivity must have been wrenched by frequent intrusions, and while his subsequent remark about "a long tragedy of early experience" probably refers to no more than minor tragedies, there occurred three family deaths during his boyhood that may have struck him with profound shock. On January 15, 1864, when he was four, his younger sister, Helen, died at the age of fifteen months; when he was seven, his father's mother passed away, and later that same year, in December 1867, his mother's father, aged seventy-seven, died in the Thompson house at Ashton. The boy was not too young for all three deaths to have affected him deeply; the agonies of childhood always seemed to knife his heart more searingly than others of his age. The first time he became separated from his mother in the street, the effect on his frail nerves loomed as a "world-wide desolation and terror," and he later compared the feeling to the first realization that a soul could be separated from God.[8]

Despite all this, it would be false to think that he shared none of the ordinary pleasures or interests of youth. A lifelong fascination with military matters, for instance, began early. "In our play-room he used to get Maggie and me to join him in mimic sieges," his sister Mary remembered, and cricket claimed so much attention that if he could get no one to play with him he would "practice bowling by himself for a couple of hours at a time." Card games and card tricks, in company with his sisters, occupied him until he discovered chess, and he threw himself into that game with such intensity, and with so many demands for quiet, that his sisters almost hated to see a game begin. For a while, art became an enthusiasm and on an improvised easel he made careful copies of Burne-Jones, but "it was only by chance that anyone else saw them." When he discovered the universe visible through a microscope, he begged an instrument of his father, and often went into the country, loaded with bottles, to bring back supplies, which he eagerly insisted on his sisters viewing while he supplied excited explanations. Often, however, his abstractions would intrude on their games. "My sport was solitary sport," he recalled, "even when I played with my sisters . . . my side of the game was part of a dream-scheme invisible to them." The dream may have been invisible, but not the dreamy manner, and "up in the moon again!" became a frequent sisterly reprimand.[9] There were also frequent strolls with his father in the countryside around Ashton, "to the accompaniment of his father's talk of buds and trees and flowers."

While it was true that, because of their religion, the family had fewer friends than might have been expected, their separation was by no means absolute, and the Church itself provided some society. One of his friends recalled Thompson's rather noisy advent as an altar boy at St. Mary's about 1872:

> He asked if he could not have a red cassock. He was told he could not, he was too tall, and the candle bearers were the only ones in red. He admired James Clayton's cassock (a pretty purple one) but Clayton was the boat bearer (the smallest boy) and walked with the thurifer.

Stamford Street, Ashton-under-Lyne, at the turn of the century. The Thompson home, at No. 226, was about three blocks down on the right.

With bad grace Thompson donned a black cassock and surplice. The first day passed over very well, but the following Sunday quite unexpectedly he seized a long metal taper holder, went on the side altar and began to light up the big candles.

Frank MacFarlane, head clerk, rushed on and took the taper from him, or the whole of the candles and sticks might have been spread about the altar. Later on I was promoted to be thurifer, with Clayton still as boat boy. But Thompson used to tell us at low mass that he was a nobody and had nothing to do. The thurifer spent much time in the vestry keeping his charcoal in good condition, sometimes dropping the lid of the thurible to swing up the light. Thompson quite unexpectedly came off at the side of the altar, and saw me revolving the thurible. In a minute he had hold of it, opened the thurible, and ere I could protest he was whizzing it round. He caught the floor and all the charcoal was scattered over the vestry floor. I ran to the housekeeper's room and she came with a shovel, stamped out what she could and carried away the rest, while I was heating more charcoal. When I returned Thompson had gone back to his seat on the altar.

The friend, a boy named Byrne, supplied other bits of information that show Thompson was often indistinguishable from his more prosaic chums. They are the everyday things of his boyhood, which have largely

Francis Thompson at the age of eleven.

been ignored by biographers in their search for the gloomy foreshadowings of the poet:

> Clayton and I used to spend hours in Thompson's kitchen, and Mrs. Thompson, a handsome lady, used to ask us how Thompson was getting on. She told us we must not call him "Frank." Francis was his name. Until his mother put a stop to it, he had become a keen reader of my penny books, "The Boys of England," and "Young Men of Great Britain," which he used to pass on to his sisters. Thompson would spend hours in Church Street, watching my grandfather (Edward Wall) sole and heel shoes. A great favourite of his was an old clockmaker, a fat man, opposite Thompson's back door. The old man used to hang clocks on the outside wall and Thompson was never tired of watching the man work, but he was evidently privileged for few boys dared breathe when passing the clockmaker's place. The boys used to play cricket etc., at the back of Dunham Terrace, but Charlie Murray was by no means impressed by Thompson as an athlete, and used to say that "Francis ought to be a monk." I remember that Thompson felt he had lost a pal when Charlie Murray was sent to Stonyhurst to qualify for a commission in the Army. A favourite playground of Thompson's was Park Parade and Knott's Steps. Whenever he dared venture he would go into Man Kemp's fields. I say with all respect that Booth Street and Park Parade neighbours used to rush off to Wood Street to inform Mrs. Thompson "Your Francis is on Park Parade again." The emancipation of Thompson from his trammels may be attributed to the late James Duffy, who used to take Thompson on the Moss and teach him "piggy" playing, taw ring, etc., and how to charge, prime and fire a gun.[10]

With all his later eccentricities, and in spite of some degree of intellectual isolation, it is evident that Thompson knew a good deal of the joys and strifes of any normal boy. He even appears to have taken part in amateur theatricals at neighborhood churches.[11] Later, there was a local girl, Lucy Keogh, who held his attention, and who eventually found immortality as Lucidè in *Dream Tryst*.[12] Thompson afterwards journeyed far from home, and returned only twice, but he did not forget; some nostalgic lines entitled *To Daisies*, found among his papers, perhaps hold memories of lazy days in Kemp's fields on soft summer days in Ashton:

> These hands did toy,
> Children, with you when I was a child,
> And in each other's eyes we smiled:
> Not yours, not yours the grievous-fair
> Apparelling
> With which you wet mine eyes; you wear
> Ah me, the garment of the grace
> I wove you when I was a boy

The commoner realities were thrust upon Thompson on the very day he first left home for boarding school. At the age of ten years and nine months he was to receive his initial taste of formal education, having till then been tutored at home, and in the train that took the boys from the Manchester area to Ushaw College in Durham, he was silent and withdrawn. His reticence attracted the more boisterous in the crowd and in the resulting horse-play, a bag of jam tarts he was carrying in his pocket was crushed.[13] The slight incident was remembered by the older student who had charge of the boys on the train, and in his later telling of it there was a hint of jocularity; for Thompson, however, it was one of the first signs that the world provided no comfortable niche for its dreamers.

St. Cuthbert's College at Ushaw prepared boys for the seminary as well as for secular pursuits, but it was with an eye on the priesthood that Thompson was sent there. "He wished to be a priest from a little boy," his sister recalled,[14] and it is hardly surprising that he began early to have visions of himself clothed in the vestments of the altar. The aura of piety and religion that hung round his house had been greatly intensified by his mother, a gentle, understanding woman who, in her own youth, had once briefly retreated to a convent.[15] Few precise facts about her remain, but in a school essay by Thompson, written when he was fourteen, there occurs a passage that must certainly be a portrait of his mother, and which sufficiently reveals the influence she held over her son. In the essay, as the boy views scenes of his past life in a magic mirror, a picture of his mother's room appears:

> But who is the lady, sweet and graceful, in all the first bloom of youth and beauty, and who is the child with his fair golden hair, and open smiling countenance, who is standing with his little hands upon her knee, while her arm is twined lovingly round his shoulder. See, her head is almost touching his brow, and her long, fair hair surrounds him with a golden halo, whilst she breathes into his ear lessons of love and piety, which take root in his heart, and will bear fruit in after days. Look, she rises, and points to the old crucifix which hangs on the wall; they kneel down, and she joins his little hands, and together they pour forth an earnest prayer to the agonized Redeemer.[16]

The scene is a touching illustration of Thompson's later remark that the religious spirit of some of his work was "no mere medieval imitation, but the natural temper of my Catholic training in a simple, provincial home."[17] Perhaps inevitably, the simple, provincial home had brought his religious strain into dominance, and thrown back into shadow his more profound yearning for literary things.

At Ushaw his private world of dreams suffered a devastating invasion. Sometime in the opening weeks, in front of a crowd of laughing students, "a capacious whin-bush . . . occupied his undivided attention," and when the paddling was over he was dubbed "Tommy." But such incidents did not produce the expected sense of camaraderie, and his merry companions would undoubtedly have been shocked could they have seen into the heart of the sad-eyed youth: "The malignity of my tormentors was more lacerating than the pain itself," he wrote many years after, "it seemed to me—virginal to the world's ferocity—a hideous thing that strangers should dislike me, should delight and triumph in pain to me, though I had done them no ill and bore them no malice . . . these malign schoolmates who danced round me with mocking evil distortion of laughter . . . were to me devilish apparitions." The spirit that could react with such raw ferocity to a school initiation could not hope to find peace in new surroundings and the result, inevitably, was further withdrawal. An atmosphere of melancholy was quickly noticed by his teachers, and his sense of separation was plain even in his walk: "He sidled along the wall and every now and then he would hitch up the collar of his coat as though it were slipping off his none too thickly covered shoulder blades." The other boys thought him "mooney," and began to see him as "frail and abnormal." Concentrating on his studies,

The Thompson home in Ashton-Under-Lyne as it looks today (center, with the flagpole). A jewelry store occupies what was the front parlor.

by the end of his initial year he had obtained first place in English and second in Latin.[18]

Thus passed, in hurt and homesickness, Thompson's introduction to Ushaw. But contrary to much that has been written, the seven years he spent there were not a dreary stretch of unhappiness and rejection. After the first rough encounter, he managed gradually to find a niche for himself, and eventually he was even granted a certain intellectual pre-eminence by the other students. The mistaken notion of his permanent misery at Ushaw stems from the biography published in 1913 by Everard Meynell, a generally capable, devoted work, but the source of much of the present distortion of Thompson's life. In this book Meynell failed to make clear just what caused Thompson's distress or how long it lasted, and the impression given is that the unfortunate young man was subjected to long years of isolated suffering. Meynell was the first to quote, in this connection, a passage from Thompson's *Shelley* essay which highlights the petty persecutions that overclouded Shelley's schooldays, and since then no biographer has failed to make the comparison. Often they linger fondly on one deft sentence in which Thompson sketched the young Shelley: "So beset, the child fled into the tower of his own soul and raised the drawbridge." Thompson, they assert, did the same, thus accounting for his later separation from ordinary life. But, despite some resemblances, Thompson was not another Shelley; after the first savage confrontation, his school life was, for the most part, contented and satisfying. It was not the rudeness of his schoolmates or the negligence of his masters that turned him inward and gave a fatal, grotesque twist to his later life. Opium did that.

"Frank gives the greatest satisfaction in every way," the school reported to Thompson's parents in September 1871, and from then on the boy seems to have felt reasonably at home. "He was as happy in his own way, as any of us," one classmate recalled, "we saw much of him, listened to his talk—and he talked far more than any of us . . . he was not a lonely lad . . . What time he did not spend in the library was spent with his schoolfellows."[19] Making necessary allowances for the pangs of maturing creativity, seldom noticed or remembered in crowds of boys, that assertion fits the facts; he might still carry jam tarts in his pockets, but the lads who wrestled for them were no longer devilish apparitions. There was much talk, amounting, it seems, almost to garrulity, in which he retailed the results of his reading. There were frequent walks in the surrounding woods in all weathers. There were sports, especially handball and "cat," and, though it is not mentioned, there must have been cricket. At handball, in particular, he displayed better-than-average ability and was often on the courts. There was also a pirate band which he, surprisingly, was the means of forming. "Their contraband came from Mrs. Pearson's," a fellow conspirator recalled, ". . . and this was cached in the old stone wall to be called for as occasion required, and to be assimilated probably in school." Characteristically, the piracy is connected with the reading of such writers as Marryat and Ballantyne.

In the classroom, success in English came almost without effort, and by the spring of 1872 one of his teachers could report unusual attainments: "His master was speaking to me about him yesterday, and said that his English composition was the best production from a lad of his age that he had ever seen in this seminary."[20] Efficiency in Latin and Greek was also reported, though the effort cost him some restless nights; at least once he managed to disturb the dormitory with feverish Greek and Latin recitations in his sleep. About his fourth year at the school, he enjoyed a heady triumph, when one of his essays was declaimed on College Speaking Day, with passages from Macaulay and Gibbon to give it a framework. The piece, a stirring description of an incident in Napoleon's Italian campaign, along with others in which he displayed a taste for military matters, enhanced his position among the students and earned him the nickname "l'homme militaire."

He made his formal decision to continue for Holy Orders in 1874, and for the next two years happily prepared himself for ordination, but already there were telltale signs of broadening interests in literature, and what was even more significant in view of his character, indications of spiritual involvement with the priestly life were strangely lacking. "He did not betray any singular piety," recalled one friend, nor did he show more than ordinary interest in theological subjects.[21]

Though he had been an incessant reader of poetry on the highest level for years, his sensibilities had remained largely on the surface. At Ushaw, he pored over Crashaw and the Metaphysicals, Spenser, Scott, and Shakespeare, as much for the lulling music as for thought or imaginative splendor; his sense of the deeper realities of poetry was quiescent. Development came suddenly in 1876, "with a leap and a rush," and it was then that he experienced the first light straining of the tension that would ultimately strip him of all desire for the priesthood and leave him, in his own words, "a boy of 17 . . . devoured with literary ambition."[22] Looking back on those years from the vantage point of a quarter century, perhaps with something of a wondering nostalgia, he remembered how his first passionate perceptions had finally burgeoned in his sixteenth year, and how he had conscientiously studied meter from that time on, while his "young heart beat prophecy." The piracy, the handball, even walking and talking were forgotten, and during his free hours he would customarily retreat to the library, "with a thick manuscript book under his arm, and there sit reading and copying poetry, nervously running one hand through his hair."[23]

Robert Frost once observed that the poet develops in the manner of waterspouts at sea, beginning as a cloud of all the other poets he has ever read, and for Thompson the description is apt. Effortlessly, he drew in the varied music of Coleridge, Shelley, Keats, Wordsworth, Donne and most of the other seventeenth-century poets, Spenser, and even Poe. The only examples that have survived of his juvenile verse are the nine poems contained in the *Ushaw College Notebook*.[24] One of these pieces, derived from Shelley's *Indian Serenade*, could hardly have lent assurance regarding his priestly aspirations:

> My window is open for thee, sweet love,
>   My window is open for thee,
> The bindweed rope on the tree doth move,
>   As the breezes come and flee;
> Wert thou here, wert thou here, I would cast away fear,
>   And descend to the garden to thee . . .

Thompson's mother in 1877.

Another fragment betrays his reading of Keats:

> Full in a spot which the glad sunlight laves
> There spreads a wood, where undulating waves
> Of foliage thick shine in the moving light
> Which shifts from tree to tree along their height . . .

Another, entitled *Spring,* is redolent of Wordsworth, four rousing pieces sing of martial valor in satisfyingly competent meter, and in *The Song of the Neglected Poet*—quite obviously inspired by *Alastor*—he confesses that in "poesy divine" he has a "treasure not the banded world can take." But it is all very schoolboyish and there is yet no sign of the slumbering genius.

It is always a disconcerting thing for a young man to find himself suddenly and strongly pulled away from a path he has been for years contentedly pursuing. Anxiety, guilt, even fear, would mix their dark hues with the bright pleasures of awakening creativity, and there is evidence that Thompson underwent just such tortures. "Before he left College he had entered into a strange mental struggle which caused much anxiety to his superiors," said a writer in the college magazine a few years later.[25] Mistaken vocations, however, are a fairly common occurrence in any seminary and the signs are well understood, or many of them are, so it could have occasioned small surprise when, in April 1877, such doubts were openly discussed:

> I spoke to Frank the other day and he tells me that he is quite well and that his own inclinations in regard to the priesthood are not altered, but that his confessor has doubts as to his vocation. He is as he has always been, a very good boy; and I still hope that he will become a good priest. In the meantime I hope that you will not be uneasy about him, as I am sure that his vocation will not be decided precipitately.[26]

Understandably reluctant to turn his back on six years' preparation, or on his family's hopes, in his confusion Thompson held fast to the life he knew, and it is possible that he even entertained the idea of combining poetry with the priesthood. In any case, by July the decision was made; he was not to become a priest.

The legend of the rejected seminarian—the "spoiled priest"—pursuing his lonely way in a world in which he did not belong and from whose materialities he recoiled, has clung to Thompson from the beginning. It had some currency even while he lived. The reality, however, is different, and his tortured life has no need of spurious sentimentality. Thompson deliberately rejected the priesthood in the only way that counted; he lagged in his duties, and neglected his obligations, knowing well the penalties for doing so. Again, it was Everard Meynell who fastened the "spoiled priest" legend onto the Thompson story, though it is evident that he performed the office with some reluctance. He records the supposition that Thompson's "life-long trouble was that he failed in the attempt to be a priest," and that "his failure in the seminary was with him an acute and lasting grief." But he quietly refers that opinion to a Thompson relative.[27] His own comment takes the form of rather weak agreement: "There is nothing to throw substantial discredit on such a reading of his career." In another dissenting and seldom-quoted remark he is bolder: "It is probable that while his family were solicitous for him to enter the Church, he recognized the justice of his confessor's opinion."

Thompson at fourteen, with his sisters Mary and Maggie.

But a number of the more revealing of his opinions never reached print. Buried in his original manuscript are such frank phrases as: "The disappointment was not Francis'; he knew himself too well to wish to put on the cassock." And again: "He seems early to have realised . . . that he had no vocation for the priesthood."[28] No statement so forthright appears in the published book; instead Meynell allowed the sentimental notions of others to guide his pen.

Nowhere does Thompson himself say anything explicit on the subject, not even in the privacy of his notebooks. But it is just possible that in some random remarks made twenty years later he refers to his days at Ushaw: "If it be true that the poet is not made, it is unfortunately true that he can be unmade—or at least balked of his complete making, whether that unmaking take the form of compulsory ecclesiasticism or compulsory journalism."[29] At the time he wrote those words he felt he had, in a way, been forced into journalism. Perhaps there was an echo of earlier difficulties in that "compulsory ecclesiasticism."

Father Tate to Dr. Thompson, July 1877:

> With regard to Frank . . . I have been most reluctantly compelled to concur in the opinion of his director and others that it is not the holy will of God that he should go on for the priesthood . . . I quite agree with you in thinking that it is quite time that he should begin to prepare for some other career. If he can shake off a natural *indolence* which has always been an obstacle with him, he has ability to succeed in any career.[30]

With a sound education and a deepening tendency to "indolence," Thompson returned to Ashton-under-Lyne, uncertain about his future, but with poetry swarming in his head.

Where stood Jerusalem, the fallen towers
Of Babylon, the eternal pyramids,
                    . . . and dead men
Hang their mute thoughts on the mute walls around,
He lingered, poring on memorials
Of the world's youth

Alastor

2

TOWERS OF BABYLON

IT WAS PERHAPS INEVITABLE THAT THOMPSON SHOULD HAVE BEEN
pointed in the direction of a medical career. In the dozen years his father
had been practicing in Ashton, despite his adherence to the narrow doc-
trines of homeopathy, he had gained a position of respect, even of affection. Notwithstanding the son's flair for literature, medicine must have
seemed an obvious choice, especially since one of England's leading
medical schools was within easy commuting distance, at Manchester. It
is more difficult to guess why Thompson went along with the idea, but
it is a fact that he offered no demur, and in July of 1877 he sat for his
entrance examination at Owens College. Honors in Latin and Greek
could not cover his deficiencies in the sciences, however, especially
mathematics—a difficulty that might have been foreseen, since he had
shown the usual poet's aversion to such subjects at Ushaw. But he was

accepted for a make-up course, and on September 27, 1877, he signed the Owens College Register, listing his father as "surgeon"; the following year he was admitted to the Medical Department for both summer and winter studies.[1] Still two months short of his eighteenth birthday, his affairs may have seemed under control at last: with only a hazy notion of the courses in chemistry, anatomy, physiology, and pharmacy that awaited him, perhaps he honestly believed that poetry could also be served. But his road had taken another wrong turn. "An intellectual temperament less adapted to the career of a doctor and a surgeon could not be imagined," summed up an Ashton neighbor who knew him well.[2]

At first he must have been regular in attendance and studies. The accepted picture of him abruptly turning his back on the classroom in order to forage in Manchester libraries, galleries, and museums is a false one—the rules of the college would not have permitted it. Attendance at lectures was registered and students were warned that all breaches of discipline and absences would be reported to parents.[3] That Thompson managed to continue at the college for six years argues that he met the minimal obligations—though he, no doubt, now and then found means of avoiding the lecture room undetected. It is possible to believe, in fact, that, were it not for two tragedies that fell across his life at this time, he might even have somehow successfully stumbled through the four-year course at Owens, though, admittedly, it is quite another question as to whether he could ever have actually practiced. To consider these two events in their proper light it is necessary to return to Everard Meynell's biography.

> In 1879 Francis fell ill, and did not recover until after a long bout of fever. He looks stricken and thin in photographs taken at his recovery, and it is probably at this time that he first tasted laudanum. It was at this time, too, during his early courses at Owens College, that Mrs. Thompson, without any known cause or purpose, gave her son a copy of *The Confessions of an English Opium Eater*. It was a last gift, for she died December 19, 1880 . . . That she, "giver of life, death, peace, distress," should thus have confirmed and renewed her gifts was a strange thing to befall. From her copy of *The Confessions of an English Opium Eater* he learnt a new existence at her hands.[4]

That passage, describing two of the pivotal events of Thompson's history, has been accepted by every subsequent writer. In reality, it constitutes one of the central problems of Thompson biography, for it is by no means certain that things happened in just that way.

Meynell, it is clear, did not know the nature of the supposed 1879

Thompson's father in 1877.

illness, nor was he quite certain as to when Mrs. Thompson gave her son the *Confessions*. A close reading of the passage shows only that he believed in general that there was some connection between an illness, the drugs, and the gift of the *Confessions*. He has treated them together, but has carefully avoided linking them in any time sequence or causal relationship. Where did he get his information to begin with? Almost certainly it was from his own father—and a more unreliable source for such data can scarcely be imagined. Wilfrid Meynell was a generous, talented man, whose warm heart and home had later provided Thompson's chief moral, and often financial, support, but he was not interested

in strict biographical truth; approximation and a glossing over of anything unpleasant constituted his approach to the life of his friend. Aside
from his son's contention, there is no record of Thompson suffering any
serious illness in 1879. On this whole question another son, Francis, has
commented frankly: "The laudanum as a medical necessity—medical
treatment—could conceivably be an invention of my father's, a benevolent invention, in order to excuse what my father would regard as a
disgraceful lapse. It would have been unlikely that father would have
invented the illness, but given the fact of an illness, and the development
of the habit, he would persuade himself that there was a connection
between the two. When it was necessary to make an explanation he
would put all the emphasis on the medical necessity in order not to admit
a weak surrender to a habit."[5] There is proof that Wilfrid Meynell
would go even further to prevent sordidness from tarnishing his friend's
reputation: when in 1938 he turned a large amount of manuscript
material over to the Thompson collection at Boston College, he did so
with the stipulation that anything unpleasant should be burned.[6]

It is not likely, at this date, that it will ever be known precisely how or
when Thompson was first impelled to drug addiction. The indications
are, however, that he took to experimenting with laudanum simply and
solely as a result of his reading of De Quincey, and that his mother gave
him the *Confessions* only because he had already been captivated by the
book's visionary grandeur and talked incessantly of it at home. It is
unlikely that he could have discovered De Quincey at Ushaw, but it is
equally unlikely that he could have visited Manchester and haunted its
bookshops and libraries for any length of time without doing so. The first
biography of De Quincey was published, in two volumes, in 1877; thus
in the very year Thompson began at Owens, De Quincey's work and life
were again occupying the attention of literary circles. Norbert Thompson, the poet's half brother, has asserted that "After Francis went to
Owens College (Manchester University) to study medicine, he spent a
large part of his time in old bookshops and it was there that he picked up
De Quincey."[7] That he talked about his new enthusiasm at home is
testified by his uncle who later recalled that the *Confessions* was his
nephew's favorite book: "We had often said his experiences would
surpass those of De Quincey,"[8]—a remark not quite clear in its implications, but which serves to demonstrate the extent to which his family had
noticed his involvement. That his mother's gift of the book followed this,
possibly for his birthday in 1879, is most likely. She had, it might be
noted, already presented him with a bust of Shakespeare because of his
early interest in the plays.

An element certainly as important as any of the above, in considering how Thompson fell into addiction, was the fact that the laudanum so alluringly described by De Quincey was as available in Thompson's time as it had been earlier, and even more so in Manchester, where the cotton workers were known for its use. Technically a tincture of opium (90 per cent by volume of alcohol), laudanum could then be bought cheaply by anyone at any chemist's shop even more freely than codeine-based medicines can be purchased today. Quite simply, laudanum was the most widely used medicine and painkiller in a time that knew little of the vast pharmacology that has come into being in the last fifty years. And Thompson had yet other means of access, since his own father kept a supply of it, as did the laboratory at Owens. In addition to all this, the patent medicines of the day often contained insidious quantities of both opium and cocaine.

Addiction, it is now well understood, is not merely a matter of consuming a sufficient quantity of drugs. It results from a complicated pattern of physical and emotional factors, interwoven with social and family pressures. Despite the great amount of attention the subject is even now receiving, however, there is still no large understanding of its treatment and prevention. It is only within the present generation that the problem of addiction has been openly recognized and studied at all, and there can be little hope of uncovering the precise reasons for Thompson's failure when batteries of present-day scientists, scrutinizing living examples, cannot isolate the fundamental, correctable basis of drug addiction. Perhaps it is enough to realize that Thompson, caught between his extreme involvement with imaginative literature and the frustrating demands of his uncongenial college routine, had arrived at a danger point: given some basic defect in his emotional pattern, the situation had made him, in the modern phrase, an addictive personality, susceptible to whatever escape mechanism could lay its potent grip on his heart. In all this, one fact should be kept in view: throughout the nineteenth century laudanum was an ever-present social danger, and the incidence of addiction of the milder sort was appalling. In the United States, for instance, just prior to the imposition of control over the public sale of drugs in 1914, the known rate of addiction was about one person in four hundred, and in 1964, with drugs and drug-based medicines under strict supervision, the percentage had decreased to one in four thousand. In other words, when laudanum and similar preparations were freely available, ten times as many people, a good proportion of them housewives, were habituated to their use.

If Thompson succumbed to drugs through the *Confessions*, what, exactly, did De Quincey have to say on the subject? The answer, surprisingly, is that De Quincey vacillated in his attitude. In extravagant language he praised the powers of opium, but balanced the praise with equally strong expressions of condemnation and regret. Writing at a time when even the medical profession knew almost nothing about drug addiction, he assured his readers in hypnotic prose that opium is no more unlawful or immoral than drink, that at least four months of steady indulgence are needed to cause dependence, that he himself had toyed with it for years without contracting an undue craving, remaining all the while in the best of health. Then, quite abruptly, in the middle of a calm analysis of the steps leading to addiction, he bursts out: "Oh heavens! that it should be possible for a child not seventeen years old, by a momentary blindness, by listening to a false, false whisper from his own heart, by one erring step, by a motion this way or that, to change the currents of his destiny, to poison the fountains of his peace, and in the twinkling of an eye to lay the foundations of a life-long repentance!" Seventeen; just Thompson's age when he read that passage—yet its blazing regret did not forestall him from listening to the false whisper that was beginning in *his* own heart. What entrammeled him, of course, was not any academic discussion of the drug itself, but the visionary dreams and the masterful manner of their recounting. Traces of the overwhelming effect that De Quincey's dream sequences had on the young medical student lingered in some of his later remarks on the *Confessions*: "The crowning glory of it is the dreams . . . passages of such vaporous sublimity, in the true sense of that abused word, such ministerial grandeurs of style, as we know not where else to look for . . . The mere architecture of the sentences in some of the chief passages is to the literary student an astonishment."[9] His feeling for his Manchester predecessor "soon came to be that of a younger for an elder brother," and characteristically, the younger brother adopted a De Quincey habit as his own, from this time on using the old-fashioned "ȳ" in place of "the" in his manuscripts.

In June 1879, after two years of study, Thompson went to London for the Oxford Local Examinations given by the General Medical Council. It was his first time in London, and he stayed with his cousin, William Costall May, a surgeon, who lived at 52 Tregunter Road, Fulham. After the examinations he attended the opera, and, with the *Confessions* resounding in his ears, it is hard to believe that he did not go in search of the gaunt house at "the northwest corner of Greek Street . . . nearest to Soho Square," in which De Quincey had spent so many miserable nights.[10] He also visited the South Kensington Museum to view the golden treasure brought back from Troy by Schliemann, noting particularly an unusual two-handled cup identified as the *Amphicypellon* of

Homer, which would later provide him with the first title of his longest poem.[11] Back in Ashton, a few days later, the results of the examination reached him: he had failed.

Even if he had expected failure, the reality must have been disheartening to him and a blow to his father. What explanations he made are not known, but he was back at Owens for the summer session soon after, and seems to have made an attempt to apply himself at home in the evenings as well. Though perhaps not yet a confirmed addict, he was certainly still dabbling with the drug. Then the second tragedy of his youth struck: soon after his return from London, Mrs. Thompson came down with a liver ailment and six months later, on December 19, she died.[12] The only echo of this sad event is a poem by Thompson, which remained unpublished until after his own death. Though it was probably not written until years later, it still affords a painfully vivid insight into the soul of the bereaved young man:

> Son of the womb of her,
> Loved till doom of her,
> Thought of the brain of her,
>   Heart of her side:
> Joyed in him, grieved in him,
> Hoped, believed in him—
> God grew fain of her,
>   And she died.

> Died; and horribly
> Saw the mystery,
> Saw the grime of it—
>   That hid soul;
> Saw the sear of it,
> Saw the fear of it,
> Saw the slime of it,
>   Saw it whole!

> O mother! mother! for all the sweet John saith,
> O mother, was not *this* the Second Death?[13]

"After my mother died it was I who looked after him," Mary Thompson told the Meynells, "you know he required looking after almost like a child, though he was the eldest of the family."[14] Mrs. Thompson was fifty-eight at her death. She was buried in Dukinfield Cemetery, a short

Medal won by Thompson for excellence in English at Ushaw.

walk from the house in Stamford Street. It is not too much to say that her son's last chance for a normal life was buried with her.

II

Thompson's first published poem did not appear until he was twenty-eight, and the reasons for the belated start seem, on the surface, to have been due to nothing more complicated than a late-maturing intellect and a consequent total lack of serious subject matter. The urge to write was straining his mind, but he lacked the thought to which he could harness himself; only when his own experiences gave him material for meditation was he able to produce anything of original worth. But on a deeper level, the tardiness may also have resulted from an inability to reconcile his religious upbringing with the natural bent of his genius. His response, like that of all authentic artists, was to essence, to spirit; but his constant emotional need to measure himself against the teachings of his faith, constricted him to the point where he became a victim of artistic inertia. He was held motionless, on the one hand, by his desire to loose his imaginings without regard for dogma, and, on the other, by the necessity of cleaving to his strong Catholic heritage—which, in the England of the second half of the nineteenth century had small use for any art not immediately related to instruction. In the first of his prose writings, some years later, he was still concerned with this situation and voiced a protest that throws some light on his early frustrations. "It would be a mistake to suppose," he insisted, "that literature makes for good only through the comparatively narrow medium of professedly religious writing. On the contrary the most powerful moralizing influence is exercised in the long run by the purely secular literature which is widely read, which never makes direct reference to either religion or morals, but which insensibly insinuates the *ethos* that laves it, as our bodies are insensibly permeated by the viewless constituents of the air that we breathe."[15] Shortly before writing those words he had jotted down another exuberant comment that succinctly expresses both the dilemma and his own inclinations: "The tree, but by putting on greenness, preaches louder than if it cried 'Praise Heaven!' "[16]

Essentially, of course, all of this was the groping for identity which, in some form, confronts every creative mind. With Thompson it assumed the proportions of a struggle between background and aspiration —one moreover which he was never permanently to resolve, his efforts short-circuited by opium. When he did begin to write seriously, it was because he had temporarily solved his dilemma, and his solution, or compromise—dearly bought and dearly paid for—was to impose literary taste on religious forms. He was not always to be successful in this, of course, but when he did succeed he produced some of modern poetry's most striking and original work, culminating in one of the world's great lyrics.

In private and in silence, during those six increasingly furtive years at Owens, he continued to fashion verses. The *Notebook of Early Poems*[17] contains about twenty examples that can confidently be assigned to these years, but in none of them is there more than a hint—a phrase here and a word there—of the later Thompson. One sonnet embedded in the unpublished fragment *Ode to the Delian Artemis,* is interesting in its display of early descriptive power. The verses describe the passage of Diana through the forest:

> My vision grows intense; no haze bedims
> The sight which passes ere these eyes have winked!
> I see her as she goes; her moving limbs
> White-gleaming through the dusk; her robe succinct
> Streams into fluttering folds; one hand enrims
> Her outstretched bow; the other, shown distinct
> By the rays dripping from her argent crest,
> Flings back the windy trammel of her scarf;
> The eager, tremulous lips are half-apart,
> And to the chase the flashing eyes addressed;
> Lessening in gloom as of a Stygian wharf,

> Fades the brief dream into the forest's heart:
> Around her glittering form in its quick flight
> The agitated air reels, giddy with delight.

This is imitation, but it is the highly competent imitation of real talent working its way toward the light and the importance of such experiments, of course, lay almost entirely on the technical side. The originality, the new note, would come later.

"Until I was twenty-two," he afterwards recalled, "Shelley was more studied by me than anyone else," indicating that about 1883 he turned elsewhere for inspiration. Though he nowhere says to whom he turned, it was probably Dante Gabriel Rossetti, who died amid dark rumors of drugs and madness in April 1882, and whose life and work were much discussed in the following months.[18] The choice is not surprising; the intensely personal, highly colored verse of the poet-painter must have had a very special appeal for Thompson, whose subtle ear could hardly avoid being charmed by Rossetti's musical sinuosities, and whose devotion to both Shelley and Keats would only have sealed the attraction. Though Rossetti's influence waned perceptibly once Thompson had found his own voice, it was strong during his middle and late twenties, and out of it came his first undeniably fine poem, *Dream Tryst*.

Rossetti's sonnets attracted him strongly and a third of the tentative verses in the *Notebook of Early Poems* are in this form. Particularly interesting is an unpublished sequence of four, clearly modeled on Rossetti's *Willowwood*. They display an increased sureness of touch and an early facility that later enabled him to produce a half-dozen sonnets of high worth. The verses, and their derivation from *Willowwood*, have so far been overlooked, ever since a few garbled lines from them appeared in the 1913 biography. Entitled *On the Anniversary of Rossetti's Death*, they were written, probably, in 1883–84.

I

> This was the day that great, sad heart,
> That great sad heart did beat no more,
> Which nursed so long its Southern flame
> Amid our vapours dull and frore.
> He said a thing in English verse,
> He made our English painting young,
> He taught our lingering lips to speak
> As Giotto spake in Tuscan tongue.

Through voice of art and voice of song
   He uttered one same truth abroad—
Through voice of art and voice of song—
   That love below a pilgrim trod;
He said through wondrous eyes, "How long!
   Love's other half's with God!"

II

He taught our English art to burn
   With colours from diviner skies,
He taught our English art to gaze
   On nature with a learner's eyes:
That hills which look into the heaven
   Have their firm bases on the earth;
God paints his most angelic hues
   On vapours of a terrene birth.

This first was he in all Time's girth
   Who painted Sadness crowned and fair—
He only, in all Time's wide girth—
   With royal eyes and glooming hair;
In this poor day's ungod-ed dearth
   The one divine thing left to her.

III

He gave our art his poet's mind,
   He gave our North his Southern song,
He gave our verse his painter's eye
   And Dante's soul to Shakespeare's tongue.
Sad Dante sang a flowerless love,
   And lost what never had been his:
He, more unhappy, knew too well
   The sweetness of the vanished kiss.

He had embraced his Beatrice,
   And tamed the plumes that soon grew cold;
He had embraced his Beatrice!
   And if his heart were early old,
It yearned for the remembered bliss
   Clasped in death's fleshless fold.

Annie Thompson, the poet's stepmother.

IV

If he were weak, forgive it him;
  Be mindful only of his power:
Remember all God dowered him with,
  And how to us he gave that dower.
Kindler of colour, fiery heart
  Of deep, imaginative design,
He trod the vintage whence we draw
  Our modern painting's richest wine.

May God his locks with glories twine,
  Be kind to all he wrought amiss!
May God his locks with flories twine,
  And give him back his Beatrice,
This day that sad heart ceased to pine,
  I trust his lady's beats at his,
And two souls flame in single bliss.

Not only "dawn's grey eyes" of *Dream Tryst,* but also its theme of reunion with a lost love may be traced to the *Willowwood* sonnets. A number of other verses in the *Notebook of Early Poems* attest the strength of the impression made by Rossetti's recurrent lament for his lost love, despite the fact that there seems to have been no truly devastating female entanglements in Thompson's life to this point.[19]

III

Three times Thompson failed his medical examinations: the first in 1879, the second in 1881, and the last—taken at Glasgow instead of London because it was thought the Scottish examiners were more lenient—probably in 1884. On the surface a sorry record of wasted opportunity, his later advice to the aspiring poet reflects his own attitude at this time: "He is not to sow profligately; he must not fear to leave his mind her fallow periods. Strictly speaking, he should not sow at all; his mind is under the Equator and has but to teem with the seeds that fall broadcast from the wasteful hand of Pan." The idea remained with him through life: "Great poetry cannot be written without abundant leisure," he insisted long afterwards, meaning that unfettered freedom is also needed by the poet in embryo. His belief that "Vacant moments are the fallow-field of literature," sums up the triumph of the years at Owens as well as their tragedy.[20]

Many of his own most vacant moments were spent in one or another of the half-dozen galleries, museums, and libraries of Manchester. In one of these, in particular, there stood the bust of a nameless female who, for some reason, threw over his spirit a peculiar thralldom, and which he described in a later essay. The passage affords a fine illustration of the misty, half-unrealized mental landscape in which he roamed during this time:

> . . . with her leaf-twined locks, she seemed some strayed Bacchante, indissolubly filmed in secular reverie . . . This indecipherable significance, I slowly discerned, lurked in the singularly diverse set of the two corners of the mouth; so that her profile wholly shifted her meaning, according as it was viewed from the right or the left. In one corner of her mouth the little langorous firstling of a smile had gone to sleep; as if she had fallen a-dream and forgotten it was there. The other had drooped, as of its own listless weight, into a something which guessed

at sadness . . . on the full countenance those two expressions blended to a single expression inexpressible . . . Thither each evening, as twilight fell, I stole to meditate and worship the baffling mysteries of her meaning: as twilight fell, and the blank noon surceased arrest upon her life, and in the vaguening countenance the eyes broke out from their day-long ambuscade. Eyes of violet-blue, drowsed-amorous, which surveyed me not but looked ever beyond . . .[21]

That he learned something at the College is shown by the scientific allusions in his work, but these are veiled days in his history; no clear picture remains of the medical student commuting daily to Manchester. His later letters contain casual references to the "varnish I used for ringing microscopic slides," an admission that he more than once employed a dissecting scalpel in place of a razor to shave himself and, in conversation, a confession of physical repugnance for the dissection of corpses and the sight of flowing blood, but such details of memory are meager. The College still stands but nearly all trace of him has vanished from its records; there remain merely a few register entries. Only in some incidental memories from Ashton can the young man be seen carrying the double burden of poetic abstraction and deepening addiction. At home in the evenings he displayed a tendency to increased withdrawal, often shutting himself up in his room. Other days he would remain late in the city, attending concerts or listening to music at the home of an unknown friend (was the friend also an addict, perhaps, and was this combination of drugs and music a deliberate emulation of De Quincey? Thompson later recalled the "musical dreams" of this period[22]). His abstracted indifference to his surroundings was also coming more into evidence; neighbors remembered the dragging shoelaces of the young man who passed their doors on Stamford Street, and "the quick, short step, the sudden and apparently causeless hesitation or full stop. Then the old, quick pace again, the continued muttered soliloquy, the frail and slight figure." His erratic walk was emphasized, it appears, by some peculiarity in the gait, which at one time among the small boys of the neighborhood had earned him the nickname of "Elasticlegs."[23]

By the summer of 1884 he had failed out of Owens, and during the next year and a half he drifted through at least two jobs and a short stay in the army. There can be no adequate explanation of his remarkable listlessness at this time (aside from the drugs) except his own later admission that he had "none of a boy's 'mistaken' ambitions. I did not want to grow up; did not want emancipation from parental control, fine clothes, dissipation, freedom and worldly pleasures. I did not want responsibility, did not want to be a man. I did not much want even fame,

*Thompson's signature in the register of the Royal Infirmary, Manchester,
where the medical students from Owens College did their laboratory work.*

and soon abandoned it as hopeless . . . Toys I could surrender (with
chagrin) so I had my great toy of the imagination, whereby the world
became to me my box of toys."[24] This, of course, was nothing more or
less than the despair of frustrated ambition. For ten years the lure of poetry had led him on, but at twenty-four he had written nothing of any real
worth, had not achieved the publication of even one poem; at the same
age, he knew, Shelley had won immortality. Disheartened, he shrank
from a world in which he could not find adequate expression for the
disturbing beauty that shone on him out of the past, from his own heart,
from the heavens. Above all there loomed the specter of the drugs which,
for all he knew, was throttling his infant muse in her cradle. "It was only
in his later years," said Everard Meynell, "when he was delivered of his
poetry and beheld it emerge unmarred by his former surrender to the
drug, that he found peace of mind."

Thompson's listlessness could hardly have given his father reason to
hope that his son would finally get at the serious business of earning a
living, but the effort had to be made, and the initial attempt was
undertaken with a manufacturer of surgical instruments, a logical choice.
Though the name of the company is not known, opportunities in this
line for an ex-medical student were numerous; in the Manchester area
alone the directories of the period list nine such firms. It made little
difference which it was, for within a few weeks he had lost his ap-

prenticeship. There followed some time as an encyclopedia salesman, and that idea presents a picture so impossible to visualize that Everard Meynell brushed it off lightly: "It took him two months to read the encyclopedia, and then he discarded it, unsold." That he tried to join the army soon after this seems to be well established; he spoke in later times of the dullness of barracks life and the weariness it was to march and drill. It was in order to build up his frail body to the required strength and weight that the marching and drilling were performed, probably over a period of a month or so, but "he returned from it late one night, silent." The drug addiction, rather than any serious lack of inches or pounds, presumably brought about his military failure. If the two jobs and the enlistment occupied about six months, then the first ten months of the following year, 1885, are a total blank. No more is heard of Thompson until the Sunday on which his father's anxious hopes and his own silent fears exploded in rancorous argument and accusation. During the night following that disagreement, Thompson stole unnoticed from the house, never really to return.

It is difficult to know what irritant precipitated the trouble on November 8, 1885. Everard Meynell says that Dr. Thompson accused his son of drinking, because of his frequently flushed appearance, and that Thompson, knowing the cause was opium, denied his father's charges. It has also been said that the elder Thompson not only discovered his son's addiction but accused him of stealing laudanum from his own supplies.[25] A third possibility, until now suppressed, centers on the remarriage of Dr. Thompson. "The second marriage was in prospect when Francis left home," wrote Mary Thompson in a letter which the Meynells left unpublished, "and may, for all I know, have been the cause of his departure . . . My father may have given Frank some reason for thinking that he would be in the way if he was not earning his own living after the intended marriage, but at that I can only guess."[26] From some remarks in additional unpublished correspondence, it appears that Thompson's own version did, in fact, concern an ultimatum given him by his father. Mary's guarded statement about the second marriage was prompted by an inquiry on the part of Meynell, in which he was checking Thompson's claim, a fact that is evident from a passage in another letter of Mary's: "I forgot to ask you more particulars about Francis' leaving home on account of my father's projected marriage. I should much like to know what he said on the matter."[27] No word of all this found its way into the 1913 biography and a comment on that book by Mary is revealing. "The first pages, those concerning his life at home," she wrote to Meynell on reading the book, "and his departure thence, seemed to me a bit constrained, as if the writer had not said freely all he would like to say . . . he had a delicate task and has erred on the side of restraint . . ."[28] But three years previous to the publication of the *Life,* Everard, in an article on Thompson which he wrote for the *Dictionary of National Biography* in 1910, had openly stated that "His father's reproaches at his failure to earn a livelihood led him suddenly in November 1885 to seek his fortune in London."

There is no way to choose with certainty among these reasons, and the probability is that each played its part. But, in any case, there was a certain inevitability to it all; the situation had simply become too tangled for serenity. There was, too, a final barrier in the differing temperaments of father and son; they did not, then or afterwards, really understand each other. De Quincey has described the gulf that lay between him and his own unfeeling mother and his words apply with equal justice to Thompson's case: "My mother was predisposed to think ill of all causes that required many words; I, predisposed to subtleties of all sorts and degrees." A silent man, even if an ordinarily amiable one, the elder Thompson simply had the misfortune to be standing in the way of genius. Many years later, Mary Thompson, then a nun in a Manchester convent, while listening to a radio broadcast about her brother, in which the father was portrayed as dictatorial, exclaimed aloud before the assembled nuns: "It isn't true! Father was kind to him!"[29] The outburst was sincere. In a letter she had written nearly fifty years before, she indicated the lengths to which Dr. Thompson's patience and understanding had gone:

> To you I think I may speak without fear of misunderstanding, or of lessening your opinion of Frank—and it will show you how very unsuspecting we all were of anything wrong—how much we all trusted and loved Frank. You asked me if he had all he required at home, and I replied in the affirmative. But I did not say how often he asked for and was given money for use in connection with his studies, and which he never used for that purpose. Many a time he asked my father for £3 or £4 for dissecting fees; so often that my father remarked what a number of corpses he was cutting up, astonished somewhat, yet never doubting and always giving what Frank asked for. Then again, when going to London for examination, he was believed and trusted by us regarding the amount and mode of paying the fees required. Frank said he had to take it with him, £5 or £7—I forget exactly the amount. Of course, he must have used the money—I know it cost my father about £10 each time he went for his supposed examination. I feel sure he must have spent an amount on opium in those days even, though he probably expended some of the money on other things,

Thompson at the age of seventeen

such as cricket bats, balls, and wickets, music books, etc., which he brought home with the most wonderful tales of their having been given to him. Whatever he told us we believed. And I think that all these things he was never reproached with, unless in a general way when it was first found out.[30]

It was perhaps while remembering such things that Thompson later absolved his father of blame in the severance with home and family. After her brother's death, it was Mary who supplied out of her own heart, the last and most appropriate comment: "You ask me if I am not proud of bearing my brother's name," she replied to a question from one of the Meynells. "Yes, I am, but that pride is duly kept under control by the great pain which such talent caused both to him and to us."[31]

The dawn of the day following the fatal Sunday brought with it the solution of all problems at home: a note was found on Margaret's dressing table in which Thompson bade goodbye, saying he was on his way to London. It is usually affirmed that he went to the metropolis with no set purpose, but the significance of this "running away" as it is usually termed—inappropriately for a twenty-five-year-old man with a dozen years of higher education behind him—goes deeper than mere rebellion or hopeless retreat. Thompson may have not fully realized it himself, but his precipitate action was in reality a decision to return once more to the struggle for literary fame. He had, for more than a year, gone through a period of despondency, and then, in one desperate moment, had recommitted himself, impelled, as he said later, by his "latent belief in a destiny."[32] He knew instinctively that he could not continue at home, that he must strike out blindly into a world which would either mangle him or make him a poet, more probably both. He had, again, the example of De Quincey, who had also thrown himself in desperation upon London. "I set off on foot," related the older writer, "a favourite English poet in one pocket, and an odd volume, containing about one-half of Canter's *Euripides,* in the other." When Thompson crept out of the sleeping house he, too, had a favourite English poet—Blake—in one pocket, and a classic of the ancient world—Aeschylus—in the other.

As he trudged the ten cold, dark miles from Ashton to Manchester,[33] he must certainly have been aware of the beginning of a new phase of his existence; he undoubtedly understood the significance of his leaving home, and of its likeness to the drama of his predecessor's life. What he could not have foreseen was that he was indeed going down into the cruel jaws of London, "like some dreadful mouth of Acheron," and would suffer torments beyond the most terrible of De Quincey's dreams.

At length upon the lone Chorasmian shore
He paused, a wide and melancholy waste . . .
and silent death exposed,
Faithless perhaps as sleep, a shadowy lure,
With doubtful smile mocking its own strange charms

Alastor

3

THE LONE CHORASMIAN SHORE

THE INNOCENT LETTERING OF TWO THEATER SIGNS MOCKED THOMPSON'S arrival in the capital: *Dark Days* was announced at the Haymarket, while the marquee of the Olympia proclaimed *Alone In London*,[1] and the solitary young man could hardly have missed seeing both of them when he arrived in the West End about November 15. More than a week had passed since the argument with his father, but he had paused after reaching Manchester, and had lingered a few days in correspondence with home. It had at length been agreed that his train fare to London would be supplied, as well as a small weekly sum—enough for subsistence, but with nothing left over for opium. Thus, with a measure of support from a father who perhaps hoped that his son was at last showing some decision, Thompson made his entrance on the crowded stage of London.

One of his first acts was to inform his sister Mary where she was to send the weekly seven shillings, a reading room in the Strand, probably Gillig's.[2] His next must have been to look for a job since he seems to have quickly found work, although menial work, as a collector for a bookstore. Everard Meynell, who was familiar with the book business of the time, said that his first efforts at gainful employment "were made with a sackful of literature upon his shoulders, the day's orders of a general bookseller. His journeys would be laborious and slowly accomplished, and his turn in all probability the last served at the counters where he called out the list." Though the work was undemanding, and though such positions were rather easily obtained at one or another of the city's seven hundred bookstores, Thompson soon drifted from even this slight anchorage, as he had from the instrument maker and the encyclopedia firm. During the first half of 1886 he becomes an indistinct figure flitting through the noonday shadows of the bustling populace in pursuit of whatever odd jobs he could find, and subsiding in opium dreams into the gray evenings and the dark nights.

The Guildhall Library, the only free library in London at that time to which he could gain admittance, allowed him to feed his unabated desire for knowledge and imaginative release, but eventually even this door was closed on him. There has been a good deal of hand-wringing over this episode, beginning with Everard Meynell's "He was willing to tell of the poets he had read in the Guildhall library, until the police, being, as he said, against him, barred the entrance." But the truth is that libraries to which the public was allowed unrestricted access were a new and still rare thing in the London of the eighties. As soon as the Guildhall opened its doors in 1872 it had become the target of a large number of the town vagabonds, who found its hearty oak solitudes a pleasant haven from the streets. It was not unusual to encounter in the Guildhall a dozen ragged readers dozing behind their books or newspapers, and they were tolerated until their condition began to offend or interfere with serious patrons. Into this category Thompson fitted, and it must have been on some particularly threadbare and unwashed day that he was refused further admittance. The man who barred the way was a young attendant named Bernard Kettle, who later explained that Thompson "got into such bad straits, and was so poorly clad that it fell to my lot to have to perform the painful duty of asking him to forego his visits here. He always came in with two books in his pocket. One, I think, was Sophocles; and had I known that I was entertaining an 'angel unawares' I should perhaps have been more reluctant to reject him."[3] No revengeful fury descended on Kettle for his act, and in time he became head librarian.

If the libraries were closed to him, the museums and galleries were

not. He spent much of his time in the National Gallery where, surrounded by the world's great art, he was for a while able to forget
himself. Once, in frayed and wrinkled trousers and a bedraggled coat
that barely hid the soiled shirt underneath, he overheard two women at
the gallery, in puzzled discussion before Ghirlandaio's picture of Christ
pausing on the way to Calvary. He stopped and listened and at length
became so perplexed by the women's "exotic ignorance" that he burst in
with "Is it possible that you have never heard of Veronica? Do you not
know Our Lord is wiping his face with her handkerchief?" The women
looked at the speaker and drew back, and it was some moments before
Thompson realized that his appearance invalidated any information he
had to offer.[4] During this, or a similar visit he saw for the first time one
of Rossetti's best-known oils, *Ecce Ancilla Domini,* and was moved to
write a sonnet, as Rossetti himself had so often written sonnets on pictures.[5] Though the poem presupposes some knowledge of the picture, it
was a definite advance on anything he had done before, and shows that
poetry continued to struggle beneath the drugs and the gathering despair. In its picturesque handling of its religious theme, it also shows that
he had begun to come to terms with his artistic dilemma. Rossetti's
painting depicts the Blessed Virgin kneeling on her bed and staring
expectantly at a white-robed angel whose hand offers a lily, while a dove
is seen through a window in the background:

> This angel's feet, winged with aspiring light,
>   That kindles its own image in the floor;
> His gravely noble face, serene in might
>   From gazing on the Godhead evermore;
> This lily shining from the lilied hand,
>   Making a breath of heaven in the room;
> Yon dove, whose presence tells how near at hand
>   The mystical conception of her womb:
> Were these the things that roused from holy dreams
>   To holier waking the elected maid?
> Absorbed in all the great to-be she seems,
>   With pensive eyes that yet are not afraid.
> Soon her low voice shall ratify heaven's will,
>   And hell's gate groan, and death's stern heart
>   stand still.[6]

To his hopelessness there was soon added hunger and even exposure
when his bed had to be made out of doors, and his descent, though
gradual, was swift. Perhaps by July 1886 he was living wholly on the

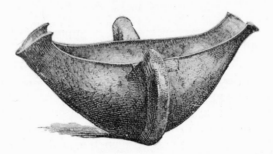

A sketch of the gold cup from Troy, the Amphicypellon *of Homer, which provided Thompson with the first title of* Sister Songs. *He saw the original in June, 1879, at the South Kensington Museum. (From Schliemann's* Ilios.)

streets and finding in his daily efforts only enough money to buy the necessary bottles of laudanum. Had it not been for a large-hearted, evangelistic Protestant he might have sunk too far beneath the surface ever to make his way upward again.

John McMaster, owner of a bootshop at 14 Panton Street, just off Leicester Square, and a prominent member of the church of St. Martin-in-the-Fields, occasionally offered a chance for rehabilitation to some unfortunate of the streets who happened to catch his eye. A number of times he had noticed Thompson—perhaps in the Square or on the Strand or even passing the shop—his frail hands proffering boxes of matches for sale. At last, in early August, McMaster spoke to the wan-faced young man, opening the conversation by inquiring if his soul was saved—and was met by the reply that he was speaking to a Catholic. His effective retort, no doubt developed out of similar encounters, was: "If you won't let me save your soul, let me save your body." After contacting the Ashton police and receiving assurances as to Thompson's background, McMaster found a room for his charge in Southampton Row, had him examined by a doctor, supplied him with fresh clothes, arranged for his daily food, took him into the shop to learn the bootmaking trade, paid him, in addition, the sum of five shillings a week, and noted with satisfaction that "He soon looked very different and he tried his best to please."[7] The arrangement lasted for six months but it was doomed to failure. The bootmaker at first was unaware of his charge's drug problem and eventually when the opium began to interfere with even the simple tasks that Thompson was assigned, McMaster let him go, later explaining: "It was impossible to keep him. I always said that he should be put away, put in a home."[8]

Before the break, however, McMaster attempted to reconcile Thompson and his family. Sometime in November he began a correspondence with Dr. Thompson which resulted in the father visiting London, accompanied by one of his daughters, probably Margaret, and it was arranged that Thompson should spend the Christmas holidays in Ashton.[9] Whatever feelings stirred in his heart on this return home are not known; perhaps he was wise enough to anticipate no change in the circumstances that had originally driven him away. And that is what seems to have taken place: "Other members of the Thompson family were adepts, like Francis, in reserve, and it was practised rigorously during his holiday . . . he volunteered no account of himself and was asked for none."[10] His father's upcoming remarriage, however, must have been talked of, since it had been scheduled for April 1887. Dr. Thompson, even at sixty-two still tall and straight and considered nearly handsome, had been a widower for six years. With his two daughters reaching an age where they would be making plans of their own (Mary had already decided to enter the convent) his long friendship with a thirty-three-year-old spinster named Annie Richardson, sister of a friend, had turned toward marriage. If Thompson had had any thoughts of resuming his life in Ashton, the presence of Annie Richardson would probably have discouraged him.

The months at Panton Street were probably the most important in Thompson's life to this time. While there, he expanded his efforts to include prose, and it was by his prose that he first won attention. Through McMaster, it is known that he wrote continually, both in the shop's slack periods, and evenings in his own room—where his employer took particular notice of a crucifix that hung over the bed.

Thompson's first real attempt at prose was the essay, *Paganism Old and New.* In this he contended, somewhat narrowly, that the ancient world knew little of true poetic sensibility despite the nostalgic appeal that some modern poets had imparted to it. It was Christianity, he claimed, that made sensibility flower in men's hearts. The idea had probably been caught from De Quincey's *Modern Superstition,* but in working it out he followed his own typical bent. He showed that in describing womanly beauty the ancient world tended to grossness, almost never referring, especially, to the spiritual power of women's eyes. To support the contention, this lonely, drug-captivated youth made casual allusion to Aeschylus, Sophocles, Homer, Cicero, Horace, Virgil, Tibullus, Catullus, Propertius, Ovid, Martial, Pliny, Statius, and Juvenal, and against these, balanced quotations from Chaucer, Morris, Rossetti, Tennyson, Wordsworth, Shelley, Coleridge, De Quincey, and Collins, as well as some random remarks of Heine and Blake—all from memory. The style of the essay is pure, unhurried artistry: "On the wings of Christianity came the great truth that Love is of the soul, and with the soul coeval . . . passion, in putting on chastity, put on also tenfold beauty. For purity is the sum of all loveliness, as whiteness is the sum of all colours." The beauty seen by moderns looking back toward Greece and Rome, he insisted, was largely a delusion:

Bring back, then, even the best age of Paganism, and you smite beauty on the cheek. But you *cannot* bring back the best age of Paganism, the age when Paganism was a faith. None will again behold Apollo in the forefront of the morning, or see Aphrodite in the upper air loose the long lustre of her golden locks . . . But you may bring back . . . the Paganism of . . . much philosophy and little belief . . . of poetry singing dead songs on dead themes with the most polished and artistic vocalization . . . of Vice carefully drained out of sight, and large fountains of Virtue springing in the open air . . . This is the Paganism which is formidable, and not the antique lamp whose feeding oil is spent, whose light has not outlasted the damps of its long sepulture . . . could Paganism indeed grow supple in her cere-cloths and open her tarnished eyes to the light of our modern sun—in that same hour the poetry of Paganism would sicken and fall to decay. For Pagan Paganism was not poetical.

Thus, on bits and scraps of paper, in evenings and odd moments, he doggedly fashioned his essay. It would have been a satisfying perform- ance for an established classical scholar composing at leisure in a well- stocked library; it was a remarkable accomplishment for a youth of twenty-six writing with the energy of despair. And it yielded, moreover, an unexpected dividend. Preoccupation with the topic of women's eyes quickened his own inspiration, and produced the first real sign of a poetic power above the ordinary, *Dream Tryst*. Closely modeled on Rossetti's *Insomnia*, these verses give off echoes of the *Willowwood* sonnets and the *Blessed Damozel* as well, but it is not unlikely that the poem's immediate inspiration was an actual dream, perhaps stimulated by a meeting with Lucy Keogh during his Christmas sojourn in Ashton a few weeks before.

There was no change in her sweet eyes
Since last I saw those sweet eyes shine;

There was no change in her sweet heart
Since last that deep heart knocked at mine.
Her eyes were clear, her eyes were Hope's
Wherein did ever come and go
The sparkle of the fountain-drops
From her sweet soul below . . .

Together, *Paganism Old and New* and *Dream Tryst,* along with another short poem, *The Passion of Mary,* which he had begun before leaving home, opened for him the doors to publication. That these were all written, or completed, while he was under the care of McMaster is something to be remembered in the bootmaker's favor at the moment when he finally tells Thompson he must relinquish even the simple security of the shop.

On his return to London from Ashton, Thompson stopped off in Manchester and seems to have indulged in an opium debauch (did he perhaps meet some friends of the habit from his earlier days?) and when he eventually arrived at the shop on Panton Street, began to display "periodic visitations of much more than customary uselessness . . . He would grow very restless and flushed, and then retire into an equally disconcerting satisfaction and peace of mind."[11] McMaster was aware of the drugs by this time, and he said later that he tried to influence Thompson to stop the practice, but without success. In a drugged state, Thompson caused a number of accidents in the shop, once injuring the foot of a customer, and by mid-January he was again adrift on the London pavements.

The departure from McMaster affected him almost as had the departure from his own home. If not exactly fond of the bootmaker, he certainly felt the beginnings of affection as well as deep gratitude, and now McMaster, too, had failed him. In his immediate bewilderment he wrote home for money, and when it came: "With a few shillings to give me breathing space, I began to decipher and put together the half-obliterated manuscript of 'Paganism'. I came simultaneously to my last page and my last half-penny. . . . Next day I spent the half-penny on two boxes of matches and began the struggle for life."[12] Toward the end of February 1887, he dropped a packet of manuscript into the mailbox of a small Catholic magazine on Essex Street, just off the Strand, giving as his return address the *Poste Restante* at Charing Cross Post Office. He waited in small hope, and when the weeks lengthened into months without an answer he ceased to call for his mail. When, finally, a letter of acceptance was sent from the magazine he had disappeared into the London underworld.

Thompson at the age of nineteen.

II

The unfortunates of the streets have always had ways of earning the few pence needed for daily subsistence. In Thompson's time it included such things as hawking newspapers and boxes of matches, helping to unload baggage at hotels, calling cabs for theatergoers and holding the reins of carriage horses (for which, of course, opportunities were many in the pre-automobile nineties). To this level he now descended. By the summer of 1887 he was just another haggard face in the city's drifting horde of derelicts.

The mere fact that he stayed alive shows that he acquired the necessary knowledge in such ways of existence, but there were many days and nights, as he later admitted, during which hunger and homelessness invested his life with unspeakable misery. He published no specific recollections of those days, and the details of such a hopelessly haphazard and unfamiliar existence must always remain largely unknown. But in the pages of Jack London's *The People of the Abyss* it is possible to conjure up the Thompson of the streets again, moving like a shadow among the other outcasts. Jack London, in order to gather an eyewitness account of destitution in the British capital, in the summer of 1902 spent some weeks tramping the streets as a down-and-out American sailor. His investigations took him over much of the city and one night in particular he spent in the heart of the West End, sleeplessly traversing the same ground that Thompson had paced little more than a decade before him. The simple directness of his description of that one night affords a picture, unavailable elsewhere, which helps to strip away the spurious veil of romance that has settled over this part of Thompson's story.

"To carry the banner," means to walk the streets all night; and I, with the figurative emblem hoisted, went out to see what I could see. Men and women walk the streets at night all over this great city, but I selected the West End, making Leicester Square my base, and scouting about from the Thames Embankment to Hyde Park. The rain was falling heavily when the theatres let out, and the brilliant throng which poured from the places of amusement was hard put to find cabs. The streets were so many wild rivers of cabs, most of which were engaged, however; and here I saw the desperate attempts of ragged men and boys to get a shelter from the night by procuring cabs for the cabless ladies and gentlemen. I used the word "desperate" advisedly, for these wretched, homeless ones were gambling a soaking against a bed; and most of them, I took notice, got the soaking and missed the bed. Now, to go through a stormy night with wet clothes, and, in addition, to be ill nourished and not to have tasted meat for a week or a month, is about as severe a hardship as a man can undergo. Well fed and well clad, I have traveled all day with the spirit thermometer down to seventy-four degrees below zero—one hundred and six degrees of frost; and though I suffered it was a mere nothing compared with carrying the banner for a night, ill fed, ill clad, and soaking wet.

The streets were very quiet and lonely after the theatre crowd had gone home. Only were to be seen the ubiquitous policemen, flashing their dark lanterns into dark alleys, and men and women and boys taking shelter in the lee of buildings from the wind and rain. Piccadilly, however, was not quite so deserted. Its pavements were brightened with well-dressed women without escort. But by three o'clock the last of them had vanished and it was then indeed lonely. At half-past one the steady downpour ceased, and only showers fell thereafter. The homeless folk came away from the shelter of the buildings, and slouched up and down and everywhere in order to rush up the circulation and keep warm . . . Now, said I, to myself; consider that you are a poor young man, penniless, in London Town, and that tomorrow you must look for work. It is necessary, therefore, that you get some sleep in order that you may have strength to look for work and to do work in case you find it. So I sat down on the stone steps of a building. Five minutes later a policeman was looking at me. My eyes were wide open so he only grunted and passed on. Ten minutes later my head was on my knees, I was dozing, and the same policeman was saying gruffly, "Ere you, get outa that!" I got. And . . . I continued to get; for every-time I dozed a policeman was there to route me along again . . .

Later on I was passing Hyde Park with a young boy of fourteen or fifteen, a most wretched looking youth, gaunt and hollow-eyed and sick. "Let's go over the fence," I proposed, "and crawl into the shrubbery for a sleep. The bobbies couldn't find us there." "No fear," he answered, "There's the Park guardians and they'd run you in for six months . . ." Among those who carry the banner, Green Park has the reputation of opening its gates earlier than the other parks, and at a quarter-past four in the morning, I and many more entered Green Park. It was raining again, but they were worn out with the night's walking, and they were down on the benches and asleep at once. Many of the men stretched out full length on the dripping wet grass, and, with the rain falling steadily upon them, were sleeping the sleep of the exhausted.

Thompson suffered through many such sleepless nights passing the dark hours in some doorway, on benches beside the Thames, or huddled out of the rain and snow under the arches of the bridges that spanned it. He scarcely needed the aid of laudanum for some unpublished lines he wrote while on the streets, and entitled *The Owl*. There is little poetry in them but much anguish of body and soul.

> The owl has eyes that bicker and gleam,
> And a hooked foul nose as may well beseem;
> And she laughs out loud with a whooping note,
> She laughs out bale from her rusty throat;
> Why doth she laugh from her rusty throat?
> She laugheth at sleep that sleepeth not.

> The Owl is the witch of the cauldron of sleep;
> And she stirs it and seeths it whooping deep;
> And she thrusts the witch-bits into it deep,
> Gendering ghosts for the smoke of sleep.
> She flings in toads from the money-dust,
> And feeds it thick with the dead fat of lust;
> Corpse-limbs of love, yet quivering new;
> And blood of the thoughts that are writhing too,
> Drawn from the place where the pang went through:

Adders of longing and fanged regrets;
Winged lizards of terror and monstrous threats—
Ah, horrible terrors, the withering threats!
And she sees with her eyes which the fires look through
Her deep sleep-cauldron, reeking new;
And she laughs at sleep, tu-whit, tu-whoo!

And so murk is the sleep-smoke of despair,
And so awful the spectres rising there,
And so fearful they throng on the calm night air,
That were not sleep as brief as deep,
It were better almost to die than sleep![13]

The awful specters were remembered. In a later book review, written in the clean comfort of a lodginghouse, he confesses that he has never been able to throw off the more terrible aspects of his dereliction: "Misery cries out to me from the kerb-stone, despair passes me by in the ways: I discern limbs laden with fetters impalpable, but not imponderable, I hear the shaking of invisible lashes, I see men dabbled with their own oozing life." With the greatness of the English tongue reverberating in the upper regions of his mind, he shrank from the dead and deadening speech of his street acquaintances, men and boys who had "almost lost the faculty of human speech; who howl and growl like animals, or use a tongue which is itself a cancerous disintegration of speech." Their conversation, he said, was impossible to describe. Even in Rabelais there was only a pale echo of it, "for there, sheer indecency is alloyed with humour, wit and other extraneous qualities: but here you have it in all its naked bestiality; its fusty, frowzy, stinking, essential, fat repulsion."[14]

There were, obviously, many days on which hunger was as much a burden as sleeplessness; days which saw not even one penny come into his hand. If there did happen to be sixpence gained from holding a horse, calling a cab, or running an errand, it was as often spent for a few ounces of laudanum as for food. It was on one such day of total penury that he found two golden sovereigns lying in the gutter, and the experience remained vivid in his mind for many years, later supplying him with one of his more memorable images. While walking along the crowded sidewalk he heard a clink on the pavement and looked down to see a coin rolling in the gutter. He picked it up thinking it was a bright new halfpenny and, when no one stepped forward, put it in his pocket. Wandering back the same way a few minutes later he saw another coin in the same place, picked it up and discovered it was a golden sovereign.

Excitedly he looked at the first coin: "That was a sovereign, too, Evi; I looked and saw it was a sovereign too!" Perhaps he was remembering this windfall, and the brief period of comfort that must have followed it, in his subsequent description of the Brownings: ". . . no poet was so mated afterwards, until Browning stooped and picked up a fair-coined soul that lay rusting in a pool of tears." (Was there remembrance of some more horrible street incident in another striking phrase: ". . . as though one stirred a fusty rag in a London alley, and met the eyes of a cobra scintillating under the yellow gas-lamp"[15]?)

He did not spend every night on the streets. When money was available he slept in a cheap bed in one of the city's many doss houses. A graphic description of these hovels occurs in *The People of the Abyss:*

> There are many kinds of doss-houses, but in one thing they are all alike, from the filthy little ones to the monster big ones . . . life in them is degrading and unwholesome. "The poor man's hotel" they are often called, but the phrase is a caricature. Not to possess a room to one's self, in which sometimes to sit alone; to be forced out of bed willy-nilly, the first thing in the morning; to engage and pay anew for a bed each night; and never to have any privacy, surely is a mode of existence quite different from that of hotel life . . .
>
> The little private doss-houses, as a rule, are unmitigated horrors. I have slept in them and I know; but let me pass them by and confine myself to the bigger and better ones. Not far from Middlesex Street, Whitechapel, I entered such a house, a place inhabited almost entirely by working men. The entrance was by way of a flight of steps descending from the sidewalk to what was properly the cellar of the building. Here were two large and gloomily lit rooms, in which men cooked and ate. I had intended to do some cooking myself, but the smell of the place stole away my appetite, or, rather, wrested it from me; so I contented myself with watching other men cook and eat.
>
> One workman, home from work, sat down opposite me at the rough wooden table, and began his meal. A handful of salt on the not over-clean table constituted his butter. Into it he dipped his bread, mouthful by mouthful, and washed it down with tea from a big mug. A piece of fish completed his bill of fare. He ate silently looking neither to right or to left nor across at me. Here and there, at the various tables, other men were eating, just as silently; in the whole room there was hardly a note of conversation. A feeling of gloom pervaded the ill-lighted place . . .
>
> I paid fivepence for a "cabin" and took my receipt for the same in the form of a huge brass check . . . To get an adequate idea of a floor filled with cabins you have merely to magnify a layer of the pasteboard

pigeonholes of an egg-crate until each pigeonhole is seven feet in height
and otherwise properly dimensioned. Then place the magnified layer on
the floor of a large, barnlike room, and there you have it. There are no
ceilings to the pigeonholes, the walls are thin, thin, and the snores from
all the neighbors and every move of your nearer neighbors come too
plainly to your ears. And this cabin is yours only for a little while. In
the morning out you go . . .

It must have been the "little private" doss houses that Thompson
knew best, and some of his later scribblings afford a depressing mealtime
glimpse into one of them:

> as beasts at feed,
> With a grudging, sidelong eye
> Disallow interruption—so these,
> With a slant and sullen eye
> Mark and not reck,
> Munching . . .[16]

When neither food nor bed was available, he would, along with the
other derelicts, often gravitate to one of the recently established Salvation Army shelters, or the Catholic Refuge in Providence Row. It was of
the latter place that Thompson supplied, evidently from his own experience, a harrowing picture: "The nightly crowd of haggard men . . .
the anxious waiting while the ticket-holders are slowly admitted; the
thrill—the almost shudder—through the crowd when the manager
emerges to pick out men for the vacant beds left over after the ticket-
holders' admission, the sickening suspense and fear in all the eyes
as—choosing a man here and there—he passes along the huddled ranks,
the cold clang with which the gates of mercy shut in those fortunate few,
but out the rest; and then the hopeless, helpless drifting off of the dreary
crowd . . ."[17] Some slight notion of who these other men were, and of
the incidents and people who filled up these interminable months, can be
gotten from the terse jottings here and there in his notebooks: "A thief
and . . . worse. 'Publicans and harlots before you.' Only once anyone
tried to cheat me. Mont. Williams workhouse, little girl outside Maiden
Lane. Reuben May. Doctor and his mode of breakfasting. My two ladies.
Murderer. Policeman who aided me. Little girl in the snow."[18] How
long a period of such doss-house misery and actual street suffering
Thompson endured remains uncertain—it was at least six months, perhaps as much as eight or nine—but the worst of it came to an end
when he was rescued from some particularly dire situation by one of the

army of harlots that infested London's West End. With this nameless prostitute he eventually entered a more or less steady relationship.

In his published work Thompson makes a number of cryptic allusions to the girl, of which the best known, veiled but memorable, occurs in *Sister Songs:*

> Then there came past
> A child; like thee, a spring-flower; but a flower
> Fallen from the budded coronal of Spring,
> And through the city streets blown withering.
> She passed—O brave, sad, lovingest, tender thing!
> And of her own scant pittance did she give,
> That I might eat and live

The first real acknowledgment of the part she played was made by Wilfrid Meynell in his obituary of Thompson. After quoting the above passage, he comments, "And how shall that final episode be turned more explicitly? There are still a few things left that cannot be uttered." But he could not hold back entirely: "This untold story transcends the mere romance of De Quincey's Ann, and might, indeed, for a moment modify Rossetti's lament over the life of 'Jenny.' "[19] When the 1913 biography was issued the story took on more substance, but the facts, meager enough, were carefully diffused throughout the narrative. Readers of the Meynell biography usually do not fully realize that Thompson, in fact, lived with this girl, and even refused for a time to part with her. It was probably while he was in some precarious position of extreme hunger and weakness that her aid came to him, and thereafter they met frequently until they became daily companions. "When the streets were no longer crowded with shameful possibilities," wrote Everard Meynell, "she would think of the only tryst that her heart regarded, and . . . would take her beggar into her vehicle at the appointed place." They would drive to the girl's lodgings in Chelsea where they "sat marvelling that there were joys for them to unbury and to share." It is not known just when they met, but Thompson would have had knowledge of many such women, and it is most likely that the two first came together in the late summer of 1887, after he had been some six months out of Mc-Master's.

In alluding to the girl, both Everard Meynell and his father used interestingly similar terms. The latter, in his obituary article, hinted that she enjoyed some sort of regeneration, "took root and flourished even in London mire, and again the fragrant petals unfolded, and the greenery grew." The son is more specific: "Weakness and confidence, humility and reverence were gifts unknown to her except at his hands, and she repaid them with graces as lovely as a child's." There is a curious passage in a fragmentary playlet by Thompson, never published, which comes so close to the sense of those remarks, that it can be taken as almost certainly modeled on actual memories. It helps to explain—if an explanation is needed—the attraction that held them together. In the extract, Quintus is Thompson:

> "But my brave girl," said Quintus, half in admiration, half in suspicion, "What motive could you have for aiding my designs? Neither in face nor form, Venus knows, am I a captivator of women; and I will aver that I do not know myself to have ever done you service."
>
> "Why do I love you, you ask?" she replied; her cheeks kindling with animation, her eyes suffused and softening; while, as she grew in passion her voice gradually rose and rang. "Why do I love you? *You;* love *You?*" The infinite tenderness of that simple iteration it is impossible to describe. "Because you are the only Roman I have seen in all this Rome who has a heart for a woman; because you are the only Roman in all this Rome who has spoken to me with human kindness, who has looked at me with eyes as if I were aught else than a chattel or an ease to lust; because you only have smiled at me in no other thought than one of gentleness and kindness; because you are the only gentle Roman in all this hard, hard Rome! And you ask me why I love you, love you, love you!" She stopped for a moment, choked by her flooding words and the mounting passion of her sobs. Quintus stood confused, astonished, moved beyond his conception . . . "Is it wonder then if I love you . . . Who besides yourself would have shown courtesy to a bondwoman, unless for an odious reason? You say you are not beautiful. I do not know how other women may see you—to *me* you are beautiful, for your face is all sweetness . . ." Recovering herself she stood before him blushing, timid, ashamed of her momentary boldness, a woman from head to toe.[20]

The possible erotic aspects of the relationship have intrigued, puzzled, or embarrassed all Thompson's admirers, beginning with Wilfrid Meynell himself. Most have felt it necessary to assure readers that the friendship was a pure one, with no admixture of sexuality. Such naïveté reached rather pathetic extremes with the solemn declaration of a Protestant clergyman, who interrupted his study of the religious content of Thompson's poetry to insist that "If there is anyone who supposes that there was anything low in the desperate friendship of that poor girl and this child of genius, and sniffs evil here, I must simply regard him as a lewd fellow of the baser sort."[21] Few, if any, of the people who have written on Thompson have cared to be regarded as lewd or base and the legend of platonic cohabitation usually passes uncontested. But the truth appears to be otherwise.

Everard Meynell, it must be pointed out, is the only one who did not feel it necessary to insist on Thompson's purity, but that fact has been obscured for fifty years. In the 1913 biography he boldly stated that, in the evenings at her lodgings with Thompson, the girl would "cherish him with an affection maidenly and motherly, and passionate in both these capacities." This could scarcely have been more explicit, and passionate associations hardly ever give rise to platonic friendships. At least once, Thompson allowed regret over some sexual transgression to creep into his poetry, though it may be doubted whether he ever intended the lines for publication. Again, it was Everard Meynell who, quite unnecessarily, put the piece into print:

> Not all kisses, woe is me!
> Are kissed true and holily.
> Not all clasps; there be embraces
> Add a shame-tip to the daisies.
> These if, O Dear Christ, I have known
> Let all my loveless lips atone.

Why daisies? Was Thompson thinking, perhaps, of the daisies he had toyed with as a child in Ashton? Did he mean that the "shame-tip" had soiled

> The garment of the grace
> I wove you when I was a boy.

Another set of lines, in the blank verse, *Orison-Tryst,* so well captures a moment of intimate knowledge that its author almost certainly must have had experience of it at first hand:

> Oh! I was then
> Like one who, dreaming solitude, awakes
> In sobbing from his dream; and straining arms
> That ache for their own void, with sudden shock
> Takes a dear form beside him . . .

In *Memorat Memoria,* written a few years later, at a time when he had become involved with another girl, he makes rather obvious allusion to sexual contact with the girl of the streets, referring to her "fragrant self" and her "soft arms." But a draft of that poem—which is really a cry of regret over fleshly transgressions—contains some lines even more to the point:

> A girl's kiss through my soul strikes echoes of ominous sin;
> I shall never feel a girl's soft arms without horror of the skin;
> At the breath of her hair, as a phantom, mine shall creep;
> You have done this to me—and I to you? It lies with Sleep.[22]

The legend of Thompson's unimpaired innocence derives directly from Wilfred Meynell, and the solicitude of this man has combined with the wishful thinking of later writers, especially among the clergy, who were, in any case, not overly anxious to probe the matter. There is one interesting bit of evidence, however, that tends, even by itself, to establish Thompson and the girl as at least occasional lovers.

The only Thompson poem which frankly treats a sexual theme is *Love Declared*. This is one of the eight poems in the sequence *A Narrow Vessel*, known to have been written about 1894–95, six years after he left the streets. But, while seven of the eight poems in the sequence were actually written at the time supposed, *Love Declared* was not—it was written, in its first form, in 1889, less than a year after he parted from the prostitute. The fact is proved by the existence of a small manuscript sheet containing an early version of *Love Declared*, in conjunction with the verses *To a Dead Astronomer*, written in December 1889, and a portion of the Shelley essay, on which he was working in the latter part of the same year. The handwriting, the ink, and the aging of the sheet show that all three pieces belong to the same period.[23] Shorter than the later version (though it may be only a part of a whole now lost) this 1889 manuscript contains these lines:

> Time's beating wing dropped down, and all the winds
> Caught up their breath, and the world's mighty pulse
> Stopped in mid-throb, the roaring train of life
> Reeled past, and left the stranded moment bare;
> Love newly alit a statued rapture stood
> Carved from a fair white silence—save alone
> Within our shaken hearts the air of passion,
> Cleft by his sudden coming, eddied still
> And whirred round his enchanted movelessness.

Such a deft description of the climax of physical love could scarcely have arisen from pure imagination; perhaps it is enough to remember that shortly before he wrote these lines he had been living, intimately if perhaps intermittently, with a prostitute. It is unlikely, however, that there was any permanent or binding arrangement. The girl was not his mistress, in the usual sense, and his whole subsequent life makes it clear that he never accepted such a way of life as right or in any way normal. She was, quite simply, his last hold on existence. It is the ultimate irony that she may also have been the cause of a final rupture with his family.

III

Dr. Thompson married Anne Richardson on April 27, 1887, in Ashton, at which time the son had been back on the streets perhaps three months. He did not attend the wedding, though he must have been told of the coming event during his holiday at home, and surely must have been invited. So much may be taken for fact; now arises conjecture. It is difficult to believe that, in all the months after Thompson left Mc-Master's bootshop, his father simply permitted him to slip out of sight, permitted his son to drift into ultimate oblivion. Yet up to the present such has been assumed. All biographers, beginning with Everard Meynell, leave the impression that Dr. Thompson, after his son's Christmas visit, washed his hands of any further concern in his welfare. But that he did not cast his son off, that he in fact went in search of him in London, is the claim of May (Mary Gertrude) Richardson, the niece of Dr. Thompson's second wife. Dr. and Mrs. Thompson, she insisted, soon after the wedding went to London to look for Thompson because he had not shown up for the ceremony and nothing had been heard from him in so many months. She could not recall precisely when they went, or if they had found him, though she was inclined to believe they had: "If Everard Meynell had inquired he would have discovered this and put it in his book," she insisted.[24] Miss Richardson shared her house with her "Auntie Annie" for a period of seven years, sometime after the death of Dr. Thompson, and claims that she heard the story many times, not only from her aunt but from Thompson's sister, Mary, as well.

If Dr. Thompson and his new wife really did go to London in mid-1887 what did they find? They would certainly have gone to McMaster's shop as the last point of contact—McMaster himself said that the poet often passed the shop in Panton Street after he left it, and it must be remembered that Thompson continued to frequent the same portion of the city as he had before.[25] Under these circumstances it is highly probable that Dr. Thompson would have found his son, and the most tantalizing question of all then becomes urgent: did Dr. Thompson's journey coincide with the time of his son's liaison with the prostitute? Some answer to that question can be provided only by indirection.

It is a fact that father and son met only once, briefly, during the six or so years in which the son enjoyed a reputation as a poet, though the two were for long periods no more than a few miles apart.[26] It is a fact that when Thompson died not one relative went to London to view his body or attend his funeral. His second sister, Margaret, who emigrated to Canada, married, and later moved with her family to Los Angeles, always kept her relationship to her poet-brother a secret, and when she died in Los Angeles in 1949, the press discovered for the first time who she was.[27] Her daughter, presently a nun in a Canadian convent, has commented frankly, "Yes, my mother did prefer to keep secret her relationship to my uncle. I think her reason was because her family considered him a failure and rather a disgrace."[28] It is also a fact that in 1891 Dr. Thompson changed his will to give precedence over Francis to the newly born son of the second marriage, and though he left one hundred pounds to his daughter Margaret, he bequeathed nothing at all—out of a gross estate probated at £1500—to the boy who had caused him such long-continued anguish.[29] This situation appears very much like total rejection and it argues some powerful cause beyond any presently known biographical fact. Did Dr. Thompson in London perhaps come upon a parent's nightmare: his son, already a drug addict, living with a prostitute?

These things may have happened. There is no direct proof that they did.[30] But the final act in the tragedy of Thompson's London sufferings, for which there is evidence, was still to be played out though on a stage but dimly lit.

Early in 1888, all hope gone, and with guilt and regret tearing at his spirit, he reached the nadir of his street existence—and there crept into his mind the whispered invitations of Death. The desperate self-loathing that burdened him at this time, making suicide possible, was thrown into some stark verses entitled *Nightmare of the Witch-Babies*,[31] an obvious allegory on himself and his prostitute friend. Sick horror rises from the lines like odor from carrion. They were never published and today it is just possible to decipher the faded scrawl of the manuscript. Though the versification is inept and the thought murky, the poem is one of the very few documents surviving from his time on the streets, and the full gruesomeness of the piece can be felt only by reading all twelve stanzas.

Two witch-babies,
  Ha! Ha!
Two witch-babies,
  Ho! Ho!
A bedemon-ridden hag,
  With the devil pigged alone
Begat them, laid at night
  On the bloody-rusted stone;
And they dwell within the Land
  Of the Bare Shank-Bone,
Where the Evil goes to and fro,
  Two witch babies, ho! ho! ho!

A lusty knight,
  Ha! Ha!
On a swart steed
  Ho! Ho!
Rode upon the land
  Where the silence feels alone,
Rode upon the land
  Of the Bare Shank-Bone,
Rode upon the Strand
  Of the Dead Men's Groan,
Where the Evil goes to and fro.
  Two witch-babies, Ho! ho! ho!

A rotten mist,
  Ha! Ha!
Like a dead man's flesh,
  Ho! Ho!
Was abhorrent in the air,
  Clung a tether to the wood
Of the wicked looking trees,
  Was a scurf upon the flood;
And the reeds they were pulpy
  With blood, blood, blood!
And the clouds were a-looming low.
  Two witch babies, ho! ho! ho!

No one life there,
  Ha! Ha!
No sweet life there,
  Ho! Ho!

But the long loud laugh,
  And the short shrill howl
And the quick brisk flip
  Of the hornèd owl,
As he flits right past
  With his gloomy cowl
Through the murkiness long and low.
  Two witch-babies, ho! ho! ho!

    What is it sees he?
      Ha! ha!
    There in the frightfulness?
      Ho! ho!
There he saw a maiden
  Fairest fair:
Sad were her dusk eyes,
  Long was her hair;
Sad were her dreaming eyes,
  Misty her hair,
And strange was her garments flow.
  Two witch-babies, ho! ho! ho!

    Swiftly he followed her,
      Ha! ha!
    Eagerly he followed her,
      Ho! ho!
From the rank, the greasy soil,
  Red bubbles oozed and stood;
Till it grew a putrid slime,
  And where his horse has trod,
The ground plash plashes,
  With a wet too like to blood;
And chill terrors like a fungus grow.
  Two witch-babies, ho! ho! ho!

    There stood the maiden;
      Ha! ha!
    Shed all her beauty,
      Ho! ho!
She shed her flower of beauty,
  Grew laidly old and dire,
Was the demon-ridden witch,
  And the consort of Hell-fire:
"Am I lovely, noble knight?

See thy heart's own desire!
Now they come, come upon thee, lo!"
Two witch-babies, ho! ho! ho!

    Into the fogginess,
      Ha! ha!
    Lo, she corrupted!
      Ho! ho!
Comes there a Death
  With the looks of a witch,
And joints that creak
  Like a night bird's scritch,
And a breath that smokes
  Like a smoking pitch,
And eyeless sockets aglow.
    Two witch-babies, ho! ho! ho!

    Close behind it
      Ha! ha!
    Ah! close behind it!
      Ho! ho!
Comes there a babe
  Of bloated youth,
With a curdled eye
  And a snaggy tooth,
And a life—no mortal
  Dare speak its sooth;
And its tongue like a worm doth show,
    Two witch-babies, ho! ho! ho!

    Its paunch a-swollen
      Ha! ha!
    Its life a-swollen
      Ho! ho!
Like the [illegible] days drowned.
  Harsh was its dream
And its paunch was rent
  Like a brasten drum;
And the blubbered fat
  From its belly doth come
With a sickening ooze—Hell made it so!
    Two witch-babies, ho! ho! ho!

It leaps on his charger,
Ha! ha!
It clasps him right fondly,
Ho! ho!
Its joints are about him,
Its breath in his bones;
Its eyes glare in his,
And it sucks up his groans:
He falls from his horse,
He burns on the stones,
And his mail cracks off in a glow.
Two witch-babies, ho! ho! ho!

Its tooth in his shoulder,
Ha! ha!
His skin dully champing,
Ho! ho!
Slimed like a snail
With that loathly thing,
His own self writhèd him
With shuddering;
His gaze grew dark
And his soul took wing
While his breath still kept its flow.
Two witch-babies, ho! ho! ho!

The picture is clear enough: armored, as a knight, with pure ideals and high ambition, Thompson comes to London, but is soon lost in "a rotten mist" of unnamed corruption, and from this he is rescued by a maiden with "dreaming eyes," who, however, is quickly discovered to be "the consort of Hell-fire." Then, tuberculosis, with "eyeless sockets aglow" and drug addiction, with "a curdled eye and a snaggy tooth," attack him and he ceases to care about ideals or ambition as the mail of his integrity "cracks off." The last stanza sighs against this living death, and Thompson seems to be asking why, if his soul has taken wing, he should continue to breathe. The poem, as it now exists, may not be complete, but the tendency of it is certainly towards self-destruction. And it is now admitted that he did, at least once, make such an attempt.[32]

The means he chose was a massive dose of laudanum, the nineteenth century's commonest weapon of suicide. As Thompson himself told the story to Wilfrid Meynell, he bought a large amount of the drug one night and went to the deserted space behind Covent Garden to take it.

Interior of the Guildhall Library at the turn of the century.

But he did not carry through his purpose, and, fittingly, it was his constant habit of literary association that saved him. Either before he put the bottle to his lips, or after he had taken some (he was familiar with the action of laudanum and knew that his stomach might reject too great a quantity all at once) there flashed on his mind the picture of Thomas Chatterton doing the same thing in the same city a century before. The recollection that help had arrived for Chatterton the day after his fatal act, forced some awareness of reality back into Thompson's clouded mind. In telling Meynell of the incident later, however, Thompson looked on it more as an actual vision, perhaps even a ghostly interposition of Chatterton's spirit. That, in any case, is how Wilfrid Meynell retold it: "He had swallowed half when he felt an arm laid on his wrist, and looking up he saw Chatterton standing over him and forbidding him to drink the other half. I asked him when he told me of it how he had known that it was Chatterton. He said 'I recognised him from the pictures of him—besides I knew that it was he before I saw him—and I remembered at once the story of the money which arrived for Chatterton the day after his suicide.' "[33] Thus the thronging host of English poets, always more real in Thompson's mind than the people he passed in the street, had at last sent some recompense. Dazed by the drug, shaken by the realization of how near he had come to death, he turned away from Covent Garden and drifted once more into the dark labyrinth.

As one that in a silver vision floats
Obedient to the sweep of odorous winds
Upon resplendent clouds

Alastor

4

UPON RESPLENDENT CLOUDS

THE NARROW, FOUR-STORY BUILDING AT 43 ESSEX STREET, JUST OFF the Strand,[1] in addition to a bookstore at street level, contained the offices of a small Catholic literary monthly named *Merry England*. Its editor, thirty-five-year-old Wilfrid Meynell, also conducted *The Weekly Register,* a chatty, work-a-day Catholic paper for the laity, published under the auspices of Cardinal Manning. *Merry England* had been in existence for four years, and though unpretentious had managed to achieve a certain respect in Catholic circles. Within its self-imposed limits, it offered its readers an approach to literature and the arts unusually liberal for the Catholicism of the time. Thompson had seen copies of it before leaving home, and once while on the streets, finding an issue in a secondhand stall which he liked, had parted with a few precious pence to obtain it.[2] It was into the mailbox of this magazine that he had dropped the packet of manuscript in February of 1887.

Meynell must have gone through the mail containing Thompson's material within a few days, but after opening the package and reading the short covering letter, had only glanced at the soiled manuscript of the essay, noted the cramped handwriting that covered both sides of each sheet,[3] then put it aside for later perusal. He had once explained that when a manuscript was not read the reason was that "the editorial eye, which is . . . practiced in gauging at a glance the quality of literary work,"[4] had given a summary decision, and there could have been little in Thompson's manuscripts to intrigue the editorial eye; it is remarkable that the material was preserved at all, especially since it was unsolicited. Something in the covering letter, no doubt, struck Meynell with just enough force to slow his galloping pace. Written on a small piece of paper, about four and a half inches square, it looks suspiciously as if it had been cut from the flyleaf of a book.[5] The handwriting is tiny and neat:

February 23/87

Dear Sir,

　　In enclosing the accompanying article for your inspection, I must ask pardon for the soiled state of the manuscript. It is due, not to slovenliness, but to the strange places and circumstances under which it has been written. For me, no less than Parolles, the dirty nurse Experience has something fouled. I enclose a stamped envelope for a reply; since I do not desire the return of the manuscript, regarding your judgment of its worthlessness as quite final. I can hardly expect that where my prose fails my verse will succeed. Nevertheless, on the principle of "yet will I try the last," I have added a few specimens of it, with the off-chance that one may be less poor than the rest. Apologizing very sincerely for my intrusion on your valuable time, I remain,

Yours with little hope,
Francis Thompson

Kindly address your rejection to
the Charing Cross Post Office.
The Editor of "Merry England."

Perhaps the casual reference to Parolles raised a flicker of interest, perhaps the hint about "strange" circumstances, perhaps the forlorn dismissal of a rejected manuscript; Meynell himself has recorded nothing on the point. Two facts, however, stand out: the note was not a haphazard thing; rather, it seems to have been carefully composed, with an eye to brevity and even a certain degree of mystery; and he was

Thompson's first letter to Wilfrid Meynell, submitting an essay and some poems.

primarily offering, not the poetry, but the prose. It was the prose, as it turned out, that interested Meynell.

All would have been well, and Thompson's story might have been very different, his sufferings curtailed, if Meynell had been moved to read the material when it first arrived at his office. Not only would a year and a half of misery have been avoided, but the entire episode with the prostitute, and even, possibly, the final falling out with his family would never have occurred. But then *The Hound of Heaven* almost certainly would never have been written. All unaware of the consequences that would flow from the simple act, Wilfrid Meynell stuffed the essay and the poems into a pigeonhole with other doubtful things to await a more leisurely moment.

II

Perhaps no home in all of London was better suited to be a haven for Thompson than the Meynells', no family was so well equipped to appreciate and foster his genius. In Wilfrid Meynell and his wife, Alice, there came together the literature of both the secular and the religious worlds, and each was given wide expression in an impressive whirl of talent and industry. From his first meeting with them in 1888 to the end of his life these two would be the center of Thompson's existence.

Wilfrid Meynell was born at Newcastle-on-Tyne in 1852, of Quaker parents, and very early inclined to both literature and religion. At eighteen he converted to the Catholic faith, entirely on his own, and by the time he was twenty was publishing poetry. About 1875 his ambitions took him to London where he soon worked his way to the center of Catholic journalism. He had quickly realized that his literary vein was neither deep nor original, though he did discover in himself a high degree of journalistic facility and an industry above the ordinary. He met Alice in 1877, and they were married the following year. In time, he came to the attention of Cardinal Manning, who in 1881 offered him the chance to edit the *Weekly Register*. The paper was to be totally his own, but he was also expected to derive his main income from it, and he had, at that time, three children to feed. One factor that decided him was his eminent fitness for the position; he was almost the prototype of the ideal editor. Buoyant and genial, of wide-ranging interests and with a compulsive love of work, he also possessed a sympathetic heart, a ready ear, and a spirit from which streamed encouragement and enthusiasm. "I know of no man," recalled his son, "and can imagine none, to whom another can so easily unburden himself of uneasiness and formalities." Another factor, certainly, was his wife's ability and willingness to make a large contribution to both writing and editing.

Alice Meynell, née Thompson, (no relation to Francis) was born in 1847, to parents who were close friends of Charles Dickens. Her father, of independent means, traveled much during her early life, a circumstance that greatly fostered her intellectual and emotional precocity. With Alice, too, a passionate interest in both literature and religion had shaped her youth. At twenty she became a Catholic—for a time going so far as to live under a strict rule of mortification—and at the age of twenty-seven published her first book of poems, *Preludes,* which included the well-known pieces *Renouncement* and *Letter from a Girl to Her Own Old Age.* It received high praise, generally, most impressively from Ruskin and Rossetti. She possessed abilities that, while they fell decidedly short of genius, were unique in style and outlook and in time she developed into one of the most sought-after literary personalities of the era. No one on meeting her remained unimpressed, though the impression was not always entirely favorable.

She moved in a peculiar blend of natural elegance and studied graces, and everything about her seemed consciously controlled. Her emotions she kept under a tight rein. Anger, for example, she deliberately robbed of its spontaneity, explaining, in a rare personal comment, that it was "when I am angry that I pretend to be angry so as to present the truth in an obvious and intelligible form." Her laughter, high and light, was something to be spun out pleasingly though not too frequently. "It would be a pity," she once coolly observed, "if laughter should ever become, like rhetoric and the arts, a habit." Never, not even in the privacy of her own home did she relax the vigil, and her daughter Viola's recollections carry a still half-incredulous note when she says that the children through all the crowded days of childhood "had never once seen her unfinished or unprepared." Somehow, she managed to wrap the preciosity in a saving sweetness and the total effect was not infrequently attractive, especially to susceptible young literary men. Richard Le Gallienne, for a time a frequent visitor to the Meynell house, described the general effect: "There was the charm of a beautiful abbess about her with the added *esprit* of intellectual sophistication . . . However quietly she sat in her drawing room of an evening with her family and friends about her, her presence radiated a peculiarly lovely serenity." The picture is softened slightly by John Drinkwater who remembered her as witty, generous, and simple, attentive to family cares and gossip as well as high-toned literary conversation.[6]

Occasionally—but only occasionally—the veil was swept aside and friends caught a glimpse of something sterner. Katherine Hinkson, one of her closest friends and intensest admirers, said that, "if she was not a saint she might have been intellectually intolerant. Sometimes, indeed, it flashed; for a moment one saw that she *might* have been arrogant."[7] The truth is that both the personality and the talent arose from the same source. In her writings, as in her manner, she seldom looked directly at life, but seemed always to be gazing beyond its fringes, discovering the charm and significance in little things. Once, while in search of essay material, she went for a ride on a London omnibus and later reported the day's events to her absent husband. One sentence in the letter forms perhaps the best brief comment on both her personality and her literary quality: "There was little to note. There was, however, the dreadful incident of a man's cutting his throat on the pavement in Shoreditch. I took note of London steeples . . . ."[8] She was extravagantly eulogized in her own day and is unduly neglected now. When Thompson first knew her she was just beginning to gather an unusual, if narrow, popularity.

In 1880 the couple founded a small literary review, *The Pen*,[9] which did not last but which broadened their associations in literary circles. In 1881 Wilfrid took over *The Weekly Register* and two years later founded *Merry England*. Husband and wife not only wrote for and edited both periodicals, but wrote and edited wherever they could find acceptance. Family connections as well as professional ones brought them acquaintance with many of the leading literary figures of the day: Browning and Tennyson, for example, as well as Aubrey de Vere, Coventry Patmore, and Sir Henry Taylor, and through them they made posthumous contact with some of the great spirits of the previous age, Wordsworth and Coleridge, Carlyle, Mill, and Thackeray. Through all this Alice longed to meet someone who had known Shelley, and in the first year of her marriage had a "memorable" visit from his daughter-in-law; later the two met Shelley's son and smiled to hear him refer to "my poor father."[10] When Thompson came into the Meynells' lives they were living at Phillimore Place in Kensington and their home had already become one of the intellectual centers of London, especially on Sunday afternoons. "Calling at that house meant arriving about half-past three, staying till midnight, and meeting in the course of the year most of the literary folk worth knowing," one of the regular guests long afterwards fondly remembered.[11]

III

Everard Meynell, in the first edition of the *Life* asserts that Thompson's manuscripts lay unread in the *Merry England* office for six months. His father, on reading this, insisted the time was nearer six weeks, forgetting that he had earlier written of the period as extending for about three months.[12] Everard solved the problem by deleting all mention of time from the revised edition of the *Life,* but the most careful scrutiny of surrounding events suggests that the period was about three months, and that Wilfrid Meynell took his first unhurried look at Thompson's poems and essay in mid-June 1887. In a fit of housecleaning, as he said later, he was consigning unwanted material to the flames, giving each item only sufficient attention to establish its worthlessness, when he came to Thompson's envelope and read the poems and the essay "with growing astonishment."[13] Within a few days Mrs. Meynell had looked the material over and agreed with her husband that it was eminently publishable, especially the essay on Paganism.

It has always been assumed that the poems sent were *Dream Tryst* and *The Passion of Mary,* but it is probable that there were more than two poems in the package. A jotting by Everard Meynell, written in the course of researching his life of Thompson, affords a clue to at least one other: "Told by AM: At 21 Phillimore Place, Mother read in bed the dirty ms. of Paganism and along with it some witch-opium poems which she detested . . ."[14] This allusion to "witch-opium poems" does not fit either *Dream Tryst* or *The Passion of Mary,* but it does fit *The Nightmare of the Witch-Babies,* already quoted. The ragged bitterness of his feelings in this poem has smothered the poetry, leaving only the naked recoil of feeling, and it may very well, as the Meynells suspected, have been written under the influence of drugs. The fact that it was submitted at all seems to argue that Thompson was still somewhat in an opium haze at the time. But "the sanity of the essay was proof enough of the inspiration of genius" and a letter was sent to the Charing Cross Post Office inviting Thompson to call to read proof.

By this time, of course, Thompson had surrendered to despair and had stopped inquiring for mail. The uncalled-for letter remained at the Charing Cross Post Office during the summer and about September–October was finally returned to the *Merry England* office as undeliverable. Wilfrid Meynell made casual inquiries, thereafter, in whatever

Wilfrid Meynell about the time he and Thompson first met.

publishing quarters he thought the name of Francis Thompson might be known, but there was little he could do. The young C. L. Hind remembered being told in the autumn of 1887 by Meynell that "a Francis Thompson sent some things of which Alice and I think very highly . . . but . . . we cannot trace him."[15] By this time Thompson was living with the girl of the streets, of course, and was thus occupying perhaps the one position totally inaccessible to Meynell's search.

By the beginning of the new year of 1888, Meynell decided to publish one of the poems as a possible way of bringing the author to the surface. *The Passion of Mary,* six Crashaw-like quatrains on the sorrows of the Virgin, simply but felicitously phrased,[16] was tailor-made for Eastertime and he scheduled it for the April issue. Thompson had written this poem before leaving home in 1885; the *L'Envoy* he probably added just before sending it to *Merry England,* and in his eyes it must have seemed more like prayer than poetry:

> O thou who dwellest in the day!
>   Behold, I pace amidst the gloom:
> Darkness is ever round my way
>   With little space for sunbeam-room.
>   . . .
> O light in Light, shine down from Heaven!

The April issue of *Merry England* reached its subscribers during the third week in March, and very soon after, Father John Carroll, a family friend stationed near Ashton, was in touch with Thompson, informing him of the publication of *The Passion of Mary,* encouraging him to visit the *Merry England* office, and sending a small sum of money to tidy himself up.[17] On April 14 Thompson wrote to Wilfrid Meynell:

Dear Sir,
    In the last days of February or the first days of March, 1887, (my memory fails me as to the exact date) I forwarded to you for your magazine a prose article, ("Paganism, Old and New," or "Ancient and Modern," for I forget which wording I adopted) and accompanied it by some pieces of verse, on the chance that if the prose failed, some of the verse might meet acceptance. I enclosed a stamped envelope for a reply, since (as I said) I did not desire the return of the manuscript. Imprudently perhaps, instead of forwarding the parcel through the post I dropped it with my own hand into the letter-box of 43 Essex Street. There was consequently no stamp on it, since I did not think a stamp would be necessary under the circumstances. I asked you to address your

answer to the Charing Cross Post Office. To be brief, from that day to this, no answer has ever come into my hands. And yet, more than a twelve-month since the forwarding of the manuscript, I am now informed that one of the copies of verse which I submitted to you (i.e. "The Passion of Mary") is appearing in this month's issue of "Merry England." Such an occurrence I can only explain to myself in one way; viz. that some untoward accident cut off your means of communicating with me. To suppose otherwise,—to suppose it intentional—would be to wrong your known honour and courtesy. I have no doubt that your explanation, when I receive it, will be entirely satisfactory to me. I therefore enclose a stamped and addressed envelope for an answer, hoping that you will recompense me for my long delay by the favour of an early reply. In any case, however long circumstances may possibly delay your reply, it will be sure of reaching me at the address I have now given.

I remain,
Yours respectfully,
Francis Joseph Thompson

P.S. Doubtless, when I received no answer, I ought to have written again. My excuse must be that a flood-tide of misfortune rolled over me, leaving me no leisure to occupy myself with what I regarded as an attempt that had hopelessly failed. Hence my entire subsequent silence.[18]

The letter was written, most likely, in the Chelsea rooms of his friend, but he avoided giving that address; the envelope he included for a reply bore the name of a chemist's shop in Drury Lane, a three-minute walk from the *Merry England* office. On receiving the letter, Meynell immediately wrote an explanation of what had happened, inviting Thompson to call for pay and to discuss further work. The note was sent by special messenger to the chemist's shop, but "the chemist's manner of accepting responsibility for the safe delivery of the letter was discouraging. He said that Thompson sometimes called for letters but that he knew little of him," which was not quite the truth since it was at his shop that Thompson bought laudanum and the chemist certainly was aware that his seedy customer was an addict.[19] After some days of silence, Meynell himself walked the few blocks between his office and the chemist's shop, to be met by an invitation to pay a Thompson debt of three-and-ninepence. He paid the money and promised an additional reward if the chemist succeeded in producing Thompson. It was "many days later" that Thompson finally materialized, and the most likely explanation for his continued non-appearance is a drug debauch undertaken with the money sent by Father Carroll, a supposition strengthened by the fact that when he did arrive at Essex Street his clothes were in the last extremity of disrepair. It was mid-May when Wilfrid Meynell, alone in his office, was told that Francis Thompson wished to see him. "I was at work in my office . . . when the door opened. A shadow of a figure half-appeared, and the door was shut again. The door was opened again, with somebody hesitating to enter, and was shut again. I got up, opened it, and there was Thompson, frightened to come in."[20] Thus Francis Meynell quotes the story he heard many times from his father. Everard's account in the *Life* is similar, describing Thompson as "a waif of a man . . . more ragged and unkempt than the average beggar, with no shirt beneath his coat and bare feet in broken shoes." The trepidation, the urgent hope, the fear of failure that gripped Thompson standing outside that door were later remembered in verse:

> Like one who sweats before a despot's gate,
> Summoned by some presaging scroll of fate,
> And knows not whether kiss or dagger wait;
> And all so sickened is his countenance
> The courtiers buzz, "Lo, doomed!" and look at him askance:—
> > At fate's dread portal, then
> > Even so stood I, I ken,
> Even so stood I, between a joy and fear,
> And said to mine own heart, "Now, if the end be here!"[21]

The nonplussed editor, faced with impressive literary erudition swathed in rags, offered his caller a seat and, at a loss for something to say, could only mutter, "You must have had access to many books when you wrote that essay." Thompson, the shyness dropping suddenly from him, replied in a tremulous voice that was unexpectedly deep: "That is precisely where the essay fails. I had no books by me at the time, save Aeschylus and Blake." Throughout the interview Thompson maintained a certain reserve, and Meynell felt that little was accomplished at this first meeting. He offered Thompson a small weekly sum, enough to give him food and a bed in order that he might spend his time writing, but this was refused (Thompson was not actually on the streets, of course, he was living with the girl and his threadbare condition, most probably, was the result of a recent opium debauch). Thompson revealed nothing of his circumstances or background, but agreed to the publication of *Paganism* in the June issue of *Merry England,* and to return within a few days to read the proofs of the essay. Meynell, however, soon knew all about his visitor; Edward Healy Thompson, discovering the name of his nephew in *Merry England,* wrote to the magazine on May 25, frankly revealing some of the background of "your poetical contributor," and asking Meynell to extend help to the wayward young man: "If you come across him you might be able to be of service to him in the way of kindly sympathy and advice."[22]

With money in his pocket, Thompson left the Essex Street office, and that night in the Chelsea room told his friend of the happy developments; "I always knew you were a genius," said the girl.[23] He was more than that. He was a man of singular power of intellect and secret strength of personality; he emerged from his time of trial with his moral and intellectual powers intact, and "neither his happiness, nor his tenderness, nor his sensibility had been marred . . . His spirit rose from the penal waters fresh as Botticelli's Venus."

During June and July Thompson continued to visit Meynell at the *Merry England* office and sometimes at his home in Phillimore Place, "where he was persuaded to bathe,"[24] but he remained reticent about his history and did not respond with enthusiasm to the gentle efforts to coax him into a more settled way of life. Even a visit to Bishop Henry Vaughan, arranged in the hope of gaining high-placed encouragement, did not move him. He seems to have written nothing during these weeks, but only compiled for Meynell a sampling of the finished poems in his possession, about thirty in all.[25]

In reality, rescue had brought with it a crisis of another sort: he was faced with the necessity of breaking off his relationship with his friend of the streets and of leaving her to the hopeless continuation of her sordid existence. The girl herself had quickly recognized the inevitable. "They will not understand our friendship," she had told Thompson, with some understatement, soon after his first visit to Meynell; he must leave her, she said, and go to them. But Thompson could not bring himself to abandon the girl who had for so long stood between him and utter desolation, even death. It was the girl herself who resolved the situation, disappearing without a word and without a trace. She sacrificed her own chances for rescue in order not to jeopardize Thompson's—but her gift was more than mere life, it was immortality, for in fleeing from Thompson she created the emotional matrix in which was born the first idea for *The Hound of Heaven.* It is perhaps to this fact that Thompson refers in a touching sonnet not published until long after his death:[26]

> Who clasp lost spirits, also clasp their hell;
>   You have clasped, and burn, sad child, sad Semele!

One half of my cup have you drunk too well,
    And that's the death; the immortality
Girt in the fiery spirit flies your lip.
    That to my deathless progeny of pain
You should be mother, bear your fellowship
    I' the mortal grief, without the immortal gain!
Not only I, that these poor verses live,
    A heavy vigil keep of parchèd nights;
But you for unborn men your pangs must give,
    And wake in tears that they may dream delights.
        What poems be, Sweet, you did never know;
        And yet are poems suckled by your woe!

In Greek mythology Semele, a mortal, was the lover of Zeus, and mother by him of Dionysius. Semele's one wish was to behold Zeus in all his glory, but when she did so immediately perished. In this sonnet, Thompson pictures his friend of the streets as the mother of his poetry, and laments the fact that the "glory" of his success has torn them apart and sent the girl to her obscure doom.

It was Everard Meynell who first glimpsed the connection between *The Hound of Heaven* and Thompson's search for his friend during August–September 1888, as well as an ultimate link to De Quincey's *Daughter of Lebanon,* which had been inspired by a similar search for a lost prostitute-friend.[27] His allusions to these things, though brief and a shade too casual, leave the distinct impression that he is drawing on conversations with Thompson himself. That Thompson did search anxiously for his friend is known, "nor would he leave the streets, thinking that in doing so he would make a final severance." That De Quincey also thus searched for his Ann, Thompson knew from the *Confessions,* and during these hectic days his memory more than once may have called up De Quincey's words: "Where was she? Whither had she gone? According to our agreement I sought her daily, and waited for her every night, so long as I stayed in London . . . She had few acquaintances; most people, besides, thought that the earnestness of my inquiries arose from motives which moved their laughter or their slight regard . . . All was in vain." In one of De Quincey's more impassioned passages regarding Ann in the *Confessions* can be seen the first miniature design of his *The Daughter of Lebanon,* and at a more distant remove, *The Hound of Heaven:*

O youthful benefactress! how often in succeeding years, standing in solitary places and thinking of thee with grief of heart and perfect love—how often have I wished that, as in ancient times the curse of a father was believed to have a supernatural power, and to pursue its object with a fatal necessity of self-fulfillment, even so the benediction of a heart oppressed with gratitude might have a like prerogative; might have power given it from above to chase, to haunt, to waylay, to pursue thee into the central darkness of a London brothel, or (if it were possible) even into the darkness of the grave, there to awaken thee with an authentic message of peace and forgiveness, and of final reconciliation!

Somehow, during these closing months of 1888, the montage of pursuit and flight in Thompson's mind found answering echoes among the great traditions of a pursuing God—traditions expressed in such documents as the *Confessions of St. Augustine,* the Psalms, especially Psalm 138, and the medieval verses, *Quia Amore Langueo,* perhaps also the *Dio Amore* of Silvio Pellico. It was in this welter of disparate but converging thoughts that the first idea for *The Hound of Heaven* was generated. The only existing reference by Thompson to the process is an autobiographical note of uncertain date: "At this time visited me the rudimentary conception of *The Hound of Heaven* . . . It was a very rudimentary conception with nothing like the scope it later took to itself: but I felt it great in suggestion—too great for my present powers of execution. Fortunately I shrank from executing it . . ."[28] Suffering malnutrition, under a daily necessity for opium, and with incipient tuberculosis sapping his strength, he was in no condition to attempt such a work. It is even likely that the idea itself was too vague to permit condensation into poetry; the heavenly pursuit had not yet found the necessary image—the hound—around which to crystallize. That crystallization would not occur for another year, and when it did, the impetus for it would come, appropriately enough, from Shelley.

Perhaps by mid-October Thompson had accepted the fact that the girl had vanished for good, but like De Quincey with Ann, he did not forget her. "Often since, I have longed to encounter her," he confided many years later, "to thank her for that graciously delicate whisper which brought such healing to my hurt, indignant heart. But I never shall, till the Day which evens all debts. It is not like that these lines will ever have meeting with her sweet, sad eyes. Could that be, I would desire she might read in them a gratitude which passes speech and the accumulated silences of many years."[29] As with De Quincey, too, the girl often haunted his dreams, and in *Memorat Memoria* he writes of meeting her "dear and dreadful face," in the "passes of Sleep." The girl was never found, nor was her name ever discovered, but a far echo of the poignant episode was sounded in 1933 when a play written around the

Alice Meynell.

incident was presented on the London stage, and Wilfrid Meynell, then over seventy, said in an interview, "One of the possibilities which has a fascination for me is that she might pass the theatre, and seeing the name of the poet on the bills, might go in and find herself, by one of the strangest transformations in history, a recognized heroine of London's literary life. Such a discovery might make it well worth while for her to have lived into her sixties."[30]

Alone, Thompson became more amenable to Meynell's offers of help. He allowed himself to be examined by a doctor, who reported that Thompson was near total physical collapse, a condition which might be hastened if the opium were denied him, but "the risk was taken, and Francis was sent to a private hospital"; to keep him busy more than anything else, he was given a book of essays to review for *Merry England.* The stay in the hospital covered perhaps six weeks and the trials of withdrawal that he underwent can be known only through his verse. It was probably in October, while still in the hospital, that he wrote *Not Even In Dream,* a direct reference to the opium which he had given up.[31]

This love is crueller than the other love:
  We had the Dreams for Tryst, we other pair;
But here there is no *we;*—not anywhere
  Returning breaths of sighs about me move.
No wings, even of the stuff which fancy wove,
  Perturb Sleep's air with a responsive flight
When mine sweep into dreams. My soul in fright
  Circles as round its widowed nest a dove . . .

By December Thompson was out of the hospital, and living in lodgings, probably in Paddington, but visiting the Meynell house in Phillimore Place almost every day.[32] What he found in this home was what he had been searching for, in a way, ever since he left Ushaw, and he must have been as duly impressed by it as was another young Meynell protégé who remembered "the literary atmosphere, the papers and books and pictures, the various things that suggested foreign travel: the names that were spoken, the easy reference to people of thrilling interest."[33] In such surroundings Thompson began to flourish.

The book review he had written while in the hospital had grown into an article on Bunyan's *Pilgrim's Progress,* and Meynell was so pleased with it that he gave it the lead position in the November *Merry England,* entitling it "Bunyan In the Light of Modern Criticism." It was essential that Thompson be kept busy, Meynell knew, so a number of projects were discussed. The then current controversy over the English translation of Zola's *La Terre,* in which French realism had brought its English publisher nothing but headaches and a large fine, offered a timely subject, and Thompson produced a short piece called "The Error of the Extreme Realists," in which he declared that "art resides not in undiscerning comprehensiveness, but in discerning selection . . . Zolaism is not artistic completeness: it is artistic excess." It was a rather superficial effort, but it fitted well the policy of *Merry England.* He was given some poetry to review for *The Dublin Review,* a quarterly with which Meynell had a connection, was also at work on a short piece for *Merry England,* called "Literary Coincidence," and was completing the copying out of his existing poems. His main effort, at this time, however, was a long discussion of the poetry of Crashaw, which he began early in 1889, probably January. Meynell, it can be seen, was having the agreeable experience of discovering that his derelict possessed not only surprising literary erudition, but the ability to turn it into forceful prose as well. It could not have been long, in fact, before he saw that Thompson was precisely the kind of author he had in mind for *Merry England,* but which he probably never really hoped to find.[34]

In the matter of poetry, there was less reason for exultation. Toward the end of 1888 Thompson had turned over to Meynell the notebook in which he had copied the poems he thought worthy of consideration. There were thirty-two in all, written over an eight-year period. They showed unquestionable facility and taste, but were largely imitative and Meynell used only one: *Not Even In Dream.* He might have used others if the requirements of his magazine had been more flexible—the five poems on Rossetti, for instance, or possibly *Her Kiss,* and *Adversity.* In any case, it was undoubtedly the prose that most interested the busy editor, while the poetry was to be left to work itself out in occasional pieces. Neither Meynell nor his wife could have expected anything like the sustained singing that was to burst from Thompson within the next six months.

IV

The new year of 1889 seems to have brought with it some relapse into addiction and Meynell, in order to put an end to the temptations that abounded in London, suggested that Thompson might retire to a monastery in Sussex, where he would have the benefit of fresh air, the kindly solicitude of the monks, and isolation from drugs.[35] By this time the older man had assumed a fatherly authority, and Thompson readily agreed to go.

The monastery chosen was that of the Canons of Prémontré, in the village of Storrington, known as the Priory of Our Lady of England. Of French origin, the small group of monks had only one building for living quarters and a tiny chapel, nestled near Kithurst Hill on the South Downs. Little English was spoken, but that was no obstacle since Thompson's French was fluent. In February 1889 he arrived at the monastery, was given a room to himself on the top floor, and was soon reporting to his benefactor:

> I am, as I expected to be, very ill just now; so that you must excuse me if I confine my letter to what is necessary. In the first place, Mrs. Blackburn spoke of forwarding me some boots. If you can do so I should be very much obliged, for those I have are completely worn out. In the second place, principally owing to my boots being worn through,

my socks are likewise beyond repair . . . Can you send me a razor? I shall have to shave myself here I think, and it would, of course, be a saving of expense in the long run. Any kind of razor would do for me; I have shaved with a dissecting-scalpel before now. I would solve the difficulty by not shaving at all, if it were possible for me to grow a beard: but repeated experiment has convinced me that the only result of such action is to make me look like an escaped convict . . . I am not at present capable of writing; but it would be an absolute mercy to have any books. At present there is nothing to keep my mind from dwelling on itself. I may say I shall want even a Shakespeare for the *Dublin* article, since I believe they have not one here. I could easily find distraction for my mind there. And with regard to my illness there is nothing to be alarmed about. It is severer and more obstinate than I had hoped would be the case; but it is a mere matter of holding on. And in that kind of passive endurance I am well practiced. I daresay this week will see the end of it . . . I think I shall like this place when I begin again to like anything. The want of books is the principal drawback so far as I see at present. Let me say that I keep on my legs and force myself to go out as much as possible . . . Please accept my warmest thanks for all your kindness and trouble on my behalf. I know this is a very perfunctory-looking letter, but until the first sharp struggle is over, it is difficult for me to write in any other way. Once again, however, there is no cause at all for uneasiness on that account.[36]

Some dim notion of the sufferings that accompanied his courageous defiance of his addiction can be gathered from an autobiographical passage in a later essay, in which he makes veiled reference to a poet passing through a period of seclusion and interior gestation; it shows that his miseries included hallucinations. "On a day when the skirts of prolonged darkness were drawing off from him, he walked the garden inhaling the keenly langorous relief of mental and bodily convalescence; the nerves sensitized by suffering. Pausing in reverie before an arum, he suddenly was aware of a minute white-stoled child sitting on the lily. For a second he viewed her with surprised delight, but no wonder; then, returning to consciousness, he recognized the hallucination almost in the instant of her vanishing."[37]

Before he went to Storrington, his review of three books of poetry for the *Dublin Review* had earned him an invitation to submit further ideas, and agreement had settled on a discussion of *Macbeth*.[38] As soon as the "first sharp struggle" was over he was hard at work, and the lengthy closely reasoned article, replete with quotations, was finished by mid-May. With quiet exultation he reported his pleasure in the fact that he had been able to complete such a sustained effort: "At first I could not get on at all. I tried regularly enough to settle myself to writing; but my brain would not work. Then gradually, after long pushing, my brain slowly began to move. It has not gone very fast since, nor gone willingly, but I have been able to make it go regularly . . . If I have indeed begun to acquire the power of working in the teeth of nerves and mood and bilious melancholy, then the fight is half fought. And I think I have . . ."[39] Indeed he had. Very shortly after writing that letter he was at work on the *Ode to the Setting Sun*, the poem which would reveal a far loftier ability than anything indicated by his previous work.

He found the idea for the Ode in Coleridge's *Hymn Before Sunrise*, but it is possible that the immediate spark came from a rereading of his own essay on Crashaw which was written in January and which reached him at Storrington in the May issue of *Merry England*. There are obvious links between the essay and the Ode, especially in the discussion of Coleridge's "numerous versification," and the quoting of Crashaw's sun-images. By May he had reached a point of recuperation in which he must have been anxious to put his poetry to a real test: he had by then been without opium for five or six months, at least, and could write, moreover, in the comfortable knowledge that his work would receive serious attention. It was in such a receptive frame of mind that he heard one day at sunset the music of three itinerant musicians floating across the countryside, while he was standing beside a life-size crucifix in a field owned by the Priory. There stirred in him thoughts about his past life, about the hard novitiate demanded by his calling as poet, about his uncertain future, and as the lowering sun tinted the skies to multicolored hues over Kithurst Hill, he felt "soul, sky, and music bleed together." Under the shadow of the crucifix he began his Ode.[40]

> Alpha and Omega, sadness and mirth,
>   The springing music, and its wasting breath—
> The fairest things in life are Death and Birth
>   And of these two the fairer thing is Death.
> Mystical twins of Time inseparable,
>   The younger hath the holier array,
>   And hath the awfuller sway:
>   It is the falling star that trails the light,
>   It is the breaking wave that hath the might,
> The passing shower that rainbows maniple.
>   Is it not so, O thou down-stricken Day,
> That draw'st thy splendours round thee in thy fall? . . .

Composition occupied, altogether, perhaps a month, and was done mostly out of doors. Though the writing seems to have gone steadily, during that time he was not entirely free of "nerves and mood and bilious melancholy," a fact indicated by his interruption of the ode to dash off a sonnet in which he mentally writhes in the pains of opium withdrawal—though he cannot at the same time withhold expression of his wonder and awe as he realizes that true poetry has begun to flow from him: [41]

> . . . The pulses sicken, hearkening through the gloom.
> Afar the thunders of a coming doom
> Ramp on the cowering winds. Lo! at the dread,
> Thy heart's tomb yawns and renders up its dead,—
> The hopes 'gainst hope embalmèd in its womb . . .

As the ode progressed, the usual echoes from other writers slipped unnoticed into his lines; the Book of Job, Coleridge's *Hymn Before Sunrise,* and Henry Vaughan's *Vanities,* for instance, came together in the series of rhetorical "who" statements. Blake's *Tyger* crept into the lines:

> Who hast with life imbued
> The lion maned in tawny majesty,
>   The tiger velvet-barred,
>   The stealthy-stepping pard,
> And the lithe panther's flexous symmetry . . . ?

The meter, modeled on Coleridge's *Christabel,* through Thompson's deft orchestrations and careful fitting of sense to sound acquired nearly symphonic qualities. Seemingly pagan in spirit because of its fervent praise of the life-generating powers of the sun, as with Coleridge's *Hymn Before Sunrise* the real purpose of the Ode becomes apparent only in the closing lines:

> O blessed Sun, thy state
> Uprisen or derogate
> Dafts me no more with doubt; I seek and find . . .

> Thou dost image, thou dost follow
>   That King-maker of Creation,
> Who, ere Hellas hailed Apollo,
>   Gave thee, angel-god, thy station,
> Thou art of Him a type memorial.
> Like Him thou hang'st in dreadful pomp of blood
> Upon thy Western rood . . .

The sun, the most wonderful object in all of material creation, the

Storrington Priory. Thompson's room was on the third floor, extreme left. The buildings at the rear were added later.

Ode proclaimed, gave glory to God by its mere existence, and in its rising and setting symbolized daily the central facts of human life, the Crucifixion and the Resurrection. Perhaps inevitably, as he finished, his attention came back to himself and to the crucifix in whose shadow he had begun; he realized that, for him, at least, poetry had been born in sorrow:

> O, this Medusa-pleasure with its stings!
>   This essence of all suffering which is joy;
> I am not thankless for the spell it brings,
>   Though tears must be told down for the charmed toy.
>
> No; while soul, sky, and music bleed together,
>   Let me give thanks even for those griefs in me,
> The restless windward stirrings of whose feather,
>   Prove them the brood of immortality.

Sometime in July, while pacing the soft turf of Kithurst Hill and with the bright sun overhead, he completed the poem. Within a few days a fair copy was made and sent off to London.

The Meynells, busy with their wide-ranging journalism, and engaged as well in the construction of a new house,[42] were doubly unprepared for the Ode's splendor of imagery and easy mastery of phrase—though their astonishment was tempered by an occasional straining and a "violence of diction" evident in such phrases as "foizon in her tilth,"[43] as well as the almost frenetic rush of images. But the poem was ample proof that its author possessed ability of no ordinary kind. "It was a revelation," remembered Viola, and the Meynells, while on a visit to a nearby friend in July, went to the Priory at Storrington and voiced enthusiastic praise and encouragement to the young poet. The poem was inserted in the September *Merry England* accompanied by some remarks in which Meynell enthusiastically confessed that "An editor seldom has so great a literary pleasure as falls to my lot this month in giving to the public the Ode printed in the present number. Its appearance is nothing less than an event in the annals of English poetry . . . A singular personality in modern poetry is the young writer whose work—still perhaps in need of the recollection and dignity that will come in time—must needs be hailed with delight by Ushaw, and by the Professors to whom he owed his training." He was, of course, allowing too much to Thompson's Ushaw training; the religious spirit, the Catholic atmosphere of the poem had been acquired as much in his own home as at Ushaw.

Delighted and perhaps slightly overwhelmed by the chance that had brought him into relationship with a poet whom he had begun to regard as destined for greatness, Meynell now went a step further in seeking recognition for Thompson. Knowing that the circle of readers reached by *Merry England* was a narrow one, early in September he sewed together tear-sheets of the poems and the prose that had so far appeared in both *The Dublin Review* and *Merry England* and sent these makeshift booklets to various people, including both Tennyson and Browning, for comment.[44] Tennyson, just turned eighty, replied noncommittally through his son: "Thanks for letting us see the vigorous poems." The seventy-seven-year-old Browning, however, who had been something of a friend to the Meynells as well as a visitor in their home, replied warmly on October 7: "I hardly know how to apologize to you, or explain to myself how there has occurred such a delay in doing what I had an impulse to do as soon as I read the very interesting papers written by Mr. Francis Thompson and so kindly brought under my notice by yourself. Both the verse and the prose are indeed remarkable . . . Pray assure him, if he cares to know it, that I shall have a confident expectation of his success if he will but extricate himself—as by a strenuous effort he may—from all that must now embarrass him terribly . . ."[45] Scarcely two months later Browning was dead, and Meynell published the letter in the January 1890 *Merry England* as an example of the older poet's generosity toward an unknown writer. In thanking Meynell, Thompson was much struck by the idea "that in the closing days of his life my writings should have been under his eye, and he should have sent me praise and encouragement." Such notice from a poet whom Thompson—in opposition to much of the criticism of his time—unhesitatingly placed with the immortals, did much to blow away any last dark, lingering doubts about his surging ambitions.

A fragile lute, on whose harmonious strings
The breath of heaven did wander—a bright stream
Once fed with many-voicèd waves

Alastor

5

THE BREATH OF HEAVEN

MELANCHOLY WEIGHED FITFULLY ON THOMPSON THROUGHOUT THE long months at Storrington, finding now and then an outlet in both prose and poetry. It was a time of mingled joy and misery, as well as physical suffering, in which he could at one moment assure Meynell that he had learned to bear his fits of depression, and in the next cry out, "How good and kind and patient you are with me! Far more than I am with myself, for I am often fairly sick of the being that inhabits this villainous mud-hut of a body."[1]

Within a few days of completing the *Ode to the Setting Sun*, however, he began work on a short story, probably at the suggestion of Meynell, who wisely was not allowing his charge too much time in which to brood. Predictably, Thompson's own life furnished the theme of the story, and the style, also perhaps predictably, was a peculiar amalgam of De Quincey, Poe, Sir Thomas Browne, and even Oscar Wilde. The story, *Finis Coronat Opus*,[2] tells of a poet named Florentian who makes a pact with the Devil, in which he will be given fame as the leading poet of the realm, displacing a worthier rival, in return for the sacrifice of his sweetheart. In a surprisingly lurid scene, Florentian kills the girl by stabbing her to death, and the Devil keeps his promise. Later, half repentant that he has allowed literary ambition to interfere with more homely desires, Florentian insists that he has not lost all tender feelings:

> I met a child today; a child with great candour of eyes . . . She had been gathering wildflowers and offered them to me . . . I was inexpressibly touched and pleased, curiously touched and pleased. I spoke to her gently and with open confidence she began to talk . . . Of her school, her toys, the strawberries in her garden, her little brothers and sisters—nothing, surely, to interest any man. Yet I listened, enchanted. How simple it all was; how strange, how wonderful, how sweet . . . All this exquisiteness is among the commonplace of life to other men . . . like the daisies they trample under blind feet . . . knowing not what daisies are to him whose feet have wandered in grime . . .

Obviously allegorical in its picture of literary success bought at the price of normal life, the story is contrived and feverish and shows little promise of ability in the form, but the incident quoted was an actual occurrence, which gave rise to one of his most charming poems, *Daisy*.

He had made friends with a little girl of about seven or eight, named Daisy Stanford, one of nine children in a family that lived near the monastery, at Cootham. She and her sisters passed the monastery every day going to and from school, and Thompson sometimes walked with them. The girls spent much of their time in summer gathering berries on the South Downs in the vicinity of Kithurst Hill, and it was here one day, probably in August, in an unusually pensive mood, that Thompson encountered them in search of wild raspberries. "He helped me fill my basket, and child-like, any extra-fine one I got I'd give him to eat," Daisy recalled years later, adding that "I certainly did not know that I, as a child, had made any impression on him."[3] These unexpected moments of innocent companionship, precious to Thompson in his isolation, ended abruptly when the little girl left him to return home for the day. But she had caught him unawares, making his troubled heart "fly down to her little hand" and perhaps putting him in mind of the two sisters who had shared his own boyhood.

Storrington Chapel as it was in Thompson's day.

> She went her unremembering way,
> She went and left in me,
> The pang of all the partings gone
> And partings yet to be

The incident is interesting for reasons beyond the wistful poem it inspired, for it is one of the few times when Thompson can be glimpsed, so to speak, in his workshop. The emotional tone of *Daisy* is very touching, and to readers unfamiliar with Thompson's story it is effective, but it is out of all proportion to the incident it commemorates, and its strong Wordsworthian cast indicates a conscious and deliberate attempt at imitation. That he succeeded so well was a tribute to his growing artistic control; every reader of the little poem is put in mind of Wordsworth's "Lucy" verses, yet no exact echo can be traced.

The article on *Macbeth*, which appeared in the July *Dublin Review*, brought an invitation to submit further work, and by November, Thompson had decided to try an essay on Shelley, "Principally because I remember more of him than any other poet," as he explained to Meynell. But it is probable that he had more personal reasons for selecting Shelley as a subject, reasons that arose out of the brooding to which he had been prey ever since his arrival at Storrington. The texture of Shelley's genius he had always felt to be like his own, and in analyzing Shelley, he may have felt he would be looking into his own heart: if he could explain

Shelley, characterize him, capture his elusive spirit in words, then he would in some measure come to a better understanding of himself. A number of times in the essay a hint of just such an attitude comes to the surface. Treating the material circumstances of Shelley's life he remarks: "His lot was one that many a young poet might envy. He had faithful friends, a faithful wife, an income small but assured. Poverty never dictated to his pen . . . yet he wailed that he could lay down like a tired child and weep away his life of cares! Is it ever so with you, sad brother; is it ever so with me?" Discussing Shelley's ability to express the material and the immaterial in terms of each other, he declares that no poet could rival Shelley in this, and adds: "Hardly will any poet rival him as regards it in the future"—and twice during the writing of the essay he interrupted his work to attempt just such rivalry. Both *The Song of the Hours* and *Buona Notte* are so Shelleyan as to be hardly more than imitations. *The Song of the Hours,* especially, reveals his attitude at this time: directly inspired by the chorus of the Hours in *Prometheus Unbound,* which Thompson quotes in the essay, it contains many borrowings from Shelley's great work.

By mid-September he had begun the essay, and until the end of the year it was his main occupation. As it grew under his hand he felt the unmistakable surge of originality in its mounting levels of poetic prose and the audacity of its seething imagery. It was composed, he said later, "with quite agonizing pain and elaboration. It might have been written in tears and is proportionately dear to me."[4]

For several reasons this essay stands among the most important products of Thompson's genius, despite its unevenness. Parts of it deserve to rank with the best of De Quincey—particularly those that illustrate Shelley's aerial spirit—but too much of it betrays his immaturity. While it is inadequate as a rounded picture of its subject, it does make at least one valuable contribution to the understanding of Shelley: it demonstrates vividly the part played by the uninhibited, spontaneous enthusiasms of childhood in the shaping of his imagination, and shows how these qualities gave rise to the myth-making powers on which he drew for *Prometheus Unbound.* The notion of Shelley's childlikeness was not new, but Thompson did not merely state the idea, he succeeded in presenting it with compelling force. Both as man and as poet, he asserted, Shelley was essentially a child: "Know you what it is to be a child? It is to be something very different from the man of today. It is to have a spirit yet streaming from the waters of baptism; it is to believe in love, to believe in loveliness, to believe in belief; it is to be so little that the elves can reach to whisper in your ear; it is to turn pumpkins into coaches, and mice into horses, lowness into loftiness, and nothing into

everything, for each child has its fairy godmother in its own soul; it is to
live in a nutshell and count yourself the king of infinite space . . ."
Shelley, he explained, retained this idiosyncrasy of childhood even in
maturity, because his isolation at school had shielded him from the
abrasive experiences that usually modify the growing boy. At Oxford
"the encysted child developed until it reached years of virility . . .
then, bursting at once from its cyst and the university, it swam into a
world not illegitimately perplexed by such a whim of the gods." Only
from such a poet, thought Thompson, in which the heart of a child fed
its impulses into the brain of a man, could such luminous poetry come. A
phrase he had written earlier—"the king of infinite space"—came back
to him, suddenly and with penetrating suggestive force, as he attempted
to describe this unique union:

> Coming to Shelley's poetry, we peep over the wild mask of revolu-
> tionary metaphysics, and we see the winsome face of the child. Perhaps
> none of his poems is more purely and typically Shelleian than *The
> Cloud,* and it is interesting to note how essentially it springs from the
> faculty of make-believe. The same thing is conspicuous, though less
> purely conspicuous, throughout his singing; it is the child's faculty of
> make-believe raised to the nth power. He is still at play, save only
> that his play is such as manhood stops to watch, and his playthings are
> those the gods give their children. The universe is his box of toys. He
> dabbles his fingers in the day-fall. He is gold-dusty with tumbling amid
> the stars. He makes bright mischief with the moon. The meteors nuzzle
> their noses in his hand. He teases into growling the kennelled thunder,
> and laughs at the shaking of its fiery chain. He dances in and out of the
> gates of heaven; its floor is littered with his broken fancies. He runs
> wild over the fields of ether. He chases the rolling world. He gets be-
> tween the feet of the horses of the sun. He stands in the lap of patient
> Nature, and twines her loosened tresses after a hundred wilful fashions
> to see how she will look nicest in his song.

The finished essay ran to some ten thousand words; both the opening
passages and the closing ones were deliberate additions designed to make
his sympathetic view of Shelley more palatable to the Catholic audience
of the *Dublin Review.* Even with these passages, however, Thompson
was somewhat apprehensive in submitting it. "The sober, ponderous,
ecclesiastical *Dublin,* confronted with poetic prose," he ventured to
Meynell, "must be considerably scared. The editor probably cannot make
up his mind whether it is heavenly rhetoric or infernal nonsense." By
March of 1890, the Meynells had read it, pronounced it "splendid," and
sent it on to the *Review,* only to have it eventually rejected—a fate that,

The crucifix at Storrington Priory, beside which Thompson began his Ode to the Setting Sun.

considering subject and treatment, should have been anticipated. Though he carefully preserved the manuscript during the rest of his life, and even drew on some of its phrases for articles and reviews, he never again submitted it anywhere, and it was not published until after his death. Despite this, it occupies a central position in his career, for it was during the writing of it that the idea for *The Hound of Heaven* returned to him, finally to be vitalized in a mental atmosphere quickened by three months of freewheeling contemplation of Shelley's poetry. In the breathless originality of its cosmic passages, the essay is in reality Thompson's first quick sketch for *The Hound of Heaven*. It was the indispensable effort necessary to bring to the upper levels of conscious art the latent concepts of flight and pursuit that his search for the girl of the streets had generated.

II

Toward the end of 1889, while he was finishing the essay, and with his mental and physical well-being to some extent restored, Thompson began to feel increased dissatisfaction with the rustic atmosphere of

Storrington. "The removal of the opium," he explained later, "had quite destroyed my power of bearing the almost unbroken solitude in which I found myself."[5] With his imagination heated to a continuous glow by his work on the essay, and hungry for intellectual companionship, he gruffly dismissed his stolid Sussex neighbors as "sprung from the illicit union of a mowing machine and a turnip . . . If this were the condition of man before the Fall—O! maligned Eve, blessing on thee!"[6] Hills and trees denuded by winter, the sunless sky, he felt were all incapable of healing ministrations. Country life had begun to pall on him, and nature, he felt, spoke only as an echo: "You think you hear the throbbing of her heart, and it is the throbbing of your own." Beside a pond near the Priory, which had become one of his favorite haunts, he sat one evening in December working on another essay. In it he describes his surroundings and his mood:

> As I write, a calm, faint-tinted evening sky sinks like a nestward bird to its sleep. At a little distance is a dark wall of fir-wood; while close at hand a small group of larches rise like funeral plumes against the tranquil sky, and seem to say "Night Cometh." They alone are in harmony with me. All else speaks to me of a beautiful, peaceful world in which I have no part. And did I go up to yonder hill, and behold at my feet the spacious amphitheatre of hill-girt wood and mead, overhead the mighty aerial *velarium*, I should feel that my human sadness was a higher and deeper and wider thing than all.[7]

It was on a day in December, perhaps on just such a day as he here describes, that he began to write *The Hound of Heaven*.

For more than a year the elements of the poem had floated freely in his subconscious. Now and then during the preceding months, individual images had broken loose to find tentative expression in the lesser poems and some of the prose,[8] but it was not until he made the daring leap to the concept of God as a relentlessly pursuing cosmic hound that everything fell into place. It was the totally unprecedented coupling of this animal with the notion of a jealous God that struck life into the dormant idea. Though he had no precise scriptural or traditional warrant for such boldness, he could point to approximations, similar though more conventional, in early church writings[9]—still, it was a concept that succeeded only through the artistic reticence that confined the word "hound" to the title; it is never referred to in the poem. Almost certainly it was while he was still occupied with the essay that inspiration came to him in its fullness; in *Prometheus Unbound* he could have encountered the prototype of his transtellar hound:

Once the hungry hours were hounds,
    Which chased the day like a bleeding deer,
And it limped and stumbled with many wounds
    Through the nightly dells of the desert year

Hounds, in fact, fascinated Shelley, and *Prometheus Unbound* also provided "Jove's tempest walking hounds," and more significantly, "Heaven's wingéd hound," as well as making contrary reference to "the hounds of hell" and "the hell-hounds' clamour." Whatever was the actual spark, it brought surging to the front of Thompson's imagination all the speculations of the previous year, unbounded in scope and thronged with lofty imagery. It was, he noted later, "much like the *ginn* freed from his vessel by the Arabian fisherman."[10] With the release of inspiration, however, and the avalanche of thought that came down, there intruded the inevitable echoes from other writers, the one unfailing, almost unavoidable, phenomenon of his work. He was in full control of his art this time, though, and the echoes were either held in balance or put through so fine a process of assimilation that the end product in almost every instance became immeasurably more expressive than the original. The really astonishing fact about this poem is that, while so much of its thought and imagery can be traced to other sources, it still manages to live a life of its own—a singularly original, unified, and powerful entity. The sources were not—could not have been—brought consciously together; they streamed unbidden from the murk of memory and were fused in the crucible of his silently flaming imagination.

The first stanza affords a good example of the way in which the process operated. The marvelous opening lines:

I fled Him, down the nights and down the days;
    I fled Him, down the arches of the years;
I fled Him, down the labyrinthine ways
    Of my own mind

seem to be traceable, mainly, to both Shelley and Byron.[11] In the well-known fourth canto of *Childe Harold*, Byron shows his hero contemplating the Coliseum in Rome and at one point exclaiming

Arches on arches! as it were that Rome,
Collecting the chief trophies of her line,
Would build up all her triumphs in one dome,
Her Coliseum stands . . .

But when the rising moon begins to climb
Its topmost arch, and gently pauses there;
When the stars twinkle through the loops of Time . . .

Thompson refers to Byron three times in the Shelley essay and even alludes to the Coliseum. It is more than likely that Byron's "arches on arches" and his "loops of Time" have coalesced to form Thompson's magnificent "arches of the years," though there may also be in that phrase something of the misery found in the night under the arches of the Thames bridges. (And the notion is irresistible that a phrase from De Quincey's *English Mail Coach,* second dream-fugue, has also played a part: "mighty mists which grouped themselves into arches and long cathedral aisles.") The most striking word in the first stanza, "labyrinthine," provides another thread. Far from coining this word, as so many believe, he was in reality surrounded by it, and variations of it. In *Childe Harold* Byron wrote: "For he through Sin's long labyrinth had run," and the appositeness of the phrase to *The Hound* can hardly be missed. But the actual word "labyrinthine" occurs no less than seven times in Shelley's poetry, twice in *Prometheus Unbound* alone, as well as in Masson's *Life* of De Quincey, which Thompson assuredly had read, and in William Watson's poem, *The Raven's Shadow,* which appeared as Thompson was writing. An even more immediate source for the word, as well as the arches and the wild grandeur of the opening lines, is a letter of Shelley's describing the Baths of Caracalla, a letter which was present to Thompson's mind as he wrote:

I think I told you of the Coliseum and its impression on me, on my first visit to this city. The next most considerable relic of antiquity, considered as a ruin, is the Thermae of Caracalla. These consist of six enormous chambers, above two hundred feet in height, and each inclosing a vast space like that of a field. There are, in addition, a number of towers and labyrinthine recesses, hidden and woven over by the wild growth of weeds and ivy. Never was any desolation more sublime and lovely. The perpendicular wall of ruin is cloven into steep ravines . . . At every step the aerial pinnacles of shattered stone group into new combinations of effect, and tower above the lofty yet level walls . . . in one of the buttresses that supports an immense and lofty arch, which "bridges the very winds of heaven" are the crumbling remains of an antique winding staircase, whose sides are open in many places to the precipice . . . These woods are intersected on every side by paths . . . which wind to every side of this labyrinth . . . the paths still wind on, threading the perplexed windings, other labyrinths, other lawns, and deep dells of wood and lofty rocks and terrific chasms.

Thompson credits the Baths of Caracalla with having stimulated Shelley's imagination in the writing of *Prometheus Unbound*,[12] and it seems likely that the vast, phantasmagoric atmosphere of *The Hound of Heaven* came in some measure from the same place. In fact, if the passage in Thompson's essay on Shelley describing the older poet's aerial wanderings, quoted above, is superimposed on this word-portrait of the Baths of Caracalla, the whole basic setting and action of *The Hound of Heaven* starts into life.[13]

The multiple-source nature of the first stanza continues in its closing lines:

> Up vistaed hopes I sped
> And shot, precipitated,
> Adown Titanic glooms of chasmèd fears
> From those strong Feet that followed, followed after.
> But with unhurrying chase,
> And unperturbèd pace,
> Deliberate speed, majestic instancy,
> They beat—and a Voice beat
> More instant than the Feet—
> 'All things betray thee who betrayest Me.'

In this can be heard not only Shelley and Blake, but the St. John of the *Apocalypse* as well. Shelley, in *The Cloud* (a poem to which Thompson refers warmly in the essay) has:

> And wherever the beat of her unseen feet
> Which only the angels hear . . .

which perhaps hooked onto Blake's memorable "What dread feet?" And these same Feet stalk in mystical fashion through much of the *Apocalypse*, making dramatic appearances a half-dozen times.

Though Shelley is the one constant influence, Thompson's imagination ranged over much of English literature in giving body to his thoughts. A roll call of some of the purely literary sources so far identified include Herbert, Blake, Byron, Tennyson, Keats, Wordsworth, De Quincey, Milton, Rossetti, Collins, Swinburne, Southwell, Coleridge, and P. J. Bailey, as well as Isaias, St. John, and the Psalms. There is even a passage picked up from a biography of Robert Browning which he was reviewing at this time;[14] and the very effective and now well-known phrase, "deliberate speed," though he may well have coined it himself, seems to owe something to—of all places—the English Courts of Chancery.[15] In almost every case, however, the use he made of his sources transcends anything aimed at by the earlier writers. Whether he

The summit of Kithurst Hill, Storrington, where Thompson composed parts of his Ode to the Setting Sun *and* The Hound of Heaven.

was expanding a suggestion or condensing an image, his own lines became something splendid and new. This can be seen most strikingly, perhaps, in the use he made of an obscure passage in Bailey's forgotten epic, *Festus*. Bailey wrote:

> The lightning steed,
> On air which pastures, the pre-ultimate sign
> Of the divine destruction of all worlds;
> The sparkles of whose hoofs in falling stars,
> Struck from the adamantine course of space,
> Stream o'er the skies . . .

And Thompson, with the flashing ease of genius, condensed this to:

> They clanged his chariot 'thwart a heaven
> Plashy with flying lightnings round the spurn o' their feet.

Two or three times, it must be admitted, rather too much of the original remained. When he claims

> I knew how the clouds arise
> Spumèd of the wild sea-snortings

he is making almost word-for-word use of Shelley's

> The clouds that are snorted
> From the sea's broad nostril

lines which he had earlier quoted as prose in the essay. When he asks: "the pulp so bitter, how shall taste the rind?" he is merely remembering Swinburne's *Dolores:*

> Too sweet is the rind, say the sages,
> Too bitter the core

And when he has the Voice say

> Ah, fondest, blindest, weakest,
> I am He whom thou seekest!

The nearness to *Epipsychidion* is unfortunate:

> O thou of hearts the weakest
> The phantom is beside thee whom thou seekest[16]

These are, however, the only instances of undigested borrowings to be found. Usually his memory and imagination worked together to better purpose, a fact that is evident in the use he made of Scripture. St. John says, "I heard a voice from Heaven like the sound of many waters," and for Thompson this becomes: "That voice is round me like a bursting sea." Isaias intones: "In the shadow of His hand He hath protected me"; the Psalmist repeats the idea: "The Lord is thy shade upon thy right hand," and Thompson fashions:

> Is my gloom, after all,
> Shade of His hand, outstretched caressingly?

It was, appropriately, from the mystic seventh angel in the *Apocalypse* that he drew his most profound and original inspiration. It provided the figure on the battlements in the culminating passage of the poem, perhaps the finest he ever wrote:

> I dimly guess what Time in mists confounds;
> Yet ever and anon a trumpet sounds
> From the hid battlements of Eternity;
> Those shaken mists a space unsettle, then
> Round the half-glimpsèd turrets slowly wash again.
>   But not ere him who summoneth
>   I first have seen, enwound
> With glooming robes purpureal, cypress-crowned

The trumpeter on the battlements[17] is neither Christ nor a personification of Death—the two possibilities that have so far occupied critics—but a divinely appointed herald who announces the coming of the Kingdom of God into the fugitive's soul; the figure serves the same purpose in Thompson's poem as it does in the *Apocalypse*. In composing those lines, Thompson's imagination leaped back twenty years to the time when St. John's vision had entered, with "the pageantry of an appalling dream," into his boyhood, and when he had first come into contact with the majestic trumpets of Heaven. St. John had written:

> In the days of the voice of the seventh angel, when he begins to sound the trumpet, the mystery of God will be accomplished . . . And the seventh angel sounded the trumpet; and there were loud voices in heaven saying, "The Kingdom of this world has become the Kingdom of Our Lord and of His Christ, and he shall reign for ever and ever . . . And the temple of God in heaven was opened, and there was seen the ark of his covenant in his temple and there came flashes of lightning, and peals of thunder, and an earthquake, and great hail.[18]

The sound of trumpets rings clear throughout a large part of the *Apocalypse,* the word itself occurring about fifteen times, and it is beyond doubt that Thompson's majestic trumpeter arose in the first instance from its pages. But, as usually happens with Thompson, St. John must share credit with two other writers, William Collins and De Quincey. In the Shelley essay, both Collins and his *Ode on the Passions* are prominently mentioned, and the *Ode* has one passage that could hardly avoid linking itself with St. John:

> With a frown
> Revenge impatient rose:
> He threw his blood-stained sword in thunder down,
> And, with a withering look,
> The war-denouncing trumpet took,
> And blew a blast so loud and dread,
> Were ne'er prophetic sounds so full of woe!
> And ever and anon he beat
> The doubling drum with furious heat

The urgent quality of this strikes vividly across St. John's vague, half-lit grandeur, and the phrase "prophetic sounds," of course, refers directly to the seventh angel in the *Apocalypse*. De Quincey's influence is a double one. In *The Daughter of Lebanon* he provided Thompson with another celestial tableau to set beside that of St. John:

First page of the manuscript of The Hound of Heaven. *The notations at top and bottom are by Wilfrid Meynell.*

The evangelist, pitying her sorrow, turned away her eyes to the clear blue sky, which the departing vapours had exposed . . . Immediately the blue sky parted to the right and to the left, laying bare the infinite revelations that can be made visible only to dying eyes . . . as thus the child of Lebanon gazed upon the mighty vision, she saw bending forward from the heavenly host, as if in gratulation to herself, the one countenance for which she hungered and thirsted . . .

And in the third dream-fugue of *The English Mail Coach,* in which De Quincey dreams he is pursuing a child, he supplied still another mystic trumpeter, even more mysterious than the seventh angel, who comes to life on a stone sarcophagus:

Solemnly, from the field of battle he rose to his feet; and, unslinging his stony trumpet, carried it, in his dying anguish, to his stony lips—sounding once, and yet once again; proclamation that in *thy* ears, oh baby! spoke from the battlements of death. Immediately, deep shadows fell between us, and aboriginal silence.

Ultimately, the greatness of *The Hound of Heaven,* and its unique power as a work of art, depend to a large extent upon its exhilarating cosmic sweep, especially in the sense of unfettered soaring and a kind of prodigiously enlarged spatial existence. From the first word of the poem, the universal vast is implicit and it surges through almost every line. Flight and pursuit, pursuit and flight take place out of time and beyond any recognizable landscape, in the lofty vagueness of "dim transtellar things." It begins somewhere in the unimaginable reaches of outer space and ends by transcending the verge of the finite. Though the theme was supremely new in the use Thompson made of it, it was not without precedent; whether or not he was entirely aware of it, in *The Hound of Heaven* he achieved the ultimate expression in the long tradition of cosmic imagery. The "tyrannous expansion of space and time" in the poem was not a result of opium dreams or withdrawal fantasies, as it has more than once been charged, but the latest flowering of a tradition that had lain deeply embedded in English literature for more than three centuries.*

The poem, or more probably a draft of it, was finished late in February 1890.[19] Thompson knew very well what he had wrought, later calling it "certainly, with all its faults, the greatest of my odes." Aside from its matchless imagery and technical virtuosity, he was well aware that it embodied "a world-wide experience in an individual form of that experi-

---

* See Appendix: Thompson's Space Rapture.

ence; the universal becoming incarnated in the personal."[20] He knew that he had expressed, as no one ever had before, the aching tensions in the human heart between love of the spirit and love of the world, between desire for God and desire for the things He has created.

From destitution, despair, drugs, and desolation; out of licentiousness, over broken lives, and through the mouth of prophecy; with the fabric of its vision stretched across the urgent utterances of twenty centuries, the foremost religious poem of modern times had, indeed, come into being along strange paths.

6

A TREACHEROUS CALM

THOMPSON RETURNED FROM STORRINGTON TO LONDON, IN MARCH OF
1890, confident of expanding powers, but determined as well to take an
active part in the Meynells' bread-and-butter journalism. For over a
year he had been living on the bounty of Wilfrid Meynell, and during
this time, to speak in practical terms, he had produced only some half-
dozen articles and five published poems. It had cost about fifty pounds
in board, lodging, and miscellaneous to keep him at the monastery, and
his own work could not have earned even half of that.[1]

Though he must have been aware that he was no more cut out for the
demands of daily journalism than he was for medicine, he was resolved
to make the attempt. Residence in London, necessary under the circumstances, had been agreed on, though both he and Meynell had felt some
uneasiness at the thought of renewed access to drugs. Thompson,

however, conscious of increased vigor, both mental and physical, reassured his friend: "Nor need you fear the opium. I have learned the
advantage of being without it for mental exercise; and (still more
important) I have learned to bear my fits of depression without it.
Personally I no longer fear it."[2] The unclouded atmosphere thus envisioned was to prevail for more than two years, while Thompson's days
became a mixture of assiduous journalistic toil and the most unhindered
poetic flight.

On his arrival in London he went to the Meynells' house, remaining
there a few days until rooms were found for him at No. 25 Third
Avenue, Queen's Park, Kilburn.[3] This was a narrow, quiet street of
identical two-story, attached houses of reddish-brown brick that breathed
a cozy charm despite the unbroken repetition of doorway and window
along both sides of the avenue and into many of the branching streets.
Here he continued work on *The Hound of Heaven* as well as *Finis
Coronat Opus,* the short story begun the previous fall. Suffering from an
attack of influenza—"sufficient to leave my digestion very disordered,
myself easily tired, and my head apt to get sodden after an hour or so of
use"[4]—he completed the poem sometime in May. Meynell, submerged
as usual in his editorial labors, on receiving the poem dropped Thompson
a card calling it "very fine," though, ironically, both he and his wife seem
at first to have regarded the then unpublished *Buona Notte* as superior to
it.[5]

Thursday was press day for the *Register,* and Thompson made an
earnest effort to become part of the ordered confusion of the library at
the Palace Court house every week, "elbowing with other workers at the
close-packed table"—under which, very often, the Meynell children
crouched in an office of their own, editing a paper of their own, emerg-
ing now and then to run an errand or make a dash to the mailbox. It was
soon apparent, however, that the newest member of the staff lacked the
required attitude of sober concentration: "Set him to write and there
would be endless conversation on nibs and paper, of what was advisable
to write, what to ignore, of his reader's susceptibilities, and his care for
the paper's circulation." Obviously, he was trying hard to descend from
the rarefied heights in which his mind had roamed freely for a decade,
but it appears he was struck by a kind of giddy delight at finding himself
again in contact with sophisticated intelligences, after his year in the
rustic solitude of Storrington. He later settled down to the point where
he and Alice Meynell between them could turn out an issue, when
Wilfrid was on vacation ("Francis and I kept our noses to the grindstone
all yesterday. He is *extremely* good."[6]) but during these first months he
was generally left to be

> biting
> My pencil, inviting
> Inspiration and plighting
> My hair into elf-locks most wild, and affrighting,

He was not quite ready for regimentation, but that fact has been allowed to obscure his admirable achievement, from mid-1890 to mid-1892, of working steadily and continuously on both the creative and journalistic levels, often, in fact, performing both tasks simultaneously. During that period he wrote some thirty poems, including *The Poppy, Corymbus for Autumn, A Fallen Yew,* and the 1271-line *Sister Songs;* reviewed at least sixteen volumes of verse, including books by Swinburne, Kipling, and Henley, wrote over a dozen other book reviews and articles, and produced a 25,000-word study of the work of St. John Baptist de La Salle, which occupied the entire April 1891 issue of *Merry England.*[7] He may have been a hindrance at the Meynells' crowded library table, but in the seclusion of his own quarters, or the quiet of the British Museum Reading Room, he was a serious and disciplined writer.

On occasion he could even drag his reluctant muse into the service of journalism. Twice Wilfrid Meynell asked him for some obituary verse: the first occasion followed the death of Cardinal Newman in August 1890, and though Thompson felt that writing verse to order precluded all chance of its being poetry, he sat down immediately and within a few hours had "knocked off three little stanzas,"[8] which appeared in *The Register* on August 16. The second time, on the death of Cardinal Manning in January 1892, despite Thompson's misgivings about poetry written to order, he produced the memorable *To the Dead Cardinal of Westminster.* Manning died on January 14, and Thompson's poem appeared in the February *Merry England,* which means that the forty-four exquisitely carved stanzas were composed within the space of three or four days. They are clearly modeled on Herbert's *Discipline*—the spare precision of which Thompson perhaps felt would match the Cardinal's well-known character—but the short lines and brief stanzas achieve a marvelous flowing impetus far superior to Herbert's halting rhythms. The difference between the pallid Newman verses and the throbbing lines on Manning lies in the fact that Thompson felt a personal interest in the latter, having met him once for ten minutes and in that short space having been overwhelmed by the divergence between their lives, and by the mystery of human relationships to the Infinite. It was, again, in the perturbation of his own heart that poetry was born. He asks Manning in Heaven to send some assurance that a poet's sufferings are not wasted:

>   . . . are his great desires
> Food but for nether fires?
>   Ah me,
>   A mystery!
>
> "Can it be his alone,
> To find, when all is known,
>   That what
>   He solely sought
>
> "Is lost, and thereto lost
> All that its seeking cost?
>   That he
>   Must finally
>
> "Through sacrificial tears,
> And anchoretic years,
>   Tryst
>   With the sensualist?"
>
>   . . .
>
> So ask; and if they tell
> The secret terrible,
>   Good friend,
>   I pray thee send
>
> Some high gold embassage
> To teach my unripe age.
>   Tell!
>   Lest my feet walk hell.

These were not just words with Thompson; they came from the deepest part of his soul, touched somehow by the death of the austere Cardinal. Though the poem was written in a surprisingly brief time, it did not come easily; at some point when he had come up against a temporary block, he broke off composition to complain helplessly to Meynell: "I don't know what I shall do, or what you will do. I haven't been able to write a line . . . I am more in a condition to sit down and go into hysterics like a girl, than to write anything. I know how vexed and impatient you must feel to hear this from me, when you had expected to have the thing this morning."[9] A few weeks later, after the poem had appeared to high praise, he refers, in a letter to Alice Meynell, to "those Manning verses which I do not like to read again. You know that I

Thompson's London lodgings, at No. 25 Third Avenue, Queen's Park, Kilburn, where he completed The Hound of Heaven (*the corner house*).

believe eternal punishment; you know that when my dark hour is on me, this individual terror is the most monstrous of all that haunt me. . . ."[10] Both he and the Cardinal, Thompson felt, were in pursuit of the same thing, despite the vast difference in their circumstances: could it be possible then, that one should be saved and the other lost? A mystery, he says—but the poem implies his belief that his feet would not, after all, walk hell.

Not everything he wrote during this London period achieved publication. A long article reviewing Catholic advances in the literary field over the previous fifty years, a commission he had received early in 1890 from *The Tablet,* was rejected soon after his return to the city, because its coverage of the subject was inadequate and unbalanced. *A Threnody of Birth,* a short essay packed with high-wrought imagery which attempts, in the manner of Sir Thomas Browne, to describe the human life span, was submitted to *The National Observer* but it was not accepted, and the *Observer's* editor, W. E. Henley, also rejected a later, similar effort, *Modern Men: The Devil.*[11] In August 1890 the *Dublin Review,* after pondering for three months, finally declined the *Shelley* essay and the disappointment to Thompson must have been acute; his joking in a letter about it carries an edge; "I am not surprised myself. What is a poor ecclesiastical editor to do when confronted with something so *sui generis* as this . . . The editor feels himself out of his latitude. He is probably a person of only average literary taste; that is he can tell the literary hawk from the literary handsaw when the wind is southerly. The poor man feels that discretion is the better part of valor. The thing may be very good, may be very bad. But it is below or beyond his comprehension. So he rejects it. Twelve years hence (if he lives so long) he will feel uncomfortable should anyone refer to that rejection."[12] Not twelve, but eighteen years later Thompson's prediction came true, when the *Review* was offered a second chance, printed the essay posthumously in July 1908, and promptly had to reprint an issue for the first time in its seventy-five-year history.

The most dazzling achievement of this period was *Sister Songs*, the lengthy poem in which Thompson consciously made a trial of his strength, pushing his image-making power to the limit. It was Wilfrid Meynell who, inadvertently, planted the seed. In March of 1890, on the night of Thompson's return to London, there was some talk at the Meynell home of his Storrington acquaintances. Monica Meynell entered the room while the two men were talking of the little girl, Daisy, the original of the poem. Meynell inquired if Daisy was taller than his daughter, and explained to Monica: "Mr. Thompson has a friend called Daisy, and he has written some very beautiful poetry to her, which I wish had been written to you, my dear!" That casual remark seems to have struck a spark that smoldered for a time, flared up briefly in May, was purposely smothered, then ignited a blaze of inspiration that lasted for some three months, during which the poem expanded far beyond the original conception. The story of its beginnings was related by Thompson in a letter when the poem had only just gotten under way:

A fourth poem which I might have written and did not has got me in great disgrace. It was to have been as long as, or longer than, the "Hound of Heaven." But there was prose waiting to be written, and I thought that my duty to Mr. Meynell imperatively required I should sacrifice the poem, since the "Hound of Heaven" had already engaged me longer than I had looked for. During a week I struggled with the impulse, which was so strong as to prevent me from writing prose, though I would not yield to it. Then at last I stifled it; and as a result I can write neither prose nor poetry, and have made myself unwell. Mrs. Blackburn strongly disapproved of what I had done. Poetry was the special gift that God had given me, and when I had the impulse it was my duty to work it out. "Ah! if I stood alone" I said, "but it is injustice to Mr. Meynell." She rejoined that she could quite understand that consideration making me unhappy; but if there was loss now it would be repaid ultimately . . . I acknowledged that I had a strong impression that the poem would be for mere beauty—not for power or thought—the best that I had done. "Then write it, by all means." "I can't now; the impulse is past." "There, you see!" she said. Then I confessed that it was to have been addressed to two of Mr. Meynell's children; and she was downright vexed. "Oh, I wish you had written it," she said. "Oh, you horrid boy! To think that those creatures should have been so near immortality. I hope it will come back to you." I shook my head and said that if it ever did, it would not be while this weather lasted; it would need air and sunlight to rekindle the poem. She has informed me since that when Mrs. Meynell was told of it she "simply wrung her hands"; and Mr. Meynell said that I had acted very foolishly, and was never to do such a thing again. "I told them you had a good scolding for it; and so there was no more to be done," said Mrs. Blackburn. I had no idea that it would give them any particular pleasure, or I would not have throttled it. I thought I should be consulting only my own selfish pleasure in writing the poem. Now I am miserably endeavouring to resuscitate it; neither able to write it or leave it alone."[13]

His feeling that the poem would be about the length of *The Hound of Heaven* changed drastically as he wrote, for the completed *Sister Songs* is seven times as long as the other work, and the feeling is inescapable that *Sister Songs* was for Thompson what *Endymion* was for Keats, "a leap into the sea." Behind him stretched a year of strenuous effort in which he had completed about a dozen poems, seven of which had already been published and two of which carried the credentials of greatness. It had become obvious to him, as well as to the Meynells and other interested readers, that his real power and originality lay in his remarkable power of imagery, his inexhaustible and unerring figurative inventiveness, rare in English literature and certainly unequalled in his own day. It was through imagery, he must have felt, that he might produce something of true worth and, if he was to continue challenging Shelley, it would have to be precisely in that area. The projected poem, he had said in his letter, would be notable for "mere beauty," not for thought, and in saying that he seems to be openly declaring his decision to rival his great master. He was ready to leap into the sea, and the chance remark of Wilfrid Meynell, concerning as it did a subject so near to his heart, gave him the needed push. An added factor, not difficult to understand, may have been his joy at the realization that the opium had not damaged his talent, a joy that could easily have prompted a desire to discover just what heights he could reach with a sustained effort;

knowing, at last, that he was a poet above the ordinary, he wrote *Sister Songs* to determine how far above. He said almost as much in the letter sent to the Meynells with the finished poem: "One way or another, it will be an effectual test."

Having finally succeeded in resuscitating the stifled idea about the latter part of July, and having been urged by Meynell to spend on it all the time needed, by the end of August he could report considerable progress, "though as to the quality of what I have written I am in the dark." He was making a tremendous effort, with most of his waking moments devoted to the poem, and it was natural that he should have now and then drifted afar off. "I called at Palace Court on Friday, and finding you were gone," he apologized to Meynell, "I started to follow you to B. & O's. Unfortunately I fell into composition on the way; and when I next became conscious of matters sublunary, found myself wandering about somewhere in the region of Smithfield Market, and the time late in the afternoon. . . ."[14] Working steadily—though not without interruption[15]—he finished the poem sometime in early November, then held it back until he could present it to the Meynells at Christmas. Sitting in the library at Palace Court on Christmas Eve, he watched the exchange of gifts, enjoying the glow of "the one happy Christmas I have had for many a year," and, when all were gone from the room, placed the penny exercise-book containing the final manuscript of *Sister Songs* on the mantelpiece where he knew it would be found. Despite the holiday hubbub, the Meynells read the lengthy poem in the next few days, for on the last day of the year Thompson was replying to their enthusiastic praise:

Warm thanks for your letter. I only hope there may be a quarter as much merit in the poem as you incline to think. I do not fear your sincerity; I fear only that you may let your feelings bias your judgment. Above all, do not suffer me to think that I have wrought a beautiful bracelet (if such be not the case), merely because you never saw so many jewels set in the same place before. *That* of itself will not secure a beautiful bracelet, as you know, and I know. And do not treat me as did Dr. Todhunter the other day at Chiswick. Wishing to ascertain the impressions of a favourably disposed man new to my poetry, I mentioned the objection which had been made against me that I accumulated imagery until I became obscure and inartistic. He hesitated—a tell-tale hesitation—and then said, "Well, but what a splendid fault! and your imagery is often so unexpected and surprising." Perhaps you could hardly say a more dangerous thing to a man. How can you expect that he will keep a very severe guard upon a "splendid fault"?

. . . None of this correction-and-sugar, please. If my Muse rouges, tell her so; though she vow and protest that it is no more than all fashionable Muses use.[16]

Doubts about the success of the poem were thus early set in motion and it is probable that Alice Meynell, after the first reaction of excitement and gratitude, settled to a more stringent criticism, unerringly pointing out the failure of the work as a whole, perhaps suggesting revisions. Something of the sort must have happened, for the poem remained unpublished until 1895, when Thompson had already achieved a reputation, and even then it was only at the insistence of Wilfrid Meynell that it was put into print. The truth is exactly what Thompson himself and the Meynells suspected: *Sister Songs* is no more than an exotic jewel box. It lacks a unified structure, as well as a reasonable development of ideas, contains autobiographical allusions puzzling to the unready reader (in Thompson's day, in fact, no one but the Meynells and their friends could possibly have grasped the meaning of these passages), is often wire-drawn and repetitious, its imagery does not always succeed in making the invisible visible, and, again inevitably, it is studded with borrowings. Its theme is not easy to identify: it seems to be a hymn to the wonder of girlhood, as well as a memorial to his love for the Meynell children, but it is also a lamentation over the price in suffering that must be paid by poets, and himself in particular. One passage, on the human soul, while interesting, intrudes philosophical considerations that rudely strain the poem's already erratic progress.

In spite of its failure as a total work of art, however, *Sister Songs* can never fade to obscurity, for its "splendid faults" assure it immortality. In pushing his imagination to its limit, Thompson achieved, if only for moments, a perfect blending of thought and expression found only in the greatest poets:

> I remembered not
> The subtle sanctities which dart
> From childish lips' unvalued precious brush,
> Nor how it makes the sudden lilies push
> Between the loosening fibres of the heart

he says of the memories that little Madeline Meynell's impulsive kiss awakens in him, and the lines shake the mind with a gentle abruptness that reverberates softly back through the quiet centuries. He explains that Monica's love rules him

> As the innocent moon, that nothing does but shine,
> Moves all the labouring surges of the world

Alice Meynell with her daughter Monica and her husband Wilfrid (directly behind Alice). About 1900.

and somewhere above the clouds, Shakespeare must have read the lines aloud to savor their distinctive quality. Cosmic imagery, too, frequently found a place beside the details of earthly existence, one passage of which is among the finest he ever wrote in the category:

> Thou wert to me that earnest of day's light,
> When, like the black of a gold-mailed saurian
> Heaving its slow length from Nilotic slime,
> The first long gleaming fissure runs Aurorian
> Athwart the yet dun firmament of prime.

The poem remained in Meynell's hands until its publication in 1895, though he made no secret of its existence, frequently reading it aloud for visitors to his home. The two little girls who had given rise to it were often present at these sessions, more as exhibits than honored guests. "Of course," recalled Madeline many years later, adding a touch of reality to the picture, "as children we were utterly bored by that!"[17]

II

Glimpses into Thompson's personal life at this time, notwithstanding his association with the busy Meynell circle, are rare. His habits of isolation and seclusion were too strongly fixed on him by now, making him content to spend his days between Palace Court, the *Merry England* and *Register* office at Essex Street, the British Museum Reading Room, and his own quarters, with regular forays into the neighborhood parks. He met few new acquaintances and usually declined invitations, or, more often, merely ignored them.

It was always easier for him to make friends with children, since in their uninhibited give-and-take, they imposed no undue emotional strain. In the fall of 1890 in a letter to Wilfrid Meynell, he reported such a casual acquaintance struck up in Queen's Park. As with the little girl, Daisy, at Storrington, Thompson's concern for such friendships is surprising only until it is remembered what constant aloneness chilled his waking hours.

> The dearest child has made friends with me in the park; and we
> have fallen in love with each other with an instantaneous rapidity not

unusual on my side, but a good deal more unusual on the child's. I rather fancy she thinks me one of the most admirable of mortals; and I firmly believe her to be one of the most daintily supernatural of fairies . . . Of course, in some way she is sure to vanish; elves always do, and my elves in particular. This individual little elf is a Catholic, by the way; which partly accounts for the celerity of our mutual confidence. And her kinsfolk see the *Register* every week; which ought to throw for you a new and appreciable light upon elfland . . .[18]

More about this little girl he jotted down in a rough passage in one of the notebooks, which indicates she was very young, probably no more than five or six. Once, it seems, she mistook a catkin for a worm and when Thompson delivered a mock reprimand for the mistake, "she disdainfully turned aside, and clearly thought me mad;—an opinion unaccountably shared by the human frequenters of the park, who partially heard my sagacious and paternal counsel."[19] The Meynell children were frequently entrusted to him, especially for recreation in nearby Kensington Gardens. A skating party on the ice of the Round Pond, in January 1891 left him with such a glow of well-being that on reaching his rooms he immediately sat down to write a note of thanks for the confidence shown in allowing him to take care of the children: "Or shall I say entrusting me to them? For on reflection, I have a haunting suspicion that Monica managed the party with the same energy that she devotes to her skating." In the note he praises Monica's abilities on ice and confesses that he "raced her two or three times on even terms, and was well beaten."

This association with the Meynell children, so memorably perpetuated in his poetry, and his friendships with other children, should not be taken to mean that he possessed any special attractiveness for childish hearts. It was not his knock on the door at Palace Court that produced the excited rush of feet; to the Meynell children he was an accepted if erratic and even rather outlandish element in the household. Madeline Meynell, asked years afterwards if, as a child, she had liked Thompson, replied frankly, "I should almost have said *no* to that," and explained that in his sensitivities and silences he was not an easy person to talk to, and his uncared-for appearance gave him too strange an air. To the same question, Olivia Meynell replied more guardedly: "We certainly did not dislike the poet. But he was accepted as one of the accidents of life by us when we were young. It wouldn't have occurred to us to consider whether we liked him or not . . . he was just *there*."[20]

Of all the Meynell children it was Monica who appealed most to him, and it was during the summer of 1891, while vacationing with the Meynells at Friston in Suffolk, that the child pulled a poppy from the grass and impulsively handed it to him with, "Keep it as long as you live!" The opium-flower thus abruptly offered ended the happy mood of that day by reminding him of the "twenty shrivelled years" that had passed since he had been Monica's age. Yet, when he attempted to put his sadness and regret into verse, the underlying faith in his vocation reasserted itself, and he knew his life had value despite all its seeming waste:

> I hang mid men my needless head,
> And my fruit is dreams, as theirs is bread:
> The goodly men and the sun-hazed sleeper
> Time shall reap, but after the reaper
> The world shall glean of me, me the sleeper.

This Friston vacation, despite the mood of *The Poppy*, was not entirely wrapped in melancholy. Everard Meynell remembered Thompson measuring himself against tall thistle stalks to see if they equaled those that rose six foot out of the turf at Storrington; he recalled picnics on the Broads among pine cones and herons, and could dimly recollect the poet "coming in at the farm-gate dusty from a road still bright in the dusk." It was at Friston, too, that the children played, or thought they played, tricks on Thompson, such as convincing him that there was such a thing as a left and a right stocking (Madeline later admitted that Thompson might just have been going along with the joke.)

In May of 1891 another child, a boy, was born to the Meynells, and Thompson was asked to be godfather. The request touched him deeply: "I am utterly unable to express to you what I feel regarding it: I can only hope that you may comprehend without words. As for the quietness with which I took it on Saturday—for the premeditated utterance of emotions in speech I have an instinctive horror which, I think, you have sufficiently to understand and excuse in me . . . One can only, like Cordelia, speak by silence."[21] He did not long remain silent. The boy, named Francis, was born on the twelfth, and within a few days the Meynells received a poem entitled *To My Godchild*. Perhaps the child would be a poet, Thompson mused in the verses; "I ask you but to blossom from my dust," he wrote, perhaps revealing his sadness at the thought that he himself might leave no children behind him.

In order to lighten the burden of his isolation at this time, efforts were made occasionally to draw him into more companionable ways, but without much success. Soon after the return from the Friston vacation. for instance, Alice Meynell gave a party for poets and publishers at Palace Court. Invited, among others, were William Ernest Henley,

Aubrey de Vere, Coventry Patmore, and William Butler Yeats. "I am
trying to make Francis Thompson come," she explained in a letter to the
publisher John Lane, "but he is afraid of so many poets."[22] There is no
record that he attended this particular gathering, which is something of a
pity, since in such an atmosphere he might, if a spark had been struck,
have left a further glimpse into his unique personality. For neither his
silences nor the flood of conversational banalities and repetitions that
flowed from him at casual moments were true indications of his verbal
powers. On the contrary, his talk must at times have approached elo-
quence. "When the subject was literature he was a rich, abundant,
intemperate talker," Katharine Tynan recalled, echoing the others who
remembered Thompson's conversation when aroused. "He was one of
the great talkers," she insisted, thinking of the many hours she had spent
listening to him in the Meynell home: "He would walk up and down the
drawing room at Palace Court, clutching his dirty little pipe between his
fingers while he poured out his flood of argument." Alfred Hayes,
Wilfrid Whitten, Father Anselm, Coventry Patmore and his wife,
Harriet, among others, have all left portraits of Thompson caught up in
the heat of conversation, his face radiant and eyes aglow as he amazed
his listeners by "the inexhaustible well of literary allusion which was a
revelation to those who knew him." The grimy pipe, which he was
forever relighting, and the stem of which continually brushed his
mustache, is a fixture in the recollections of those who knew him in those
days—that, and a frayed and untidy suit of mustard-yellowish tweed that
tried the nerves of more than one of the Meynells' female visitors.[23]

One unusual gathering which he did attend was a meeting of the
famous Rhymers Club. This took place, probably in the fall of 1891, at
the house of Dr. John Todhunter in Bedford Park. The Club was a loose
association of young, ambitious poets, recently arrived in London, which
met haphazardly at various houses, or at Dr. Johnson's old tavern, The
Cheshire Cheese in Fleet Street, "for discreet conviviality, conversation
on literary matters, and the reading of their own new-born lyrics." The
membership included such names as Lionel Johnson, Arthur Symons,
John Davidson, Richard Le Gallienne, Ernest Dowson, and William
Butler Yeats, all of whom were still awaiting recognition. Thompson was
brought to a meeting by friends of the Meynells, and seems to have been
the evening's guest of honor. Unfortunately, no details of that gathering
were preserved beyond one tantalizing sentence recorded by C. L. Hind:
"Thompson sat next to Ernest Dowson, but I did not see them speak to
one another."[24] Yeats, however, remembered that Thompson refused an
invitation to contribute to the club's first anthology, the *Book of the
Rhymers' Club,* which was being put together that fall and which was

The Meynell home at No. 47 Palace Court, London.

published the next autumn. If any effort was made to bring Thompson into the Rhymers as a regular member, it failed, for he never attended another meeting. In fact in a verse comedy he was then attempting he seems to have satirized the whole idea of such an association: "I send you herewith the first scene of the comedy," he wrote to Alice Meynell, "on which I have been so long engaged . . . I have put the 'Rhymers' into it, as you will see—but glorified 'Rhymers' of whom only one figure, Bradford, bears any relation to the original (Radford)."[25] Yeats may have been right when he said that Thompson saw only emptiness in the Club's purpose. It could scarcely have been otherwise.

The one relationship that meant most to him at this time was that with Alice Meynell. Profoundly grateful to her because of her part in his rescue, he was peculiarly impressed and captivated by her personality and manner and he quickly conceived for her talents an awe that was nearly reverence. "I wonder what she does not know!" he exclaimed in a letter to his friend Father Carroll, "A mistress of poetry, an exquisite art-critic, she knows besides, music, Latin, Greek, Italian, French, German, and all kinds of multifarious things at which I can but dimly guess." His first acquaintance with her poetry had occurred soon after his initial visit to Wilfrid Meynell, who gave Thompson a copy of the out-of-print *Preludes,* and he declared that the book had kept him up all night and had drawn from him the exclamation, "Then, I, too, am a poet!" He had found, Meynell explained in telling the incident later, that she gave expression to some of his own deepest thoughts, and "it came to him as a revelation that they were sayable."[26] A few writers have interpreted this to mean that Thompson was uncertain till then about his poetic vocation, but his spontaneous remark was only the joy of one who, in some lonely exile, recognizes a kindred spirit. Many of the poems contained in *Preludes* were an attempt by the young Alice Meynell to express the sense of apartness that she felt so keenly. One of these in particular, *Narcissus,* struck Thompson with such breath-taking force that he habitually referred to it as "Past all question . . . one of the few greatest sonnets in the language." Coming at a time when he himself had just begun to find a path through the "trackless ways," the dreamy innuendo of the sonnet affected him strongly; in it he confessed he saw his own deepest moods, "whose supremely subtle pencilings we had previously thought beyond the capabilities of poetic reproduction." Himself a victim of such rapt rumination since his youth, he knew well the mental condition pictured, and later described it as "a blended twilight of intellect and sensation; it is the crepuscular hour of thought. It is a state whose one possible utterance would be music."[27]

Before long Thompson came to regard Mrs. Meynell not merely as the foremost living female poet, but felt her work was "the first among all poetry yet produced by women." Accepting without question the air of exquisite austerity that clung round the woman and her work, he tended to idealize her even further. A very human susceptibility to headaches, for instance, is made by him to rise from a more exalted source: in commenting on one of her essays he says, "I hope it was the result of her holidays because unless done under conditions of unusual health, it will have made her ill, as the production of these gems always does. That is why they are so lamentably few." In her appearance, too, she seemed to him something far beyond the average: "Her youthful portraits show a beautiful, spiritualized face, with musing, saddened eyes; the head, in most portraits, drooped, as with the weight of thought . . . A face which is a poem as beautiful as any she has written." Not even frequent association with the flesh-and-blood woman, at meals and at work, could reduce her to life-size in his regard: writer and writing were elevated, remote, inseparable, and perfect. Once, when she attempted to deprecate what she considered the unexciting quietness of her own verse in comparison with Thompson's brilliant imagery, he expostulated, "It is to me as if the moon should wonder how Messrs. Brock can have any respect for her, when they possess all those beautiful fireworks . . . Please never say such a thing again; it pains me." Formal in his approach, always diffident and deferential in her presence, it is not surprising that he was soon lavishing verses on her such as the Elizabethans had bestowed on their sovereign.[28]

The poems comprising *Love in Dian's Lap* were written over a period of about three years, beginning in August 1890. Made up largely of elaborate conceits that breathe the authentic atmosphere of the seven-teenth century,[29] they are entirely uncharacteristic of his work to this time; they have the feel of deliberate exercises, produced for an occasion —an impression strengthened by the curious fact that they are entirely devoid of the cosmic imagery that flashes incessantly through his best-known work. Notwithstanding the fervent praise of some commentators, and despite much felicity of phrase, the sequence today retains only a collateral and biographical interest. In its intensely personal and un-critical rhapsodizing, however, it is the eternal repository of Thompson's overflowing gratitude to the Meynells.[30]

<h1 style="text-align:center">III</h1>

After an abstention of more than three years, opium once more began to entrammel Thompson in mid-1892, putting an end to his long striving for a normal existence. An explanation for this second surrender might sufficiently be found in the now widely known fact that true drug addiction is rarely conquered—and Thompson, after all, had been an ad-dict for something like ten continuous years. But there were deeper reasons.

To begin with, there was the profound discouragement he must have felt over his failure to win both financial independence and a hearing from the literary world at large. Publication in *The Weekly Register* and *Merry England,* while satisfying at first, could hardly have continued to feed his hunger for recognition. There beckoned the important secular magazines as well as book publication, but both of these continued beyond his reach. "The walls of the Protestant periodical press remain still unshaken and to shake," he complained in a letter as early as May 1890, and in a passage of the unpublished *Venus' Fly-Trap,* obviously meant as lighthearted criticism of his own work, he confesses his disappointment at not finding the wide, general audience beyond Catho-lic circles to which he still felt his destiny tending: "None of his thoughts has lived into book form, and they sleep in unassured hope of a final resurrection." Despite what seems to have been a determined two-year effort, the walls of the secular press had held steady, cutting off, as well, his only possible source of income and forcing him to continue as Meynell's protégé. He had come to be regarded as a part of Meynell's "staff," but he must have realized that Meynell's financial position allowed him no such thing as a staff, and though Thompson was sincere and hard-working, his inability to achieve full care of himself must have been galling. At least once the situation led to temporary bitterness between Meynell and his wife, who resented the fact that a family vacation had to be postponed in order to pay Thompson's rent.[31] He probably knew nothing of this particular incident, but he undoubtedly guessed that his presence was the cause of some deprivation to the Meynells and their children.

Far more important in his relapse, however, was the crushing realization that his poetic powers were deserting him. From the summer of 1889 to the end of 1890 he had produced in succession, most notably, the *Ode to the Setting Sun*, *The Hound of Heaven*, and *Sister Songs*. In 1891 *A Corymbus for Autumn* was the only worth-while product for the first half of the year, though it could hardly be classed with the first three. In the summer of 1891 he wrote *To My Godchild* and *The Poppy* but nothing else deserving of mention appeared until *A Fallen Yew* toward the end of the year. *The Dead Cardinal of Westminster* was written, under pressure, in January 1892, *The Making of Viola* and *Her Portrait* followed a few months later, and then inspiration failed altogether. Thus, the poetry that had been a torrent in 1889–90 had calmed to a swift flow during 1891, and had dwindled to a murmur by the spring of 1892. He was aware, of course, of his lessening creative drive, and as early as January 1891 he had written to Wilfrid Meynell: "I am constantly expecting to wake up some morning and find that my Daemon has abandoned me. I hardly think I could be very vain of my literary gift; for I so keenly feel that it is beyond my power to command, and may at any moment be taken from me."[32] Toward the end of the year he reiterates the fear, now closer to reality:

> Though Pan may have delicious throat
> Tis hard to tolerate the goat.
>   What if Pan were suddenly
> To lose his singing every note?—
>   Then pity have of Pan and me!

The really inept *Broom-Branch at Twilight*, written about the same time, goes further; in it he laments the fact that he has lost all power of poetry—and the halting verse of the stanzas demonstrates the fact. What was happening? Why, after a bare two and a half years, did poetry forsake him? The answer usually given lies in the return to opium; quite simply, it is claimed, the drugs stifled the artist in Thompson, as they

Madeline Meynell about the time Thompson wrote Sister Songs.

had in Coleridge. But the truth is not so simple, and the fact seems to be that his genius had been deprived of its motivation by a life of relative comfort. His intensely personal gift could not flourish in an atmosphere of sedate daily effort—the deep-buried springs of his inspiration could be touched only by the direct impact of experience. Every one of the nine major poems written between 1889 and 1892 sprang from just such a personal involvement: being made godfather to one of the Meynell children had roused him; the chance connection of a child and a poppy; the cutting down of the yew tree, a memorial of his school days; a ten-minute meeting with a Cardinal whose personality clashed with his own—in the absence of any inspiration more profound these things had generated poetry; but by 1892 such incidents had become fewer and fewer, and seem, as well, to have lost their power to move him. In the verses *How the Singer's Singing Wailed for the Singer,* published in November 1892, he is reduced to writing of the one personal thing left to him: his lack of inspiration. In dim realization of the need for change, out of a mute and bewildered sorrow, he cried, in the essay *Moestitiae Encomium,* for the one remedy he instinctively felt could restore his tongue to its full utterance: "Come therefore, O Sadness, fair and froward and tender; dolorous coquette of the Abyss . . . whose harp is stringed with lamentations; whose voice is fatal with disastrous pre-science; draw me down, merge me under thy waters of wail! . . . Of thy beauty undesired am I desirous, for knowledge is with thee, and dominion, and piercing, and healing." In the midst of all the things that give happiness to human beings he was asking only for the means to write poetry, even if it meant renewed upheaval in his own life.

This striking and continual disregard for everything but poetry he was to make starkly clear in some lines he wrote a few years later when he was suffering through another period of drought. In *To the Sinking Sun,* written probably in early 1895, he complains of the sameness of his life and cries:

> O give me unprevisioned new,
>   Or give to change reprieve!
> For new in me is olden too,
>   That I for sameness grieve.
> O flowers! O grasses! be but once
>   The grass and flower of yester-eve!
>
> Wonder and sadness are the lot
>   Of change: thou yield'st mine eyes
> Grief of vicissitude, but not
>   Its penetrant surprise.
> Immutability mutable
>   Burthens my spirit and the skies.

Only from the unexpected looming of experience, he knew when he wrote those words, could there come to him the longed-for "penetrant surprise" that sparked inspiration. In 1892 he may have been less conscious of that truth, but he knew it instinctively.

It was precisely the same impulse that had led him to reject the priesthood, to disdain his medical studies, and to steal away to an uncertain future in London—except that now he *knew* he was a poet. Thus, uncertain how to revive his flagging powers, he turned to opium as to an old friend, for comfort and forgetfulness. And the opium drove the wedge still deeper.

By the middle of 1892 he was aware that the drug had begun to grip him with its old mastery, and in his helplessness he asked those near him for their prayers, but for reasons left vague.[33] Gradually, however, his plight became evident, and his friends awoke to the disturbing realization that he was also visiting the Palace Court house under the influence of laudanum. "On that hearthrug once," Wilfrid Meynell later told an interviewer, "when I came into the room, I found him outstretched in a sort of sleep. Alarmed, I knelt beside him, whereupon, to reassure me, he uttered the one word 'opium!' "[34] Few details regarding this time of trial have been recorded by the Meynells; they have understandably preferred to leave it obscure, though Wilfrid once further admitted, in an unguarded conversation, that "he took opium again, after he left Storrington, and went back to his life in the London streets, but not again to the

slums."[35] There are in existence, however, some unpublished letters
that throw a ray of light on this period of Thompson's pathetic relapse.
They make it clear that it was Alice Meynell's patience that gave out,
and they indicate that it was probably an intractable stand by her against
having a drug addict mixing freely in her household and with her
children that terminated this period of Thompson's London life. The
story told by the letters is fragmentary but sufficiently revealing.[36] They
date from September–October 1892.

Thompson to Alice Meynell:

My Own Dear Lady and Mother,
 How did it come about that what began between us in confidence
this afternoon, ended, somehow, in constraint and reticence? I could
not understand it at the time; I could only feel that, while I was
tenderly grateful for your dear kindness, I had somehow fallen out of
touch with you after the first moment. And I was miserable to feel it.
I have now come to the conclusion that the fault was all on my side.
Though I said otherwise at lunch (for I hate parading one's private ills
before strangers), I had slept little last night, eaten nothing in the
morning, and was able to eat little at lunch. So that I felt utterly spent,
and unable to stand the strain of emotion, or to respond to your spirit
with the instinctive perception I am accustomed to have for it. I trust
you, honour you, and love you more than ever,—O believe me, it was
simply that paralysis of the heart and emotions which follows a prolonged strain upon them. Pardon me, and do not let it rest here.
Confidence has gone too far not to go further, or die altogether. Give
me an opportunity tomorrow, if possible; at any rate the sooner the
better. And I will open to you if you wish it, my most secret soul; that
on my side you may never misunderstand me through distrust or want
of knowledge. That I promise you. On your side be all exactly as you
will . . ."

That letter, so full of anguish and doubt over some unnamed falling out
between them, becomes understandable in the light of two other letters,
written about the same time, from which the fumes of his opium misery
rise unmistakably.

Thompson to Alice Meynell:

 I at least did not on Tuesday night adopt the attitude that you had
no reason to be angry with me. On the contrary, I told you that I was
very sorry I had lapsed from my word to you. It is a minor matter, but
I had not again broken my promise on that Tuesday when I spoke to
you. I had broken it the day before, and was bitterly remorseful for
having done so. You had lightened my heart and strengthened me im-

mensely in that night's interview: for I thought that you had taken what was indeed the true view of the matter. Namely, that under a weight of suffering of which you had not, nor even can have, any conception, I had lapsed from my word for a single day; but having got relief from God when my burden was becoming beyond the strength of human nerves, I had resumed my courage and was going forward again in the path that I had promised you. You had, I thought, taken this true and merciful view; and instead of visiting me with your anger were going to pray that I might be sustained, and to encourage me by your affection and sympathy. I went to bed comforted and praying that God would help me on my side to cooperate with you, and to spare you any addition to your sorrows from me. But this morning I get your terrible letter and feel that Heaven has indeed crowned the awful trouble which has been accumulating on me for the last month, by withdrawing from me your love and sympathy, which alone gave me courage to struggle against it, and try to keep my soul from the influences which were dragging it downward. God help me, for I feel blinded and paralyzed. Before Heaven, I tell you that if you knew all as I know it, you would feel that never man had more claim on you for patience than I have; however hard it may be to extend it to me: and that I am indeed more sinned against than sinning. But I make no further claim on you. I bow to your decision. Henceforth I will only come to your house when business calls me there; and if you are brought into contact with me, it need not be beyond the ordinary formalities of courtesy. I will draw back into the hermit and leave your lives free of me; and perhaps when the curse of me is removed from the house it will settle back into its ordinary condition . . ."

The letter written, he hesitated to send it, and before he could decide, a note arrived from Wilfrid Meynell urging him to call. He replied to this note and enclosed the letter to Mrs. Meynell quoted above.[37]

Thompson to Wilfrid Meynell:

I am not fit to come in tonight. I have broken my promise to Mrs. Meynell both yesterday and today. She was wrong in thinking that I had broken it on the Tuesday when she spoke to me, nor did I guess that she thought so. I had broken it the day before, for the first, and it might have been the last time; broken by the pressure, night and day, of an extra-natural conflict in which you do not believe because— Englishman-like—it is outside your personal experience, as before that it was outside mine. But that Monday and on the Tuesday following I found myself completely delivered; as if God saw that the limits of human endurance had been passed. I was full of remorse for what I had done, and resolved never again to add to her own sorrows by giving her such pain on account of me. Then on the Wednesday morning, came her letter as a crushing blow, breaking me utterly to pieces on the top of all I had gone through. I fell into wild recklessness and carelessness about my soul; and, as I have said, I broke my word to her completely both that day and today. Therefore I cannot come in tonight. But be comforted if you can. Your little note has given me a ray of hope and comfort again; and if you can pardon and overlook what is past, I on my side will take up the task of amendment again . . . if I am only delivered from the thought that she and you have cast me off and turned against me, I can once more regain the mastery of my own self and soul.

The Meynells did not cast him off, but they did insist on a complete severance with drugs, and as the most immediate step to that end they suggested that he should bury himself in some remote situation far from London temptations. The Franciscan monastery at Pantasaph, in north Wales, presented itself as an appropriate haven since Thompson was kindly disposed toward "the bearded counsellors of God," having a number of times visited their Friary at Crawley. By the middle of October arrangements were complete.[38] Thompson was to live in a guest cottage at the monastery, and was not to have access to any money; his board and lodging would be paid by Meynell directly to the landlady, and any other little needs were to be supplied by the monks acting on Meynell's behalf. In December, he left London, not to return for over two years. In that period he would recover his lost powers—though altered in tone—would have his first brush with romance, and would even find himself, after publication of his first volume, swept suddenly to the pinnacle of fame.

7

WIND FROM THE WEST

IN A HOLLOW OF THE STORMY HILLS THAT BILLOW ACROSS THE NORTH of Wales, about a dozen miles south of the Irish Sea, there are gathered the gray Gothic buildings of the Franciscan monastery at Pantasaph. Low, iron gates front the road at the foot of a long, tree-lined lane and just within the gates stands Bishop's House, a guest cottage. To this house, in this rough, sparsely populated, wind-swept land came Thompson, late in December 1892, to renew his struggle against addiction. On the journey from London—as much to prevent any last resort to laudanum, as to ensure his safe arrival—he had been given a companion, H. A. Hinkson, husband of Katharine Tynan, who had stayed with him to Chester, where a priest from the monastery took him in charge.[1]

Though he was among strangers, he was far from alone. There were ordinarily staying at Bishop's House one or two of the monastery's temporary guests, and there was also the large family of the proprietor, Michael Brien, which included five girls and a teen-age son. The youngest of the Briens, Agnes, was eight and the oldest, Margaret Ann, a gentle, soft-voiced girl in delicate health, was twenty-four. Maggie drew Thompson's attention from the first, even while he was still experiencing the pains of withdrawal, and he mentions her in what may have been his first letter from Wales:

> Now you'll think that I'm in a state of light-hearted exhilarence, which is very improper in me, considering all I have to repent of. Therefore I beg to assure you that I'm suffering like old Nick. But when one is in this condition, one must laugh out or weep out . . . therefore I'll grin through the very biggest horse-collar I can find. Don't think though that I repent having come here: if I were in London I would simply take a header into the Thames—only that it's such a damnably dirty place for a poet to drown in. But I am in a most unconventional state at present; ready to go smash among all conventions like a bull in a china-shop . . . I have half a mind, by way of final outrage, to make love to what I think the loveliest girl I have ever seen. But I have still some convention hanging about me in a tattered condition . . .[2]

His first few days at Pantasaph were spent indoors, and early in January, when he began to long for open air and exercise, a heavy snowfall and broken shoes prolonged his confinement. *"C'en est fait,* as regards the opium," he wrote on January 4, "though I have only just taken the turning which leads out of the debility consequent on the breaking off . . . By a foolish trick before I left London, I have ruined my boots . . . so that just when I want and long for walking to act as a tonic against my debility, I am compelled to stay in the house."[3] New shoes must have been promptly sent, for, after a few days of trudging across snow-covered hills, he sends a report to Meynell that he is nearly himself again. There is a note almost of exhilaration in a letter of February: "I am very pleasantly domesticated with my agricultural family . . . My landlady is a very motherly, kindhearted woman; and the girls are all merry lighthearted creatures, which is a great Godsend to a melancholy man like myself."[4] Before long, the melancholy man was playing ball with the neighborhood children and "tearing round the garden like a schoolboy."

The walks were often undertaken with Father Anselm, a twenty-eight-year-old philosophy teacher and editor of the Order's official magazine, *Franciscan Annals*. Anselm, fully apprised of the poet's drug problem, had been loosely assigned to keep a watch over Thompson, and had called at Bishop's House to introduce himself soon after Thompson's

The Welsh hills near Pantasaph.

arrival. At this first meeting, he remembered, Thompson entered the room "with a springy step but with a certain shyness," and thereafter Anselm looked in on him every other day or so. His description of Thompson's physical appearance at this time is valuable because it captures the actuality, and avoids the unconscious deference to the Victorian ideal in the descriptions supplied by others: "He had a great and spacious forehead, a splendid pair of large gray eyes that seemed always changing into light blue, a small but definitely combative nose and the orator's mouth of no particular symmetry. About his whole appearance there was a suggestion of physical frailness, yet withal, of nervous energy and grace from his delicate features to the tips of his artistic fingers." Their conversation usually ran to philosophy and theology and Anselm was continually amazed at the range and lucidity of his companion's intellect, and he early discovered, what a few had known before him, that under mental excitement Thompson became transformed, and "would talk like an angel." Some of the talk was channeled by Anselm into the pages of the *Annals* in the form of brief articles, and there was even a pedestrian poem, on the stigmata of St. Francis, written at Anselm's special request.[5] Before that, however, poetry of some worth had begun again to flow.

The first flash of reawakening inspiration occurred at Christmastime, a few days after his arrival, with the writing of *Little Jesus,* a poem often underestimated, but which is, in its own way, one of his most complete successes. It is supposed to have been written while he knelt before the Christmas crib,[6] in the Pantasaph chapel, and this may be true, but if so it could only indicate a first draft of eighteen lines, which still exists in manuscript. The piece was afterwards elaborated to its final fifty lines by adding the tender grace notes of childhood, portrayed as operating in the life of the child Jesus. It appears to have been the total atmosphere of the monastery, and not just the crib, that engendered the poem. Thompson had been much struck by the simplicity of Franciscan attitudes on his first sustained contact with them, and soon came to feel that the Franciscan was an embodiment of what he called, in a note made at this time, the poet's ideal: "the spontaneous candour of the child with adult consciousness."[7] The phrase is so exact a description of the unique qualities of *Little Jesus* that it is no straining of conjecture to link poem and note.

After a deceptively simple and low-keyed beginning:

> Little Jesus, wast thou shy
> Once, and just so small as I?
> And what did it feel like to be
> out of Heaven and just like me? . . .

that continues for eighteen lines, he quietly inserts one of the most unusual and touching expressions of the mystery of the Incarnation in all literature:

> And did Thy Mother let Thee spoil
> Thy robes, with playing on *our* soil?

In the concluding lines of the poem he achieves an extremely subtle blending of childlike mentality and adult consciousness: the child's relation to its father and the human being's relation to God the Father.

> So, a little Child, come down
> And hear a child's tongue like Thy own;
> Take me by the hand and walk,
> And listen to my baby-talk.
> To Thy Father show my prayer
> (He will look, Thou art so fair),
> And say: "O Father, I, Thy Son,
> Bring the prayer of a little one."
>
> And He will smile, that children's tongue
> Hast not changed since Thou wast young!

The poem and a sonnet, *Desiderium Indesideratum*, were complete by the end of March, and must have given Thompson some degree of satisfaction, though he seems to have thought little of them. "I send you two bantlings in verse," was his casual comment to Meynell. But it was a slow start, and there was nothing else until late May when he wrote *Any Saint*. In the meantime, there was Maggie Brien.

A slim, rather pert-faced young woman with large, intelligent eyes and brown hair, Maggie's duties consisted of helping her mother to care for the house and its guests, so she came into almost daily contact with Thompson. Though mutual shyness kept them from any immediate involvement, by the fall there was some disclosure of feelings on both sides. Eventually, there was a somewhat hesitant declaration of love, followed by a rather painful period of courtship, and an anticlimactic subsidence into friendly forgetfulness. Though she was a girl of little education and no real understanding of literature, Maggie Brien was not merely of passing significance in Thompson's life, as the Meynells have implied. For more than two years she gave him warmth and friendship, for a while even love, and it was during this time that he began again to write poetry. It was, finally, while he was wrapped in the uneasy comfort of his first mature love affair that he composed one of his most unusual and powerful pieces, *An Anthem of Earth*.

The affair is very fully recorded in the sequence *A Narrow Vessel*, which appeared in *New Poems* in 1897, and even more explicitly in the unpublished verses Thompson called *A La Marguerite*, a title he later deleted in favor of *Wild-Flower*. Despite its importance to Thompson, however, the relationship was always a rather uneasy one, with the inexperienced, solitary poet fumbling for common ground on which to meet the country-coquettish Maggie. On February 16, 1894, he wrote to Monica Meynell: "I return your father the letter from the *Review of Reviews*. I hope he doesn't want the proof of my portrait back; because a girl at my lodgings has gone off with it. I'm sure I don't know why, for she does not like me, and keeps out of my way as much as possible. But the ways of girls are unsearchable . . ."[8] The feelings between them were never entirely free of constraint, and even when he reached the point of declaring his love for her, he could not quite overcome a doubt that the gulf separating their worlds was too great. His peculiarly equivocal and rather pathetic attitude is clearly revealed in the unpublished *Wild-Flower*.

> A little gift to me you gave,
> And for your meed a poem crave.
>   You do not know how much you ask,
> You will not know how much you have.

Such hard words here to try you! Oh,
I see you frown, and read, and sew!
  But if you know they mean "I love you,"
What matters all you do not know?

Brown eyes! that laughed in fair amaze
To learn your beauty from my gaze;
  Yet would not trust the too glad tidings
Until my mouth sware to the praise!

Age has some conscience taught my tongue,
It would not flatter you to your wrong
  Dear girl; but ah, I fear mine eyes
Are babblers still, unlearned and young!

. . .

One thought of mine has nobler art
Of love, than all your little heart;
  Which God made shallow, for He knew
Your days in joy should have small part.

And so I love you more than can
You, dearest dear, love any man.
  To your strait clod-walled days, the boon
Of love's fine sense were cruel ban.

What hardest heart could wish it you?
Nay, do, poor child, as children do—
  Love me as long as the whole space
Between two playthings leaveth you.

Love me one vast hour, more or less,
Till a lost kerchief's wept distress
  Void the weak pang; love me almost
As sweetly, Sweet! as a new dress.

Yes, play the vagrant too! For still
The child from knee to knee strays, till
  The first-forsaken pardon it
With half a laugh and all his will.

. . .

Nay, but you my deep-bended glance
Foil with insentient countenance,

And absent eyes unknowing. Whence
I know you know it with joyance.

Then my gaze mocks and the smiles grow
Just at your mouth-tip, and you glow.
　　Love-fashions, surely?—Pest on it!
But you would love ten dozen so!

. . .

With love so past your compassing
You count it but a little thing;
　　With love you shall not know again—
You do not know it now—I sing;

With love beyond your own kin's love,
Of threads too fine for your sight wove;
　　With love enough to make me sad
Seeing you have no skill thereof;

With love enough to let you make
My lips smile and my heart half ache,
　　When you grow tired, and pout, because
The toy's too strong for you to break.[9]

The playful give-and-take that was Maggie's simple notion of courtship only irritated Thompson, who could not understand the total unreason of the purely feminine in such matters. Her coyness may have been attractive at first, but he felt that such behavior had its limits, and occasionally he would run out of patience. Maggie's sister, Agnes, recalled him more than once losing his temper: "You could tell from the way he'd go bouncing around."[10] *Beginning of End* contains an unusually graphic account of exactly the type of behavior that sadly perplexed him in Maggie. He was standing outside Bishop's House one day, at the monastery gates, when she and a friend passed by without acknowledging his presence, Maggie only glancing back a few seconds later to gauge the effect of her stratagem. She could hardly have surmised the depth of Thompson's reaction:

Appointed tryst defiantly she balked,
And with her lightest comrade lightly walked,
Who scared the chidden Love to hide apart,
And peep from some unnoticed corner of her heart.
She thought not of her lover, deem it not

Maggie Brien.

(There yonder, in the hollow, that's *his* cot),
But she forgot not that he was forgot.
She saw him at his gate, yet stilled her tongue—
So weak she felt her, that she would feel strong,
And she must punish him for doing him wrong;
Passed, unoblivious of oblivion still;
And, if she turned upon the brow o' the hill,
It was so openly, so lightly done,
You saw she thought he was not thought upon.
He through the gate went back in bitterness,
She that night woke and stirred with no distress . . .[11]

With the two of them living under the same roof, the proximity seems to have led in time to something more than emotional attachment. The verses *A Girl's Sin: In His Eyes* purportedly deal with the gift of a lock of hair, but such a commonplace transaction could hardly have aroused the response Thompson describes:

> But naught were extreme punishment
> For that beyond-divine content,
> When my with-thee-first-giddied eyes

Stooped ere their due on Paradise!
O hour of consternating bliss
When I heavened me in thy kiss;
Thy softness (daring overmuch)
Profanèd with my licensed touch;
Worshipped, with tears, on happy knee,
Her doubt, her trust, her shyness free,
Her timorous audacity!

The sexual contact between them, undoubtedly slight, was probably taken by Thompson as a sign of serious involvement. But he soon began to suspect Maggie of a disturbing flippancy:

For when a girl is in the house,
    And dusts and cleans all day,
What should she take a lover for
    But a sun-bright holiday?

The shaping of a new dress,
    And what the neighbours say,
These are a girl's true interests,
    She goes to love for play.[12]

His perplexity only deepened as the affair progressed toward its close. A stray passage in a later book review reveals, rightly or wrongly, how strong was his disillusionment at the time. He is discussing Robert Burns's affair with Jean Armour:

Though we have talked of the poet's "career of seduction" . . . it was far from implying what it would imply in a higher society. The young ladies of such a community did not need much seduction . . . We are not, it is true, personally acquainted with Scottish village-life . . . Yet we do not speak out of our inner consciousness only. The reviewer has lived intimately in contact with a type of peasantry strongly analogous to that described by Burns, though more dour, less streaked with gaiety, and has, therefore, a vivid realisation of what such an environment means . . . From this same experience, we doubt the heroism which Mr. Henley imputes to Jean Armour in a certain detail of conduct. He hardly, we think, realises the extent to which such girls' sensibilities are dulled in these matters. But all this is not to be pursued here . . ."[13]

Despite this denouement, there was for a time a real attachment between them. Maggie's sister, Agnes, as late as 1964 said, in the understated manner of one who had never lost the early reticence of country life: "He did care for her . . . I used to see them talking together . . . He did think a lot of her . . . and she thought a lot of him." Mrs. Blackburn, who was well acquainted with the Briens, also serves as a witness. In 1911 she suggested to Wilfrid Meynell that a simple cross might be put over Maggie's grave, "for I know for the time of his stay here, he did love her in quite a human way. She was a good girl; he told me once she was a 'white soul' . . . She did love him for all her reticence."[14]

Insofar as it is possible to trace it, the affair seems to have lasted until the end of 1895. The two were not together in the same house all this time, however. About the middle of 1894 the Briens gave up Bishop's House and moved to Creccas Cottage, another property of the monks, located just over the hill behind the monastery, Thompson remaining at Bishop's House. In October of that same year, 1894, he quarreled with his new landlady, and went to live at Ivy Cottage, also nearby. In July of 1895 he moved in again with the Briens at Creccas Cottage, occupying a combined bedroom-sitting room on the ground floor, about ten by twelve feet, with a fireplace and a window that looked out on a honeysuckle arbor. This return to the Briens is interesting, if only because of the fact that Creccas Cottage was hardly big enough to accommodate the Briens themselves. The upper floor contained two small bedrooms, with an extra bed on the landing, and below, in addition to Thompson's room, there was only the kitchen.[15] It may have been, of course, a need for extra money that prompted the Briens to accept a boarder in such cramped conditions, one with whom they were familiar; it may also have been that all parties concerned had reason to expect something more permanent to happen.

The relationship had cooled off well before Thompson left Pantasaph, but they had drifted apart, not separated in any dramatic or sudden way, so that it was possible for Thompson and Maggie to go on living under the same roof until he departed for good in 1896. Maggie lived out her life in Pantasaph, unmarried, and died of a heart attack in 1907, just three weeks before Thompson's own death: she returned from church on Sunday, October 20, and collapsed without warning. She was buried in the monastery churchyard where she lies today, her grave still unmarked. Sometime afterward, her family discovered behind a picture in the room that had been hers the faded, yellowish proof of Thompson's portrait.[16]

II

Late in May 1893 Thompson received from the Meynells the news that the publisher, John Lane, had asked for a book of his poetry. The firm had earlier contracted to bring out Alice Meynell's essays, as well as a reissue of her early verses, and while preparation of these was under way Thompson's poems from *Merry England* had been submitted. On May 6, Richard Le Gallienne, Lane's reader and a member of the Meynell circle, reported favorably—"Would certainly publish. Rich coloured, oriental things. Remind me very much of Crashaw"—and by June, Thompson was hard at work preparing the manuscript of *Poems.*[17]

He brought together the scattered pieces he had written to Alice Meynell and labeled the sequence *Love in Dian's Lap.* Of some thirty other poems published to that time, he selected eleven and carefully combed them, line by line. Both his selections and his revisions were unerring. The original lines from *The Poppy,* for instance:

> With burnt mouth red as a lion's one
> It sucked the blood of the prostrate sun

became instead

> With burnt mouth red like a lion's it drank
> The blood of the sun as he slaughtered sank

thus doing away with the artificial phrase "lion's one," as well as softening the feverish "sucked the blood." From *To the Dead Cardinal of Westminster* he dropped half a dozen stanzas in which the reference was obscurely personal. The *Hound of Heaven* he used nearly as it had been first printed, but he made two changes that imparted to it a final perfection. One passage, in which he rightly detected the note of excess, he deleted entirely:

> I grazed
> Too closely Thy blue window as I gazed,
> Jutted a careless elbow through clear Heaven
> And gashed me with the splinters—see I bleed!

and the poem's last line became

Thou dravest love from thee, who dravest Me

where he had earlier tried both "drivest" and "drovest." The *Ode to the Setting Sun* was not included, undoubtedly because he recognized the justice of the Meynells' opinion that it suffered from "violence of diction," but also because he had himself come to realize that the poem contained too many weak passages; his revision of it for a later volume vindicated his decision. Early in July, the manuscript was finished and sent off to Wilfrid Meynell for transmittal to Lane, and during the next two months he was busily engaged in reading proof and discussing by letter minor points of composition. *Poems* was published late in November 1893. An almost-square book of eighty-one pages, it carried a frontispiece by Laurence Housman, visualizing the "hearted casement" passage in *The Hound of Heaven*. The picture earned Thompson's immediate displeasure: "the artist has overstepped the limits within which pictorial symbolism can act. To attempt to render a purely literary image such as the 'hearted casement' in black and white is a grievous mistake—the result reminds one of nothing but a half-obliterated five of hearts."[18] Otherwise, he felt, "the book is indeed beautifully got up."

Wilfrid Meynell had managed to attract considerable prepublication attention by skillful use of the Browning letter, as well as hints about Thompson's "bohemian" background, with the result that, of all the thousands of volumes of poetry that issued from London presses in the nineties, few, perhaps none, aroused attention equal to that which greeted Thompson's. It went through three editions in its first three months—earning royalties of nearly one hundred pounds in 1894, which probably afforded him the pleasure of making some repayment to the Meynells[19]—and was reviewed by every magazine or newspaper with literary pretensions. The commentary went to one extreme or the other, usually in the same article, but none of it was lukewarm. Before 1894 was half gone, Thompson's name was known in all literate circles of the English-speaking world, and the majority of the opinions agreed that a poet of the first rank had appeared.

There was much decrying of his often archaic diction, involved structure, stuffed imagery, word-coining, overly gorgeous imagination, and his Latinisms, but very often the reviewers who pointed to all of these things, ended by helplessly agreeing that, despite it all, the writer was indeed a true, perhaps a great poet. Wilfrid Meynell bundled up as many reviews as he could gather and from time to time sent them to Pantasaph, where Thompson read them in mingled satisfaction and tolerance. Only in the case of an opinion by Arthur

Creccas Cottage, Pantasaph. The window at lower left was Thompson's.

Symons, who Meynell thought was favorable, did he dissent violently. "Call you this dealing favourably with a man?" he asked in immediate anger, "Heaven save me, then, from the unfavourable dealers! If the writer and myself were not so completely unknown to each other, I should have thought it had the note of personal spite." Yet Symons' article was really a sincere and penetrating evaluation, that actually granted Thompson a great measure of lyrical magnificence, and abundant imagination. What he did not like was Symons' dwelling on the imitative side of his verse, and the opening sentence of the review perhaps robbed him of any chance for a balanced reading: "If Crashaw, Shelley, Donne, Marvell, Patmore and some other poets had not existed, Francis Thompson would be a poet of remarkable novelty." It was Symons' claim that Thompson had not sufficiently assimilated his borrowings; "thus his work, with all its splendours, has the impress of no individuality; it is a splendour of rags and patches."[20] With that sentence Symons crystallized the major point of contention in the critical discussion of Thompson's poetry, a point which has not yet been laid to rest and perhaps never will. In some measure, of course, it was this very splendor of rags and patches that prompted the unprecedented close attention and grudging avowals of worth—poetry in which there sounded so many echoes of established writers, teasing and tantalizing the memory, could hardly be overlooked.[21]

Of more importance to Thompson were the comments that touched him in a personal way. He was, for instance, accused of being "the poet of a small Catholic clique." This was not true in any conscious sense, and it was vociferously denied at the time and again in Everard Meynell's *Life*. Yet, in a way it was so, and moreover, circumstances made it appear to be truer that it was. Richard Le Gallienne, for example, had recommended publication of the poems to Lane, and had afterwards reviewed them, highly favorably, in both the *Star* and the *Chronicle*. He had been a friend of the Meynells for three or four years and had been praising Thompson's poetry since the appearance of *Ode to the Setting Sun,* so that, while his published response to Thompson's verse was sincere, and his report to Lane carefully considered, his pretending to disinterest was a distortion. At least a half-dozen other enthusiastic reviews, in the most influential London papers, were produced by close friends of the Meynells, and while all of these were sincere, to insiders the situation, nevertheless, did have the look of a concerted maneuver.

More serious were the writings in which Thompson's background was discussed, often to the detriment of his family's good name. Stories of his being cast out of home, penniless and starving, were shamefully widespread, all part of the curiosity that centered around rumors of his London destitution and his life at a monastery. Edward Bok, of *Americanization* fame, then conducting a syndicated column called *Literary Leaves,* provides a fair example of the distortions that were rife and the slanders that were blithely leveled at the elder Thompson:

An English literary friend writes me, in a most interesting manner, that the literary guild of London, that is, the more critical portion of it, is a perfect unit in regard to the fact that England has found its new poet in Francis Thompson. He is the subject of discussion at the London literary clubs, and his praises are being sung in every quarter where men and women are appreciative of mentality in literature . . . Thompson was in London three weeks ago, but only a few people saw him although he might have been feted to his heart's desire by the literary set had he but made his presence known. He is now living in Wales at a monastery . . . His life furnishes a new chapter in the history of Bohemian genius . . . From his boyhood he seemed to live in books, even against the wishes of his father, who desired his son to follow the profession of medicine. For this purpose he was sent to London when he was twenty-

The Pantasaph guest house.

four years of age. But parental wishes proved incapable of stamping out the bent for literature in the young man. Instead of reading books of medicine he would read classic poetry by the hour. This angered the father, and one day he gave his son his choice: either he must pursue the studies which he had been sent to London to take up, or all parental assistance would be cut off. Young Thompson chose the latter. The weekly stipend was cut off, and the young man was left practically penniless on the streets . . . Day after day Thompson wandered around the streets of London, barely earning enough to even pay for the poorest accommodations in the cheapest lodging houses . . . This life he continued for four whole years, and during that entire time he never ate a full meal, nor did he sleep in a comfortable bed. His meals consisted chiefly of an apple, a fish caught by him in a rural brook, and fried over a few pieces of wood on the shore . . .[22]

Bok didn't explain how the rural brook had found its way into the streets of London, but he did mention the laudanum, saying the habit was now first contracted, thus indirectly blaming the father for the addiction. Bok concluded his remarks by quoting from his English friend's letter: "I thought . . . as I looked at Thompson who was sitting only two tables from me, what must be the feelings of a father who had caused so much suffering to come into the life of that son who may yet never fully overcome its terrible inroads upon his health." It was, of course, the father himself who could never fully overcome the blighted feelings caused by such charges. Bok's column was not an isolated case; it was typical of much that was written about Thompson, in both America and England, in the early days of his fame. He was aware of all this and had feared such a result even before *Poems* was published. "I am sorry to hear about my father," he wrote to Meynell. "To say the truth, I feared he would be hurt."[23] But it was inevitable. Fame swept over the Thompson family like a juggernaut leaving permanent wreckage behind it. Some attempt to repair the blatant injustice to Dr. Thompson was made by the son in the fall of 1894, when he visited home for the first time in eight years, but no record of this meeting, beyond the fact of its occurrence, remains and, judging by subsequent events, it brought the two no closer.[24]

III

Out of the intellectual ferment created by his frequent and animated discussions with Father Anselm and the other monks, as well as abstinence from drugs, perhaps also the rehandling of his early poetry, there came afresh the urge to compose. The immediate results in the latter half of 1893 were *Any Saint, Assumpta Maria,* and *From the Night of Forebeing,* poems which heralded a period of renewed inspiration that with more or less brief intervals of dryness, was to last until the turn of the century. But it was not the Thompson of old that came to life, the soaring, prodigally gifted image-maker. The old cosmic exuberance had faded, in fact had been deliberately smothered, and in its place was a sober striving after new levels of mystical thought, and a deliberate effort to achieve a calmer, quieter, sparer expression.

It is not easy to grasp what it was that brought Thompson to the point of dissatisfaction with his earlier work, but it is clear that the change arose from causes that had been operating for some time, and did not come unheralded from association with any person or group. It seems, indeed, to have been one of those intellectual floodings, not infrequent in some creative minds, which come with a rush after a sufficient accumulation of experience, profoundly modifying previous attitudes. J. C. Reid, in his occasionally perceptive if waspish biography of Thompson, sets forth the opinion that the poet at Pantasaph felt "the crumbling about him of his cloudy towers of dream," and that he "faced challenges to his undeveloped ideas about Catholicism that left him more understanding of its mystique and dissatisfied with his own earlier liturgical debauches." This was true (setting aside the "liturgical debauches") but it was not the whole truth. The doubts were stirred, not by his changing notions of the Catholic mystique, not even by any new attitudes toward formal religion in general, but by a sudden and deeply realized philosophical hunger which overwhelmed him just as he faced, squarely and for the first time, the inadequacy of his training. He saw how his relentless pursuit of literary things had left him with a shallow and erratic philosophical foundation, for which not even "brilliant intuition" could compensate. He very early confessed to Father Anselm that he knew nothing of formal philosophy beyond a little Coleridge, some superficial

Maggie Brien (right) and her sister Agnes, taking tea outside Creccas Cottage.

Leibniz, and some secondhand Plato, "supplemented by a direct reading of the *Symposium,* into which I plunged like a duck into water. Beyond this nothing . . ."[25]

There were others at the monastery, besides Anselm, who could see that something was happening, who could recall times that Thompson revealed "the stirring of something more than the singer." Always, before, he had been content to rely on a mysterious spontaneity in the creative faculty, an impulse which seemed to speak from some unknown region of his mind, and which presented him not only with a ready-made philosophy but the themes on which to exercise it. "For what am I a poet," he had cried in his first blind resistance to the change that was overtaking him, "but that my soul's instincts may stand like lighthouses amidst the storms of thought?" At Pantasaph he awoke to the possibility that instinct might perhaps only be a beginning and that lighthouses are erected only with much labor and difficulty. Not surprisingly, his early poems began to seem like so much tinsel, barren as they then appeared to him of specific intellectual freight. Maturity, he explained a few years later, brings with it a need for meaning as well as beauty in life and art: "We are still grateful enough for mere beauty in song, as in existence. But we are more grateful for song which has both beauty and conscious significance." That the change in outlook was also at bottom a return to the professedly religious attitudes of his youth seems obvious. "He came, even to the point of silence in certain moods," said Everard Meynell, "to feel the futility of all writings save such as were explicitly a confession of faith; and also of faithfulness to the institutional side of religion—the Church and the organized means of Grace." Thus at Pantasaph he began the repudiation of his earlier belief in secular literature as the greatest influence for moral good. He was no longer content to have his poetry "put on greenness" in order to praise God. The praise itself, in the accents of ancient tradition, must be voiced. Unfortunately, as it developed, he was not one whose genius could be made to submit to conscious control in any great degree, and if he succeeded in his quest for conscious significance he did so at the cost of song. And in this, too, he was following some great predecessors, with Wordsworth as the supreme example—men who were true poets only so long as they did not try to be.[26]

While no external force brought about the upheaval in Thompson's approach to his art, it did coincide with the beginning of his friendship with Coventry Patmore, and it was Patmore who set the course of his awakening. Of all the masters Thompson could possibly have chosen, Patmore would have seemed the least likely. Any writer who, like Thompson, looked on Shelley and De Quincey as his polestars in literature, could not be expected to respond with enthusiasm to the drily cerebral, unmusical verse, and the turgid prose of Patmore. Yet this is just what Thompson did, and so thoroughly, in fact, that for a while he lost his own poetic identity. The two even became personal friends, and that, too, is surprising. Patmore's age—twice that of Thompson—his well-known intellectual arrogance, his forbidding manner, were things that might have precluded the possibility of closeness. C. L. Hind, himself very much a man of the world, recalled that Patmore "was an aristocrat in letters as in life, and he always gave me the idea that it was an honor to be in his presence . . . He could be very courteously brusque, and shall I say, pedantically off-hand."[27] That this man and Thompson became intimate, and that Patmore, against all probability, was eventually led to acknowledge Thompson's superiority, remains one of the more amusing literary quirks of the nineties. The poetry to which the relationship gave rise is still the focus of much disagreement, but it is the same type of disagreement that centers on most of Patmore's own work: critics, especially Catholic critics, debate its merits as mystical philosophy while hardly anyone reads it as poetry.

Coventry Patmore at mid-century had been one of the best-known poets in England, a position he had attained with his plodding epic of married love, *The Angel In the House*. Thereafter, his work had suddenly turned into the bypaths of mystical philosophy, abstruse theology, and metrical experimentation. His chosen form became the irregular ode, which he pared to jarring and erratic rhythms often distinguishable from outright free verse only by an occasional rhyme. Few people were interested in Patmore as a visionary, however, and during the sixties and seventies he fell into almost total obscurity and retired to his country home. In the mid-eighties his reputation enjoyed a mild revival and he returned to a limited participation in London literary society under the sponsorship of Edmund Gosse, the Meynells, and others. Alice Meynell, especially, revered him. To her, perhaps not surprisingly, his poetry was "the greatest thing in the world, the most harrowing and the sweetest. I can hardly realise that he who has written it and who is greater than his words is celestially kind to me and calls me friend." It was undoubtedly her open and often-expressed adulation of the older poet that moved Thompson to read him with a receptive mind.

His first acquaintance with Patmore's work—both the prose and the poetry—had begun at Storrington toward the end of 1889, when he read *The Unknown Eros* as well as Patmore's first collection of prose, *Principle In Art*.[28] Though his initial response had been one of distaste, by April of 1890 he completely reversed himself and was ready to accept Patmore as the "second of living poets," as well as "the great Catholic poet whom it has been the desire of [my] life to see," and the switch of opinion is certainly due to association with the Meynell circle. The avowal was hardly an enthusiastic one, however, since little trace of the Patmorean idiom can be found in the poems of this period, except for the consciously imitative *To Monica Thought Dying*, written in February 1892, and which was obviously suggested by Patmore's *If I Were Dead*. Throughout his residence in London, Thompson's view of Patmore continued to vacillate between respect for his poetry and abhorrence of certain aspects of his philosophy, particularly the sex-and-piety symbolism that Patmore had derived from the *Canticle of Canticles*, and which had become his most distinctive trait. Patmore's habit of elucidating the God-man relationship in terms of human love and sex—often slightly hysterical when not tedious—was the opposite of Thompson's etherealized way of approaching the same subjects, but there was some affinity of thought between them and a slight Patmore influence began to show itself occasionally, as in the close of *A Fallen Yew*, and even *Little Jesus*.

It was not, however, until Thompson read Patmore's review of *Poems* in January 1894 that he finally cast aside all reservations and accepted the older poet wholeheartedly in the role of mentor. "I am delighted with it," he wrote to the Meynells. "From first to last it is pre-eminently *just; and manages to combine fine praise with discriminate and illuminating criticism of defects and limitations . . . Other critics note the symptoms of one's poetic maladies, he diagnoses the seat of the disease. I have got more help and self-knowledge from his article than from anything else which has appeared."[29] Patmore's comments, of course, had not been written after one or two readings of *Poems*, as had the other reviews, but were the well-considered product of some three years' acquaintance. From the first he had felt a "proprietary interest" in the metrical side of Thompson's verse, since, as he implies in the review, Thompson evidently had followed his own highly individualistic ideas on the subject, a suggestion not true but which Thompson let pass. Patmore's praise of *Poems* was unstinted: "Profound thought, and far-fetched splendour of imagery . . . a truly splendid command of language." Thompson, he felt, was a giant among recent poets, a master of meter, and belonged "in the permanent ranks of fame" with Crashaw and Cowley. The adverse criticism was equally to the point: the ardors were too often merely intellectual and lacked the "finish from within" that came from true passion; Thompson was deficient in the necessary "feminine" traits of taste and moderation, and his cosmic moments were "cheap" because they had thrown off all reticence; his neologisms and revivals were disturbing interruptions to the smooth flow of the verse. There was nothing in all of this that could not be found elsewhere, spread through-

Thompson at the age of thirty-three, in the year when his first volume was published.

out the mass of reviews, but in Patmore it was all brought together and expressed with point and vigor. To Thompson, it was a review "which cannot but remain a landmark in my life."

A few months later Wilfrid Meynell sent Thompson Patmore's second collection of essays for review, and with the reading of this book, *Religio Poetae,* the revolution in Thompson's outlook was nearly complete; he had begun to question his whole approach to the poetic art. The last paragraph in his review of *Religio Poetae,* veiled but perfectly clear in its allusion to himself, is an illuminating, if rather sad, confession for a world-famed poet of thirty-three. "One who has had a purely literary training," he admitted, "and has afterwards passed to the treatment of such subjects as occupy *Religio Poetae,* must have experienced a disagreeable surprise. He discovers that the style of literary beauty which had been the pride of his heart, is as useless for his new objects as a butterfly-net for deep-sea fishing."[30] While writing the review he inaugurated his correspondence with the older poet and if he never entirely threw away his net, he did temporarily lay it aside in favor of the more ponderous capacities of a dredge.

It was a visit to Pantasaph by Patmore, about October of 1894, that sealed the transformation. Thompson, prepared to be impressed, was greatly struck by the older poet's commanding presence; he found him "a striking figure; of great height, increased in appearance by his extreme gauntness; large-boned, with imposing forehead and powerful nose; the skin of his face was somewhat flaccid and innumerably wrinkled, the eyelids had a pendulous droop, under which gleamed a scimitarlike line of steel-blue eye. But under emotion the lid would suddenly widen, and the eye darken in a remarkable manner." The two found much to discuss, in Patmore's room, or strolling over the hills, and it was in the stimulating give-and-take of freewheeling, unrelentingly intellectual conversation, very welcome to the younger man after nearly two years in the wilds of Wales, that each found his greatest pleasure. "The contact of our ideas was dynamic," remembered Thompson; "he reverberated my idea with such and so many echoes that it returned to me greater than I gave it forth." A selection from a long string of ragged notes Thompson made on these conversations affords some notion of the topics that echoed between master and pupil:

> Nonsense verses turn out sense—Browning, value of his opinion, as exemplified in his prophecy about *Angel.* Can still laugh or cry at a stage play like any youth (wonder at his openness of mind)—*Coming Race.* 2 knobs on forehead. Started with Mrs. M's difficulties about seeing the invisible. "But you won't see it with *these* eyes."—Skeleton and flesh, for a talk on philosophy of opposites—Swedenborg mad— body in dark. Modern ps. don't get luminousness in flesh. Intense flame of life in Raphael's women—Heaven without Hell leads only to such stuff as Shelley's. You couldn't be happy in Heaven unless you could sit on green cushions and see Gladstone burning—Dreams. De-lights, Terrors, sees—in supernal beauty. Self with her face. Of Ten. no man ever had such finish from without as opposed to finish from within—Sun vibrates—fortune and giving up mistress—conversation about future of Europe—Virginity of soul in fallen woman—Supreme truths self-evident. Assertion the only method. 100 years before he is understood—Every great book should *kill* a vast quantity of books— Botticelli Venus—Many heavens and many hells which you and I would not care for—X-rays. Science will have to be stopped—is it true that Blake borrowed from Swedenborg. Yes, quite true. Where have you, etc., Well, to tell the truth, I have borrowed so much that I don't quite know what I have not borrowed. (cackle).[31]

An additional bond was the fact that Patmore could talk with some degree of sympathy on Thompson's drug problem; he had once defended Coleridge's use of laudanum, and he seems, as well, to have made experiments of his own with hashish. The friendship between these two, though it was a matter of the intellect, and carried on largely by corre-spondence, lasted until Patmore's death in November 1896, and for the rest of his own life Thompson revered his memory as "the greatest genius of the century." That surprising estimate was written to Harriet Patmore on her husband's death, so something must be allowed for the emotions of the moment, but it remains true that Thompson did tend to think of Patmore in such terms. The only adequate comment is a remark by Thompson himself on Dante in a similar situation: "Dante super-praises Arnavelt, who is thought artificial, involved, cold and mediocre . . . shows dissociation between productive and critical faculty."[32]

More than a dozen poems of some length were written by Thompson during 1894–96 which bear the stamp of Patmore's art and outlook. They have an occasional interest and power, but, despite the insistence of some Catholic critics, they remain well below the level of his best poetry (nor, according to much critical opinion, does their mystical flight rise much beyond the lower ranges—as Thompson himself admitted in a cancelled preface to New Poems). Such poems as Orient Ode, From the Night of Forebeing, and The Dread of Height can make no real claim for serious major attention; The Mistress of Vision, not ordinarily bracketed with the Patmorean poems, is yet the most Patmorean of all— the Coleridgean undertone notwithstanding—for it is an attempt, almost feverish, at mystical symbolism, and has little but cleverness left for a second reading. Of all these verses only Contemplation, perhaps, achieves a measure of sustained beauty.

While he was sincere in his attempts to reach a loftier utterance, Thompson seems never to have quite rid himself of nagging doubts about the worth of this kind of conscious endeavor in the face of a spontaneous and intuitional art such as his own. He was diligent in the effort, but even while he proclaimed his determination to advance, he wavered in the memory of what he had abandoned:

> And what hard task abstracts me from delight,
> Filling with hopeless hope and dear despair
> The still-born day and parchèd fields of night,
> That my old way of song, no longer fair
> For lack of serene care,
> Is grown a stony and weed-choked plot.
> Thou only know'st aright
> Thou only know'st for I know not.
> How many songs must die that this may live![33]

It is a sentiment many times echoed by those who have read the Ode to the Setting Sun and The Hound of Heaven with the inescapable feeling that true greatness stirred in the verses "like lightning in a cloud." Only once during his Pantasaph days, in An Anthem of Earth, did Thompson write with the full impact of his old power, and the inspirer of that moment was not Patmore, but Shakespeare.

Thompson's copy of Poems, *containing the original of* The Poppy, *and an unpublished fragment of verse.*

An Anthem of Earth is an attempt to depict the intellectual and emotional progress of Man from birth to death, and it concerns the earth only incidentally. It is the secular obverse of the theme of spiritual progress that occupies *The Hound of Heaven,* and, again, it is expressed largely in terms of Thompson's own experience. There is little on record about the genesis of this poem, but the initial spark, it appears, leaped into his mind from *Timon of Athens,* on which he was writing some commentary in April 1893. The germ of the *Anthem* is easily discerned in the lines he quotes from *Timon,* beginning:

> Common mother, thou
> Whose womb unmeasureable and infinite breast
> Teems and feeds all . . .

He calls this whole passage "an address to the earth," and concludes that it is "nothing less than an ode in miniature."[34] It is difficult to say when he began his poem, but *Timon* was in his mind again toward the end of 1893. In a letter of October he quotes his "favourite bit from *Timon,*" citing, for the "majestic melancholy" of the cadence, the lines:

> My long sickness
> Of health and living now begins to mend
> And nothing brings me all things

When he finally did turn his full attention to the writing of *An Anthem of Earth,* it was not just an effort to expand Timon's address; he had by that time determined on something more ambitious. He had always regarded Shakespeare's later blank verse as his most triumphant achievement, "but it needs an understanding as well as an ear to appreciate it; while the more smoothly linear versification of his earlier periods can be followed by the ear alone. I deliberately took it as a model, thinking that my life-long study would enable me to do what critics have pronounced impossible, what even Coleridge confessed he had tried to do and failed—i.e. catch the rhythm of Shakespeare's verse."[35] He did more than catch Shakespeare's rhythm; throughout lengthy portions of the poem he *was* Shakespeare. The peculiar aura of Prospero's "Our revels now are ended . . ." for example, lies like morning haze on the concluding lines of the *Anthem:*

> Here I untrammel,
> Here I pluck loose the body's cerementing,
> And break the tomb of life; here I shake off
> The bur o' the world, man's congregation shun,
> And to the antique order of the dead
> I take the tongueless vows; my cell is set
> Here in my bosom; my little trouble is ended
> In a little peace.

Sending the completed poem to the Meynells, he explained that it was to be considered only as an exercise in blank verse, "so it is solely for your judgment on the meter that I send it. It is my first serious attempt to handle that form, and it is not likely that I have succeeded all at once." The Meynells agreed that he had succeeded, magnificently, and they published the poem in the October 1894 *Merry England.* Despite some present disagreement, one fact is undeniable: in *An Anthem of Earth* there is revealed a brief but compelling glimpse of what Thompson might have been. In matching Shakespeare's rhythm, he had brought from the damps to glowing life, even if momentarily, the lyrical inspiration of his youth.

IV

In order to capitalize on the excitement caused by *Poems,* Wilfrid Meynell, late in 1894, urged the publication of *Sister Songs* and Thompson, though reluctant, agreed. He had become aware of some truth in the charges of obscurity and frenetic diction leveled at *Poems* and knew that the long poem he had written to the Meynell children four years previously contained a good deal more of the same. At last he acquiesced in Meynell's decision, and in December 1894 he returned to London to prepare the manuscript. The visit stretched over Christmas and into February.[36]

Sister Songs was published in June 1895, but its faults were too evident, especially when dragged through more than a thousand lines, and Thompson's hesitations proved to be well founded. Sales fell far below those of the first volume, only 599 copies being disposed of in the first six months.[37] Reviewers shook their heads either in wonderment or perplexity, though some few were able to see beyond the faults and continued the chorus of high, if qualified, approbation that had greeted *Poems*. Of these, Arnold Bennett's reaction, exhibiting the Thompson-madness that was to become so peculiar a feature with some of the poet's admirers, was typical: "I declare that for three days after this book appeared I read nothing else. I went about repeating snatches of it . . . Show me the divinest glories of Shelley and Keats, even of Tennyson . . . and I think I can match them all out of this book, this little book that can be bought at an ordinary bookseller's shop for an ordinary, prosaic crown." But the disappointing over-all reaction to *Sister Songs* did not dampen Lane's enthusiasm for Thompson's work, and he promptly requested "another collection of short poems, which I suppose you could easily do."[38] Thompson, back at Pantasaph, ignored *Sister Songs* and plunged into a period of intensive writing and revising that was to occupy him during the latter part of 1895 and the start of 1896, and out of which would emerge the manuscript of *New Poems*.

This was a time of unparalleled effort. "The whole book I look back to as a bad dream," he wrote to Meynell as he neared completion of *New Poems*, "so unexampled in my previous experience was the labour I bestowed on it. Indeed, during the last six months, over and above the rewriting upon rewriting of the poems which were ready to hand, I must have written about thirty new poems, long and short; for there were not above twenty or so when I began on the book. I hardly wrote more than thirty in the whole five years preceding my first book; so that it was an unprecedented strain for me."[39] He was, at this time, again living with the Briens and some memory of his unwonted diligence remained with Agnes Brien, who long remembered his interminable pacing, his habit of talking to himself behind the closed door of his room, and how he often called out unintelligibly in his sleep. The Brien children, lying in bed upstairs in the darkened cottage, were frightened at such unfamiliar sounds until they became accustomed to them, but it didn't help their peace of mind to hear their lodger announce one day that he had met a ghost.

Thompson had an implicit faith in the existence of the spirit world,

Coventry Patmore.

and seems at times to have felt himself in mystical contact with it; still it was with a rather light heart that he went to meet the Pantasaph ghost. The little incident was rather anti-climactic, but it provided him with perhaps his only respite from composition and revision. During 1895 reports had persisted of spirit visitations to a large abandoned mansion some distance from the monastery. There were dark rumors of shrouded carriages rolling up the driveway in the dusk, of riderless black horses led by somber-faced grooms, of stormlike noises and mysterious forces inside the otherwise silent house. In November it was Thompson's turn to come face to face with the specter. "I encountered one of the local ghosts the other day," he wrote to Patmore, "for the first time in my now considerable residence here. I will tell you of him when I am in better spirits." Regrettably no more is known of this particular ghost except that the sight of it "charged his body like a battery so that he felt thunderstorms in his hair." When, a few weeks later, two amateur ghost-hunters arrived in Pantasaph, Thompson agreed to watch with them: "I passed a pleasant night with the two. We were sleeping in a haunted house to interview the ghost; but as he was a racing man, he probably found our conversation too literary to put off his incognito."[40]

Late on April 8, 1896, without warning, word reached Pantasaph that Thompson's father lay close to death from congestion of the lungs. He had caught cold on Good Friday, grew worse over Easter, and then began to sink fast, his seventy-two years offering little resistance. Thompson borrowed money at the monastery, hastily replaced the shabby boots he had been wearing, bought a round-trip ticket to Manchester and departed. But it was already too late. On his arrival at Ashton, probably on the tenth, he was told that his father had died the night before. His stepmother, wrapped in her own grief, acutely conscious of the denigration her husband had suffered because of Thompson's fame, and perhaps accusing him of lack of concern, was bitter; she refused him a place in the Stamford Street house and he was obliged to lodge at St. Peter's Rectory in nearby Stalybridge. Brooding and silent, hardly speaking to family or friends, Thompson attended the funeral on the thirteenth, and, inevitably, was an object of curiosity. "The day after my father's funeral," wrote his sister years later, "he came here to see me. Poor boy! He said then he could see his old friends evidently were unable to shake off their former notions of him and believe him changed." During the burial, little Norbert Thompson, the five-year-old son of the second marriage, gazed at his half brother in open curiosity, being careful, as his mother had warned him, to avoid any rudeness. But he noted and remembered only the blotched skin of the mournful face.[41]

A vision on his sleep
There came, a dream of hopes that never yet
Had flushed his cheek. He dreamed a veilèd maid
Sate near him, talking in low solemn tones.
Her voice was like the voice of his own soul
Heard in the calm of thought.

Alastor

8

HE DREAMED A VEILÈD MAID

SHORTLY AFTER RETURNING TO PANTASAPH FROM HIS FATHER'S FUNERAL,
Thompson sent to Meynell the completed manuscript of *New Poems*.
He felt no enthusiasm, though, and dolefully observed that he had
"greatly lost in fire and glow. It is time I was silent. This book carries
me quite as far as my dwindling strength will allow." In a Preface
originally intended for the book he went further: "Though my aims
are unfulfilled, and my place insecure, many things warn me that with
this volume I am probably closing my brief poetic career." But less than
two months later all such somber predictions were forgotten and he
suddenly began writing poetry full of a youthful ardor such as he
had never displayed before; philosophy, theology, and arcane symbolism
were dropped and his work began once more to sing. He had finally
fallen, desperately and irretrievably, in love, and over a period of four

years the affair was to draw from him no less than twenty-five poems, only one of which was published in his lifetime.[1]

Readers of Thompson biography have always been aware of Katie King as an episode in his life, but she has so far been allowed to stand in the shadows off stage. She has, in fact, been deliberately kept there. Everard Meynell dismissed her with the brief comment that she had been "especially his friend," and it was not until nearly forty years later, when Viola Meynell published *Francis Thompson and Wilfrid Meynell* in 1952, that anything further was revealed. Viola implied that there had been something more than friendship between Katie and Thompson, but she gave it the appearance of a short and almost casual encounter. Details of the relationship were left untouched, beyond the fact that Katie's mother had not favored it, and the letters Viola supplied were edited, though without indication of the fact. Subsequently, Pierre Danchin, French devotee of Thompson and author of an exhaustive critical study of his work in French, briefly reassessed the situation in the light of some of Thompson's unpublished verse, and concluded that the poet had indeed been very much in love with Katie. He thought that the attraction might have lasted for several years, and that it might even have been Katie's marriage to another man that helped turn Thompson into a recluse and set him once more on the downward path of drug addiction. It is now time to make a final attempt, so far as it is possible, at restoring the full part played by Katie King in Thompson's life, as well as in his ultimate surrender to the bare, if industrious, solitudes of his final years.

Katherine Douglas King was another protégé of Wilfrid Meynell. In her mid-twenties she had begun a career as a writer of sentimental short stories with an appearance in *Merry England* in June 1893. Her work had no particular merit—hardly worse and no better than most of the day's magazine fiction—but Wilfrid Meynell encouraged her and during the next two years published a dozen of her stories. In 1895 she produced a novel, the first of four she was to write.[2] A charming girl, with a thoughtful cast of mind, Katie became a favorite visitor at the Meynell's house, where she spent many afternoons romping with the children and teaching them such things as candy-making, "her skirt brushing the ground as she went her eager way." Surviving portraits show her to have been an appealing, if slightly wistful, young woman, much like one of the Victorian heroines that peopled her own stories: "Her face was moulded on grave dignified lines, but her eyes were the clear open eyes of an innocent child's." Katie's original introduction to the Meynells had come through her mother, Harriet King, author herself of much pedestrian verse. Mrs. King in youth had been an enthusiast for

Elgin Avenue, Paddington. In 1890–91 Thompson lived at No. 31, located just behind the pole. During 1897–1905 he lived at No.'s 16 and 28 (now demolished), just across the street.

Mazzini, and by the 1890's had raised five children, been widowed, and had taken to an invalid's couch with no very definable illness, from which she wrote endless letters, lamenting her delicate health. Her influence over her children, however, was strong, and it was largely her hand, it appears, that snatched from Thompson all his reawakened dreams of happiness.

Thompson was at Pantasaph when Katie first entered the Meynell circle, but before their first meeting he had already developed a keen literary interest in her. "I read through all her *Merry England* stories some months ago," he wrote to Meynell in June of 1896, "and was startled by their individual and impressive note . . . There is a very striking and attractive individuality . . . If it is of any value to her, pray convey to her my sincere admiration of her true gift." It was a visit to London by Thompson, in the same month, for the purpose of discussing the manuscript of *New Poems,* that brought the two together for the first time.

Arriving on the morning of June 15, Thompson went directly to the Meynells' house. As he entered the foyer, he saw Katie sitting on the stairs with two of the Meynell children, and despite the "individuality" he had found in her stories, did not guess her identity; greeted by Meynell a few moments later, he remarked, "What a charming new nurse you've got!" Meynell introduced them and before they parted Katie invited Thompson to visit her at her mother's apartment in Cavendish Square.[3] To Patmore that evening he announced light-heartedly, "A girl I have met here, wants me to visit her; which is pretty fair for the very evening one reaches town." Both Mrs. King and Katie responded to him in genuine friendliness, and further visits, including at least one to the King home in Hale End, Essex, followed. On June 22, Mrs. King herself sent an invitation encouraging the friendship: "I am hoping that you and Mr. Meynell will be able to come here next Saturday, unless indeed it should be too great a fatigue to you . . . The garden has, I fear, just passed its highest point of beauty, but it will still be very pretty, if fine. I fear there is not much other inducement to offer you. Of course, if Francis Thompson is with you, we should be delighted to see him; but I don't know there would be anything he would care for, except that he seems to take an interest in Katie . . ."[4] It was very probably in the fading garden of the King home at Hale End, less than an hour from London, that Thompson's interest in Katie became more than literary admiration. An unpublished fragment, perhaps his first poem to her, seems to reflect a quiet moment in the country and probably dates from this time.

> A moment unforgot!
> A space our converse sunk its wing, but not
> The inward converse, that still grew;
> And like two glow-worm-lights that mix their hue,
> The liquid sphere which clothed her spread its fine
> And mantling verge until it blent with mine,
> Even as the downward sun that to a hill
> Floats, while the air doth thrill
> With much expectance, and with peace is still;
> The orb at length, ah see!
> Resting upon the peak, most sensibly
> Trembles, as does a bubble touching ground;
> And in the spirit of its light breathed round
> The extreme height
> Becomes invisible, and with the light
> One substance, and is sucked into the sun:—
> Her emanation so with mine grew one,
> Consentient, interfused, and we became
> A single effluence in a double frame,
> One being distinct in two, and yet the same;
> I felt the touch of state primordial,
> I knew the Paradise before the Fall.[5]

The references to "the liquid sphere which clothed her," and "Her emanation," were not mere symbols, since the same thought occurs in three or four other pieces, a number of times being characterized as "an aura." His preoccupation with the idea, however, may indicate nothing more abstruse than that Katie was in the habit of using some especially subtle perfume.

The friendship, which developed rapidly during the ensuing five weeks, was abruptly terminated on July 26 or 27, when Wilfrid Meynell suddenly told Thompson that he must leave London immediately and return to Pantasaph. In some considerable agitation, because of an appointment he had made to visit the Kings on the twenty-eighth, Thompson obediently departed, though he later complained in some puzzlement about the "very absurd and annoying situation in which I was placed by W.M.'s curious methods of handling me."[6] Both Katie and her mother sent regrets at his sudden leave-taking, but in the case of Mrs. King the regret was grossly insincere—for it was almost certainly at her insistence that Meynell had acted. All that can be known about the details of this incident is contained in an unpublished letter of Mrs. King to Wilfrid Meynell, dated August 30, 1896, but it is enough:

> I have had a week of unexpected fatigue since coming home: so I have not been able to snatch a moment to say to you what has been on my mind. Do not please be uneasy at the thought that you have in any way *betrayed* Francis Thompson to me. You have told me very little I did not know, and for Katie's sake ought to know. Some obvious falsehoods implied in one of his letters to me (though probably unconscious to himself) made me so uncomfortable that I felt I must have a clear explanation: but once clearly understanding I can take things as they are . . . With regard to Katie, whose position is peculiar, and might be full of many dangers, I think her greatest security lies in Francis Thompson's horror of any bond, even the slightest. He does not express this, but it is evident in his temperament. He must be utterly free, and by consequence, so must she . . .[7]

According to Thompson himself, it was on July 25 that he had accepted an invitation to visit the Kings in the following week.[8] It must therefore have been on that day or the next that Katie's mother questioned Meynell about Thompson's background, undoubtedly worried by the many stories of his drug-taking, and perhaps rumors of more sordid indulgences. Meynell could hardly have concealed everything from her, and his precipitate action points to a demand on the part of Mrs. King that Thompson's projected visit to Hale End be prevented, as a prelude to the breaking up of the friendship altogether.

Back at Pantasaph, and unaware of the sudden turn of events, Thompson found the familiar scenery dull, and the solitude depressing, and he put the feeling into verse on the very day of his return:

> The hill looks with a colder brow;
>   The silence I have made my choice
> Is doubly silent, having now
> The irreparable silence of her voice . . .[9]

Katie King.

A letter from Katie arrived within a few days, however, and he was soon busily composing in a happier mood; verse after verse fell from his pen. *To a Wind from the South* amply demonstrates the exhilaration of these days.

> Breeze that meetest her mouth,
>   Wing unto me here!
> I should know the breath you bare
>   From all breath less dear.
>
> I should know your soft fall
>   From all gales less dear;
> I should say: "My friend's breath
>   Sighs in my ear."
>
> Oh, from every meaner breeze
>   Blowing West or South,
> I should know the breeze had blown
>   Across her fragrant mouth!

During August, September, and October the writing continued. Study of the existing manuscripts, both complete and fragmentary, indicates that at least a dozen poems were produced in those weeks, many of which, if not all, were sent to Katie. Several were sonnets so reminiscent of Shakespeare that it is easy to connect them with a visit Thompson made in October to Stratford-on-Avon. Early that month he had gone to the Edgbaston home of Alfred Hayes, another of Lane's poets, to spend a week and fulfill his lifelong wish of seeing Shakespeare's home in nearby Stratford. Recalling that visit later, Hayes unwittingly preserved a portrait of Thompson in the throes of love and perhaps composition: "At meals he would sit mostly silent, sometimes quitting the table, his food half consumed, as if at some imperious mandate . . . These sudden disappearances, whose cause I never sought to discover, soon came to be expected and only provoked a smile."[10] Correspondence with Katie continued after his return to Pantasaph, and though none of this now exists it is clear that he must have begun somewhat openly to confess his true feelings. Since Katie could hardly have missed the point of such a continuous bombardment of verse and letter, it must be accepted as probable that she did not find the attention displeasing.

But Thompson could not completely shed his foreboding nature, and in the midst of his joy there was doubt. One or two poems at this time voice his fear that he is only heading into further disappointment:

> Wake not the still sad years,
> Thou canst not cure, if they should wake too sore.
> O sweet! no sweetness withers in my heart,
> For none was to impart
> What only comes from others fragrancing;
> Of pleasantness I have not any art
> In this grief-erudite heart! . . .

And the same fragment, revealingly, contains a conscious echo of *Alastor:*

> O sweet! no flowers have withered on my hair,
> For none have wreathed them there[11]

In another sonnet, *Elijah,* he compares Katie to the bird that refreshed the prophet, and says he will resume the "perilous" course of his life, but in fear of the day when "The sudden gulf goes down to dreadful doom"; *Absence,* and *Waiting,* also express this sense of a painful apprehension. Similar anxieties had troubled him even in his youth, when, in his dreams, the happiness of mutual love always hovered just beyond his reach; now, when he had finally met a girl he wanted and who was possible, such fears came back with redoubled force. And it may be, after all, that he did guess at Mrs. King's hidden disapproval—he must at least have wondered about her reaction to all the stories of his "bohemianism."

In the last week of October his fears were realized fully and with shattering abruptness: a letter arrived from Mrs. King requesting Thompson to cease all communication with Katie. He recoiled in shock, protesting illogically that he considered himself only a warm friend of her daughter's, saying that he had destroyed all Katie's letters to him, and asking Mrs. King to destroy his poems and letters. Mrs. King's answer is here printed for the first time in its entirety; it conveys a somewhat different impression than was afforded by previous edited versions.[12]

> My Dear Francis:
> I cannot help writing to you at once: you will, I am sure, excuse my writing in haste. I thank you from my heart for your letter, which makes me honour you, and value your friendship more than ever. It was a great pain to me to write and to feel your pain, and yet, I felt it was necessary. Certainly your letters and poems were open to misconstructions, though only of the most honourable kind; and I am thankful for the frank explanation. I know, from your own words, that there have been painful misunderstandings in respect of Mrs. Meynell, although your relations were circumscribed and safeguarded by the fact of her being a married woman. And I felt bound to prevent these aris-

ing in my daughter's case, both from the injury that might arise to her character, and the injustice and cruelty to you.

And in truth Katie has been placed in an invidious position, full of embarrassment and perplexity:—not so much to herself, who is very simple, as to me. I felt she was open to the charge of coquetry and of heartless trifling with affection: and that you might hereafter have cause to reproach her, if she were not cleared at once.

For, although I can only speak of this with reserve and reluctance, the matter has been talked over by others, and much more has been pressed upon her in your behalf, than you have pressed yourself. I cannot say more than this: but there seemed no alternative than to speak openly between ourselves.

I have been really miserable all this week through having been led to believe that your very life might be endangered by my plain speaking. But I am most rejoiced to meet your courage and straightforward good sense. It should make us all better friends than before: though no doubt there must be a temporary constraint from an incident of pain.

As for Katie herself, she has all along held your view simply and calmly. She expostulated at first when I told her I thought I must write in the sense I did: but she yielded to my opinion. I showed her my letter, and she made no demur to it: but she was entirely passive.

What you say about her being likely to enter a convent has been often in my own mind, though it is very painful to me.

It is not in her nature to love you: but I see no reason why some other good woman should not:—yet perhaps you are most fitted to live and die solitary, and in the love only of the Highest Lover, whom you yourself in your supremest moments feel to have espoused you to Himself. The solitary life has many advantages.

Do not please for a moment think that my friendship for you is broken: though it is poor and of little worth from many circumstances: and from hour to hour I am never sure of myself for anything, and my correspondence is necessarily intermittent.

As for Katie, she has never changed at all: she has simply submitted to what I thought right. She is at the present staying in the Convent.

Still I think, that at this moment it would be better not to re-commence a correspondence, which I believe has been dropped for some weeks: for she has lately seemed wholly engrossed in her work. But I can see no reason why you should not meet again, now that this frank explanation has been made, and no one can misunderstand.

I appreciate your delicacy in allowing me to see her letters as well as yours. I have not seen hers, not wishing at her age to invade her privacy: and I have not asked to see yours, but she has shown me *most* of them. It would seem best, as you have destroyed her letters to do the same by yours. Letters are but fugitive.

But as for the poems, they are valuable. I cannot make up my mind to destroy them. If you will allow me, I will keep them a short time longer, and then send them to you, for they are truly yours. I think you should have *time for consideration*: but I hope you will keep them and do as you think fit with them hereafter. They seem part of your earthly immortality.

As for myself I am afraid I have as little worldly wisdom as you have: I have not enough for my position: many things have forced me into the position of a recluse.

Indeed I feel that both my daughter and I are honoured by your friendship: and I could not part from it without still more pain.

Affectionately yours,
H. E. Hamilton King

"The matter has been talked over by others, and much more has been pressed on her in your behalf, than you have pressed yourself . . ." An obvious guess as to the identity of these "others" would be the Meynells, especially Wilfrid, and it must have been he who led Mrs. King to believe that Thompson's "very life might be endangered" by her frankness—that is, any grievous disappointment might turn him back to drugs. It is quite clear that the relationship between Thompson and Katie was no secret; despite a brief acquaintance of only three months, matters had progressed to the point where Thompson could entertain thoughts of marriage, and even, it seems, discuss them with the Meynells. That they were profoundly impressed with the desperate sincerity of his hopes is evident. Of Katie, it must be admitted that she not only accepted Thompson's protestations, but to some degree returned them. That she allowed her mother to intervene, and eventually turned to another, is no proof that she did not share Thompson's feeling at this period. If he possessed few of the worldly acquirements calculated to take a young girl's eye, he did nevertheless have one rare advantage: he was just then being hailed by a good portion of the literary world as the latest in the line of great English poets. In fact, an important article in the *Edinburgh Review* had appeared only two months before his meeting with Katie, to cap with high praise the two-year flow of comment on his work.[13] This, in itself, could easily have dazzled the heart of a girl like Katie, if only for a time, leading her to overlook his background and his hapless way of life. Some such superficial attraction seems indicated by the passive role she assumed in the face of her mother's action. Her feelings could not have been deep if she "yielded to my opinion . . . made no demur . . . was entirely passive . . . submitted to what I thought right." Some of her later letters reinforce the impression of a young woman captivated by her closeness to literary immorality.

The bitter anguish that followed the seemingly final break with Katie assailed Thompson all during November, and alone in the Welsh hills, he could only vent his feelings in poetry. One stark sonnet, full of a wringing despair, was almost certainly written in the first rush of his terrible disappointment:

> So now give o'er; for you are lost, I see,
> And this poor babe was dead even its birth,
> Which I had thought a young Joy born to me,
> Who had no child but Sorrow: and with mirth
> I gazed upon its face, nor knew it dead,
> And in my madness vowed that it did smile . . .

Another sonnet, existing only in an unfinished state, denies there is any joy in life and has the couplet:

> The joy to live choose he who will, not I;
> Give for my part and boon the joy to die.[14]

lines which, if Mrs. King could have seen them, might have caused her some alarm. It was fortunate that just as this time Thompson was obliged to bend his mind to the demands of some work that could not be delayed, the final proofs of *New Poems*. But thoughts of Katie intruded even on his proofreading, and his use of the traditional "Go, book," envoy shaped itself around the vision of his new volume reaching her hand:

> Go, book, thou shalt be happier
> Than I; Thou shalt approach to her
> Who is sealed up from me like Paradise,
> Shalt fall into her blissful power,
> And be the happy captive of her hand . . .
>
> And, ah, my book, retain some air
> Of me,
> Thy master, that when she
> O'er thee shall bend,
> A little touch a little while
> May her beguile,
> Half-conscious, of her friend,
> Hopeless and faithful to the patient end.[15]

Then, in the midst of his hurt and bewilderment, another blow fell: in the last days of November he received the sudden news that Coventry Patmore had died on the twenty-sixth of that month. His shock and grief he expressed in a number of verse fragments in which he reiterates his

Manuscript of a Thompson poem to Katie King.

belief in Patmore's greatness, and bewails his own devastating loss, feeling himself to be

> most like to one
> That standeth sole upon an alien beach,
> And sees the last sail of his kindred go
> Down the horizon sinking slow;
> Then, for his lids are stung
> With tears, turns blinded to the unamicable land[16]

Most of these fragments on Patmore are uncomfortably high-pitched in tone, and have a note almost of hysteria, but the reason is obvious: he is bearing a double burden of grief. His sorrow over Patmore's death has borrowed intensity from the loss of Katie, and the pain of separation from her, in turn, has been sharpened by Patmore's death. At a time when he had finally begun to realize all his dreams of poetic fame, he lost, within the space of one month, both the woman he loved and the indispensable master who, he thought, was leading him to greater artistic heights. In December, numb from the twin disasters, he reached the lowest emotional pitch of his life.[17] He had indeed entered an "un-amicable land."

II

At this point in Thompson's life all previous biographers dismiss Katie King as an important factor. It was known that there had been contact between the two afterwards, but this was looked on as the casual encounter of friends. Danchin guessed at a deeper involvement, but he was not aware of the true extent of the relationship. This situation was understandable, since nearly all record of Katie and Thompson in the years 1897–99 had been obliterated or suppressed. Yet shreds of evidence still exist, and if examined in the framework of known events, they lead to only one conclusion: Thompson did not give up Katie, but returned to London determined to pursue her.

In mid-December 1896, after more than a month of brooding, he precipitately left Pantasaph for good and descended on the Meynells in London. The move was so hurried that he left all his papers behind and Father Anselm had to forward them.[18] It was so unexpected that when his sister, Mary, in her convent heard about it, she wrote in some anxiety: "I was puzzled because I could not understand why you were in London, or why you had taken your affairs into your own hands."[19] Settled into lodgings at 16 Elgin Avenue, just down the street from his old rooms of 1890–91, he plunged during the next year or so into every sort of activity accessible to him—and contemplated at least one that might have seemed out of the question: lecturing. A tentative connection with *The Academy* he greatly expanded, doing not only book reviews, but special articles on the foremost figures of English literature; from the *Daily Chronicle* he accepted a commission to compose an ode for Queen Victoria's diamond jubilee, and later from the *Academy,* another commission to do an ode on the Boer War. With Constable, the firm that was to bring out *New Poems,* he contracted to supply the text for an illustrated book on London, and with the same firm began discussions for a fourth volume of poetry. He planned and began writing plays, despite the discouragement that had greeted his first such effort six years before. He agreed, probably at the request of Alice Meynell, to deliver a talk on poetry to the respected Society of Women Journalists, and appears to have thought of lecturing as another line to be pursued seriously. It is clear that he had not only taken his affairs into his own hands, but had resolved to break out of the pattern of dependence and seclusion that had been forced on him by the effort to conquer his addiction. His purpose could have been nothing less than a full return to normal life, and the motive for this unprecedented burst of energy, so at variance with the habits of a lifetime, can have been nothing but Katie.[20]

Once he was settled the interrupted friendship was resumed and on February 8, 1897, Katie wrote from Hale End:

> I have been wanting to write to you for a long time but I thought I would not write to you directly after my mother had written. I did not want to add as I fear any words of mine would have done to the pain of disappointment that letter must have brought you. I say disappointment because I think you must have been disappointed as well as grieved to find that after all I had apparently not understood and re-joiced in your friendship for me. But indeed I think I did understand it, and it certainly was a great joy and pride to me to know you were my friend. And I should like you to know that I was very sorry in-deed that owing to the intervention and as I think misrepresentations of others—even with the best and kindest intents—our friendship has received so severe, unwarrantable and unnecessary a check. My wish was against a letter going to you. It seemed so unnecessary and there-fore unjustifiable. I thought we—you and I—understood each other perfectly—and it turns out we did! Do you want your poems yet? May I keep them a little longer? I am so proud of them they are so beauti-ful, exquisite, *living*. My mother who alone has seen them thinks they are of all yours the most beautiful. You were *young* when you wrote them, Francis! There is the lovely freshness of all things young and ardent and beautiful. They are yours when you want them, but even then they will always be mine, too, will they not? I am a great deal at the little children's Hospital. Mr. Meynell knows the way. I know you are very busy now, you are writing a great deal and your book is coming out, is it not? But if you are able and care to come, you know how glad I shall be.[21]

It was a delicate situation and Katie's note reflects her uncertainty. Thompson having responded to Mrs. King's October letter by denying any serious romantic interest in her, the girl must have been in some initial embarrassment over his true attitude, especially when she reread his fervent poems and letters. The safest tack in re-establishing the connection, she would have felt, was to imply that her feelings, too, had gone no deeper than friendship; afterwards, things could be let to develop as they would. She did not leave the future entirely to itself, however, for she promptly, as the letter indicates, suggested a meeting and sent him a photograph of herself. For some reason he did not immediately accept her invitation for a visit at the hospital—a children's institution in Leonard Square where she did volunteer work—and late in March she repeated it, sending directions and reassuring him about the unfortunate interruption to their friendship:

> I would like you to see the little children if you would care to come down to see them. I am at the hospital Thursday and Saturday this week, but Thursday is not convenient for visitors, so would you be able to come on Saturday? The best and quickest way is to take the train at Queen's Road for Moorgate. Then the bus or train down the City Road to Leonard Street. You can *walk* down in about ten minutes. The hospital is halfway down Leonard St. in Leonard Square. Vespers are at 3 so if you could get to the hospital by half past three, that would be, I think, the best time. It takes about three quarters of an hour from Palace Court to Leonard Square. I shall be very glad to see you again and now that we are assured that we understand and trust each other in our friendship we can talk freely, without fear either of misunderstanding or of giving a pain. As for the "past" we can say it *is past* and for the present and I hope the future, we are, and always will be friends. "Ad Amicam" is more to me and to you too, I hope, than exquisite poetry!

In a postscript she also invites him to Hale End, and pointedly indicates that her mother joins her in looking forward to such a visit: "It would give us both such pleasure. Perhaps we can arrange a day Saturday." This time he responded and the two met at the children's hospital before the end of March. On the thirty-first of that month Katie wrote again:

> I have been thinking often of you since Saturday, and wondering how you are. I am afraid you may have had an attack of influenza which is so much about, and with that you must take care, and I am afraid you do not take enough care of yourself. Your visit on Saturday tells me this again! I was very glad to see you again, Francis, and see for myself from your face and know from your ready hand-clasp that we are friends—not "again" but "still," and I hope always. I count you as an old friend now, but I know now I did not really know you until Saturday. When you were by the bed of your little "genius" Harry, and the baby boy, Percy, with the white shoes, was at your knee, that was to me a revelation! I think of you now with that baby boy's serious confiding a pretty ornamental *addition*. Your personality now seems incomplete face upturned to you. It was all so *natural*. For some people a child is

without the child as the natural and exquisite finish to the whole man. Adieu dear friend.

They met fairly often thereafter, especially at the Meynells' house, where Thompson spent several evenings a week, and where Katie frequently was a guest for dinner, sometimes remaining for two or three days at a time. Katie's mother had some years previously become a Catholic, but Katie herself always remained Protestant, and though the difference in faith did not seem to bother him excessively, he did go so far as to ask his sister, Mary, to pray that Katie might be converted.[22]

During 1897 Thompson quickly developed into a highly competent book reviewer and all-round practitioner of literary journalism. He produced over two dozen reviews for the year, all of them revealing extremely wide knowledge, an effortless ability to strike just the right tone, and a less inflated, more controlled and compelling style. Charles Lewis Hind, the *Academy's* editor, quickly recognizing talent of a lofty order, assured him "I am anxious every number of the *Academy* shall have something from your pen." A confident grasp of his materials was not the least of his abilities. When Hind wished him to do articles on Browning, Shelley, and Tennyson, allowing only a thousand words for each, Thompson replied: "I am sorry that, after careful consideration, I must ask you to hand them over to someone else. Considering the importance—the great importance—of the writers I am asked to treat, I do not feel that I could do justice either to my subject or my own reputation within the limit (of 1,000 words) proposed . . . I simply cannot pledge my name to the disposal of Tennyson or Browning in about two columns." Hind promptly doubled the allowance, and, considering the chronic problems of space that confronted him, the action is a good demonstration of the esteem Thompson had so quickly earned.[23]

In May 1897, *New Poems* appeared and while the sale of the book was disappointing, it received wide critical attention. Though the reviews were mixed they were not nearly so bad as tradition has painted them since. They were, on the contrary, remarkably perceptive in that they spotlighted the very elements in his later work that still feed critical commentary and that, seventy years afterwards, remain a barrier to wider appreciation—coined words, jarring diction, erratic rhythms, obscurity, and the didacticism involved in the use of specifically Catholic symbolism. "The thought," as Thompson had observed hesitantly about one of the poems, had indeed "choked the poetry." While the reviewers were often too violent in phraseology and frequently too hasty in particular judgments, much of this was the result of the pressures of professional reviewing: where a man hadn't time to be profound he could at least be clever. None of them, however, denied him his place among the leading poets of the era.[24]

In June, within the space of a few days, he wrote his 300-line *Ode for the Diamond Jubilee of Queen Victoria,* and though he professed to look down on it, calling it "uninspired imitation of myself," it was still a powerful evocation of Victoria's reign, and for an occasional piece was an impressive feat of rhetoric. That there was nervous and physical strain during this time is evident. To Alfred Hayes, he confessed at mid-year, "I have not been at all well, and it has been as much as I could do to keep myself afloat . . . Except journalism, (chiefly for the *Academy,* to which I am now a regular contributor), I have done nothing for months." His impaired health, in particular, toward the latter part of the year is mentioned in more than one letter: a matter of dyspepsia, colds, probably influenza. In November he narrowly escaped serious injury when a hansom cab accidentally ran him down, as, wrapped in his customary abstraction, he was crossing busy High Holborn. His head was badly cut and bruised and he sustained a mild concussion; he was taken by police to the nearby Homeopathic Hospital in Queen's Square, where he asked that Wilfrid Meynell be contacted. As late as six weeks afterwards he was still worried about the effects of the accident to his head, and decrying his misfortune: "The wounds are now practically healed; and I hope that I have no cerebral consequences to fear. It has been very unlucky, throwing back my affairs just when they were in a better train than they have been since I settled in London."[25]

Yet with all this, he actually increased the tempo of his activity. During 1898, in addition to more than two dozen reviews and articles contributed to the *Academy,* he began regular reviewing for the *Outlook,* and made an appearance in both the *Athenaeum,* and the *Daily Chronicle,* doing two or three reviews for each. In April he wrote another long, commissioned ode, for the *Academy,* exhorting England to firmness against the Boers. And, despite the critical hubbub over *New Poems,* he was at the same time preparing the manuscript of a fourth volume of verse: in January 1898 he replied to a query from Constable that he had "material for a thin volume whenever, and if ever, you desire again to deal in my wares," but he warned that he would need about six months to reach a finished manuscript because of the necessary revisions and the demands of journalism.

Soon after the publication of *New Poems* he had sent Katie a copy of the book and she offered him glowing congratulations in a letter that hints at the real basis, perhaps largely unconscious, of her feelings:

How very kind of you to send me your book, indeed a most rare and much-prized gift. I found it awaiting me when I returned from London, very late indeed but even at that hour bordering on midnight I couldn't forbear to open and read, all uncut as it was and myself without paper knife. But I was so desirous!—to get to the contents, I could not put it off till the morrow. Since then I have been reading it under less difficult circumstances and have followed your advice, beginning with the Miscellaneous Poems and Ultima, most poignant and sorrowful, and the last sweet one. I cannot criticize any poetry I love, but what I have read, and I have read but little yet, makes me feel glad and proud indeed that so great and immortal a poet has deigned to choose poor me for his friend and to give me so many proofs of his friendship, this last gift of his own poems being not the least sweet proof. I thank you for this Francis, with all my heart. Do you ever I wonder, in moments when you are more detached from the interior things of your heart, look and stand amazed at the wonder and divinity of your own work? Surely these "New Poems"—from those I have read —will add a fresh lustre to your already glowing crown of fame. Do you know, I do not know whether you care about *Fame* or not! So little one knows even one's friends! Adieu.

Meetings and correspondence continued during 1898, except for intervals when Katie was away or ill in bed: through March and April she suffered with a long siege of influenza, and during August she accompanied some of her hospital charges on a vacation in Littlehampton. While there she received a letter from Thompson enclosing a photograph of himself, for which she sent thanks: "I like it really very much; to me it is not *posed* for it is very like you—in one of your moods, not a peace [sic] one but I think I like it all the better . . . I really don't know what I am writing. Five boys are writing letters all around and the chatter is incessant. My head is whirling." This was a time of high contentment for Thompson and perhaps the best illustration of his happiness was a poem he wrote on the shocking assassination of the Empress of Austria, which occurred on September 10, 1898. *The House of Sorrows* is one of the few poems in the whole body of his work that is totally without a connection to his own life. His feeling of sorrow over the murder of empress Elizabeth, and the tragic deaths of some members of her family, is authentic and shows how the power of love had begun to give him the ability to look beyond himself.[26]

Love poetry also continued, and it was a review of a book by Wilfrid Blunt, written in September 1898, which indirectly produced the only poem to Katie published in Thompson's lifetime. Blunt, a close friend of Wilfrid Meynell and a many-sided man of some wealth, passionately devoted to Arabian culture, was impressed by Thompson's opinions on his verse, and persuaded the Meynells to bring him to his Sussex mansion,

Katie King with some of her hospital charges.

Newbuildings, for a visit. This took place on October 12, 1898, and while Blunt, as his diaries reveal, was silently noting his guest's frailness and reserve, and finding it difficult to think of him as a poet, Thompson was absorbing the Arabianism of the surroundings, which he soon after distilled into the very fine *Arab Love Song*.[27] The poem, a distinct marriage proposal, if an oblique one, in which the speaker exhorts his love to "leave thy mother," and dwell in "the red pavilion of my heart," was published in *The Dome* for January 1899, and shows unmistakably that Katie and Thompson had by that time progressed well beyond the status of friends. A wistful echo to the poem occurs in a review he wrote at almost the same time. Discussing the marriage customs of the Burmese, he notes that in Burma "When a girl cannot obtain her parents' consent to her marriage, she often persuades her lover to fly with her into the woods, where they live an idyllic life, known only to some confidant, until the parents come round . . . The woods themselves supply the food needed for such a climate, while the confidant brings them further supplies; the days are steeped in sun, the nights in fragrance and moon-light." He adds: "An English honeymoon couple might well try it," and the word "honeymoon" scarcely disguises his real meaning.[28]

Another poem to Katie probably written in 1898 is the long, un-published *Nocturns of My Friend*. Consisting of eighteen unusual eleven-line stanzas, it is uneven in quality, and Thompson himself rightly considered it a failure as a whole. Several entire stanzas, however, achieve a surprising force, and when they are brought together, the result is a coherent poem of more than a little value. It is evident that Thompson in attempting to stretch the piece only spoiled it; but in a shortened version, it supplies the most mature statement available of his feeling for Katie, and also affords some evidence of her feelings for him.[29]

> The moonlight cloud of her invisible beauty
>   Shook from the torrent glory of her soul
> In aëry spray, hangs round her; love grows duty,
>   If you that angel-populous aureole
>   Have the glad dower to feel;
>   As all our longings kneel
> To the intense and cherub-wingèd stole
> Orbing a painted Saint; and through control
>   Of this sweet faint
>   Veil, my unguessing Saint
> Celestial ministrations sheds which heal.
>
>
> Tis undulous with her undulating mood;
>   Love, pity, tenderness dissolve in it
> Like honey in bright wine; and so imbued,
>   It is a thing for Jovian breathing fit,
>   That gods might have of her
>   Both cup and cupbearer,
> Immortal drink in chalice exquisite!
> Her most meteorous thoughts do burn and flit
>   In lovely clear
>   Ascent through that felt sphere;
> Nor need they words, tis thought unrobed and bare.
>
>
> She in light motion, like a cloud unbound
>   From the main vapour by a tetchy wind,
> Sandals her feet with gladness; and the ground
>   Leaps to her tread, and the trees would unwind
>   Their knitted roots, and spring,
>   To see so brave a thing!
> As brave, as straight, as swift, her unconfined
> Thoughts fearless tread along her springy mind.
>   O, to be sad
>   Beside her, leave the bad!
> Whoso hath soul of good, his heart must sing!

Read in her eyes, whoso hath soul of good!
   For like the babe within the lotus-flower,
So is her childhood in her womanhood
    Clear symbolled by their sweet wise innocent power.
      The fool shall in his folly
      The child therefrom read wholly;
Nor see there, cloistered 'gainst its fitting hour,
Grave, tender, prudent, all the woman's dower.
      And this I add:—
      Ye comfortless and sad,
Therein is healing, for those wells are holy.

But of that thing which verse cannot enscroll
   To which all these lead up by winding ways,
The very keep and donjon of the whole,
    Which all these mean, and does their purple praise
      Both justify and crown,
      What song shall give renown?
Lend me the sound of fragrance, or, a space,
The word that silence hath, nor ever says!
      Then were the merit
      Of her sole-sealèd spirit
For ever shown, and ever more unknown!

Whence comes the consummation of all peace,
   And dignity past fools to comprehend,
In that dear favour she for me decrees,
    Sealed by the daily-dullèd name of Friend,
      Debased with what alloy,
      And each knave's cheapened toy.
This from her mouth doth sweetness mend,
This in her presence is its own white end.
      Fame counts past fame
      The splendour of this name;
This is calm deep of unperturbèd joy.

Now, Friend, short sweet out-sweetening sharpest woes,
   In wintry cold a little, little flame,—
So much to me that little! Here I close
    This errant song, O pardon its much blame!
      Now my grey day grows bright
      A little ere the night,
Let after-livers who may love my name,
And gauge the price I paid for dear-bought fame,

Letter of Katie King to Thompson, July 21, 1896.

> Know that at end,
> Pain was well paid, sweet Friend,
> Pain was well paid, which brought me to your sight!

After two years of strenuous effort and hopeful courtship, and in spite of what must have appeared great improbability, Thompson seemed at last on the verge of gathering in a full share of normal life. He was thirty-eight years old, possessed the fame he had thirsted for as a boy, was established in London's highest literary circles, and he loved a woman who seemed to love him. But it was not to be. The vision must vanish and the Poet must wander on alone. From early in 1899 a curtain of obscurity descends on Katie and Thompson, and when it lifts again a year later, it reveals Katie announcing her engagement to a Protestant clergyman. Only two or three letters covering the interim remain, and they are of no particular import; a few meager facts constitute the entire basis for any effort to determine what happened. The story they hint at is clouded and dim, like some old portrait nearly faded to oblivion.

After laboring fairly steadily at his reviewing, Thompson's output began to diminish early in 1899; for a period of six weeks, from about mid-February to the end of March, nothing at all appeared from his pen. Following this unexplained hiatus, in April, Father Anselm wrote to him from Crawley and inquired "Do you hear or see anything of Miss K?" and the impression created is that Anselm had heard something to make him doubtful. In the summer of 1899, suffering from some unnamed distress, Thompson, for some unknown purpose, twice went to see Katie's mother at her home in Hale End. Mrs. King recorded the visits in a letter of September 20, 1900, in which it is evident that her attitude has become one of disdain: "He came to see me twice last year, and was absolutely *drivelling*: could only repeat over and over again miserable little physical details about himself which no self-respecting person would have mentioned at all."[30]

Almost certainly the romance with Katie had begun to fade, from whatever cause, by the time of those visits or soon after them. The tendency of the previous two years suggests that it was not, as with Maggie Brien, a simple failure of attraction. It is much more probable that the affair culminated in something like a proposal of marriage, no doubt hesitantly delivered by the shy Thompson, and that the proposal was declined. This is speculation, but it is a marked coincidence that Katie included in one of her novels written about this time a scene in which the heroine rejects a proposal from a suitor whose personality is reminiscent of Thompson's, and the passage may well be a real description of the moment in which Thompson's hopes came to an end forever. Katie's heroine is speaking:

> My voice broke. Nicolai said nothing. When I looked up again, I saw the blow had gone home. Then I knew for the first time how much this courteous, gifted gentleman . . . cared for me. I hated myself, and I never liked him better than at that moment. "I am so sorry, Nicolai," I said in a whisper, and impulsively held out my hand. He took it mechanically and held it for a moment. Then he suddenly raised it to his lips. What were his thoughts I dare not say. He accepted my refusal with an absolute conviction of its certainty that was pathetic. For a moment, he looked uncertain of himself, but never of me, or of the death-blow I had dealt to his hopes. In ten seconds his face had grown ten years older, haggard, lined and hard.[31]

In mid-1899 Thompson was living at 39 Goldney Road, having moved there after a fire the previous year in his room at 16 Elgin Avenue.[32] Quite by accident, the son of the landlady, who was totally unfamiliar with the story of Thompson's life, preserved what may be the last anguished echo of Thompson's love for Katie. "Mr. Thompson's room was on a level with the front door, at the back of the house," he explained; "I remember when I used to pass his door, which had a glass panel with a red margin, with cut glass corners, I used to hear him saying

Oh God, oh God . . ." Was it Mrs. King who defeated Thompson's suit, or had Katie herself drawn away from him, perhaps attracted by someone else? To a degree in her own mind, at least, Mrs. King felt herself responsible. In some unpublished verses on Thompson, written after his death, she confesses that she had been "compelled to wound thy heart, and give thee pain." According to Katie's daughter, Filumena Burr, Katie met the man she eventually married on a cruise, and this suggests the possibility that Mrs. King made use of the classic remedy for unfavored romances. Katie, in fact, did spend the month of September 1899 cruising aboard her brother's yacht, the *Heartsease,* through the canals of Holland, and there may be a connection between this trip, and Filumena's memory.[33]

Soon after the new century dawned, in any case, Thompson heard, probably through the Meynells, that Katie was engaged and on April 11, 1900, Katie herself wrote from Hale End:

My Dear Francis,
I have been wanting to write to you for so long; and now I find it a little difficult because one feels reluctant to speak of one's own great happiness to one whose life has been so sad and lonely as yours, even though that one should be so firm and true a friend as you have ever been to me. Perhaps you may have heard that I am engaged to be married to Mr. Godfrey Burr, vicar of Rushall near Walshall in Staffordshire; and our marriage is fixed for the early part of July. Although my new home will be far away we both hope that in time we may come to live nearer London, and I hope that my marriage will bring me not less but more in touch with my friends, amongst whom, Francis, I hope that I may ever count you as one of the first and nearest. Goodbye, dear Francis, and may God bless you.

Sufficient comment is the fact that Thompson did not answer the note; instead, he once again coined verse from his misery. There exist at least a half-dozen poems lamenting his loss, and the most direct and touching, perhaps, is this fragment edited from a rough manuscript:

> As morning eyes from sleep awakening
> Upon a shining casement, briefly glimpsed,
> Close back to darkness, but the dazzled gloom
> Still keeps the inward vision; so my heart
> Asleep to love, did open upon thee,
> And took on the sudden vision of thy face;
> And from the brief irradiant four years' glimpse
> Closing again to darkness of all love,
> Sees nothing but that face.[34]

He did not entirely understand what had gone wrong. Still preserved are scribblings in which he complains bitterly that "Women of spiritual beauty and corresponding temperament desire to be loved by the same kind of men who love their sisters, young, good-looking and glowing with physical passion. Either they fail and are miserable; or they succeed and are yet more miserable; either way they are miserable. Were they content to be loved by men of their own kind, they, and those men, would be happy." Another brooding fragment in the same notebook identifies the matrimonial disadvantage of poets as "A great and monotonous concentration of interests . . . with an undue proportion of melancholic and depressed fits." These, he concludes, are "more than most wives could bear without unhappiness."[35] On June 26, 1900, Katie King married Edmund Godfrey Burr; in attendance was the entire Meynell family, with ten-year-old Olivia Meynell serving as bridesmaid. The couple went to live at the vicarage in Rushall. Soon afterwards, Thompson confided to a notebook: "My dear friend (now removed by marriage) was a brave woman, and I loved her for it against all my wont. Perhaps because she took me by surprise—perhaps because who knows why? She was not self-reliant with all her bravery . . ."[36] The maid and the dream were gone.

9

SOME DIM CHAMBER

BY MAY OF 1900 THOMPSON WAS CONSUMING FOUR OR FIVE OUNCES of laudanum daily, but the indulgence did not prevent work and he continued to write steadily for the *Academy*.[1] While the break with Katie King must certainly be regarded as the primary cause of the relapse, a contributing factor, certainly, was the rejection of his fourth volume of poetry.

The indications are that he had submitted a manuscript to Constable, probably toward the end of 1899, containing about twenty-five poems, including many of those to Katie.[2] There were none to equal the best of his previous work, but a few were at least interesting, and some of those to Katie had caught not only a portion of his old inspiration, but a new note. Most of the collection, he considered, "should be put on record, though not representing an advance"; some few he felt were "urgent of record."[3] The reasons why this volume was rejected are not known, though they may be conjectured. Did Katie, after becoming engaged to Burr, ask Thompson to leave unprinted the poems to her? (It is known that Wilfrid Meynell, at least, continued to disapprove of their publication and that Thompson felt great disappointment at this.[4]) With the Katie King poems gone—some dozen of the best—did Constable feel that there was not enough substance remaining to go before the critics, especially following the controversial *New Poems?* The evidence points to something like this occurring in the first days of the new century, perhaps in February. In a letter of June 1900, in which he refers to the new volume, Thompson confesses "the terrible blow of the New Year put an end to that project . . . What has it all come to? All chance of fulfilling my destiny over; and I *did* (up to February) still believe in my destiny . . ."[5]

Despair had been accumulating on him for three years—the death of Patmore, the unsettled relationship with Katie, the rather mixed reception of *New Poems* and its poor sale, the final loss of Katie. He had striven valiantly through it all, but the rejection of his poetry was the crowning disaster. In the space of three years he had descended so far from a position of eminence that his work had begun to encounter difficulty in finding a publisher. The wave crested and he was submerged. "I shall never forget," recalled Wilfrid Whitten, assistant editor of the *Academy,* "when he told me, under the mirrored ceiling of the Vienna Cafe, that he would never write poetry again." That was in the early months of 1900, and the resolve to forgo poetry lasted till the end of the year.[6]

The despondent mood was obvious to others besides Whitten, and a change of lodgings that now took place was probably made at Meynell's suggestion. After living at 39 Goldney Road for more than a year and a half, Thompson moved around the corner to 28 Elgin Avenue, where Barbara Maries, the wife of Meynell's printer, kept a boardinghouse. Two other friends of Meynell were already living there, and it was probably felt that the new situation would afford a better opportunity to keep a watchful eye on the brooding poet. But Thompson's despondency only deepened, and in mid-June—a few days before Katie's wedding— he decided to give up the struggle and go back to the streets. He was, he said in a note to Meynell, a week behind in his rent: "I must go, it is the only right thing." But he had been in money difficulties before without seeking such an escape. This time it was clearly a profound emotional crisis facing him; and perhaps he felt that when Katie became the wife of Godfrey Burr, the long-drawn sorrows of his own existence would reach a crescendo. "I have never lost the intuition that my life must end as it began, in tragedy," he wrote about this time, ". . . . out of the depths I came into the world of literature, and back into the depths I must go. God only grant that the final act in the London streets, to which I incessantly look forward, may be brief in its consummating agony."[7] His mind made up, he went to the Meynells' house to say goodby and deposit his manuscripts—and was persuaded to postpone or cancel his departure. He returned to Elgin Avenue, but he was not entirely free of despondency: "I have been full of worry, depression, and unconquerable foreboding," he complained to Meynell.[8] A few days after Katie's wedding, in what appears very much like an effort to throw off his burden of despondency, he lost himself in a carnival crowd flowing through the mazes of Paddington, even allowing himself to be drawn into the merry-making. Almost gleefully, he described the scene to Meynell:

> The children won me to participation in their play . . . I cheerfully submitted my neck to be tickled or my cheek *éffleuré* by the feathery weapons of the kids . . . One charming child of 13 or 15 had a veritable *impromptu* game of 'tick' with me. Instead of making an assault and retreating, as with the others, under the encouragement of my softened look (when I saw it *was* a child) she returned to the attack twice or thrice—flying and hovering round me, till at last she allowed me to 'tick' her; and then, feeling my hand among her bright tresses, with feigned fright but dancing eyes turned back on me, fled in earnest to the shelter of her two sisters.[9]

But his mood improved only temporarily and a day or two later he was still pondering a return to the "loathsome streets."

These months were an interval of drugged and bewildered self-doubt. Fifteen years of wandering had not smothered the desire for the comforts of a home and companionship, but in mid-1900, as he neared his fortieth year, all such hopeful visions had begun to vanish in the mists of uncertainty. Before him, like the dreary vista of Elgin Avenue itself, stretched endless solitude and he was unwilling to face it. Ironically, a critical study of his work, published this same year, furthered the legend of his aloofness from common life at the very time he was still struggling bitterly to remain in touch with it. "His spirit lives within a magic crystal sphere," solemnly wrote the critic, "which gives entrance to but few of the commonplace objects of modern life and holds afar, dimly ineffectual, its crass immediacy."[10] If Thompson dwelt apart during his last years, a literary hermit, it was in no magic sphere, but a cloud of longing and regret; he did not willingly become a recluse.

The Skiddaw, a pub frequented by Thompson, located just around the corner from his lodgings at No. 28 Elgin Avenue.

Everard Meynell wrote of Thompson's later life having a deceptively "superficial look of disaster and pain," and Alice Meynell refused to class him with the unhappy poets. Both dwelt on his ready smile, his laughter, even a gaiety of spirit, citing as one indication, his voluble concern with the trivialities of daily life, between them making it seem that his troubles and tragedies were small and on the surface. But Viola Meynell —herself a writer of many short stories of subtle insight—disagreed. "It seems impossible that this opinion could have been held," she argued, "if there had been more time to survey fully such signs as were hidden in the partly indecipherable notebooks, phrases written for special moments but spreading their intimations forward and backward . . . it even seems impossible to see in all the trivial commonplaces any alleviation from his unhappy life, for to his degree of sensibility all had the ominous significance of heavy Fate."[11] Her dissent is carefully worded, but what she has done is to accuse her mother and brother of a benevolent falsification. It could hardly have been necessary for them to plod through Thompson's disordered notes to discover what his last years had been like. They could have read it frequently in his eyes, his manner, the tone of the living voice. The truth is that, in order to shield the distress of their friend's last troubled years from the too-close stare of posterity, they freely glossed and distorted. They emphasized his innocence, his muddled abstraction, the withdrawn unworldliness, the immateriality of his needs and desires. Working together on the 1913 biography, they smoothed the ragged story of Thompson's final years: "You will think Everard's last two chapters most beautiful," Alice wrote to her husband, "just right in sincere feeling without too much of the illness which, as you know, I think ought not to be for the public."[12] Not only the nearly constant complaints of illness, but the full picture of the heavy and ever-deepening addiction of the last years, was thought by the Meynells to be "not for the public." When Everard Meynell does refer to the constantly drugged state of Thompson's last years, he does so in extremely vague terms, entirely without details of chronology or place. Because of the Meynells' reticence, understandable as it may be, the last decade of Thompson's life has always had about it the unreal atmosphere of a silent film, and it is almost too late now to recover any of it.

One story they left untold was Thompson's ambitious attempt once again to follow in De Quincey's footsteps, by writing a "narrative of personal experiences as an outcast in the London streets." This was undoubtedly designed as his personal *Confessions of an English Opium Eater,* and perhaps was intended to create a sensation, so that he might have readier and wider access to the world of British periodicals. It was started soon after Katie King's wedding, and, judging by the many fragments that remain scattered through the notebooks, was composed in an utterly frank and abandoned strain, touching everything from the early unhappiness of his Ushaw days, through the estrangements at home, the drugs, the prostitute, his sordid dereliction, and the meeting with the Meynells.[13] His mood at the time was despairing, and the "narrative" had in it something of a final gesture, for he had made up his mind for the second time to sink back to the blurred existence of street life until his fortunes changed. His three-year struggle to earn a living, even one so close to the margin of subsistence, had drained his resilience, while laudanum was sapping the will power needed to produce regular book reviews. He had made attempts to expand his creative outlets by again taking up play-writing, even asking William Archer for an opinion —which came back a kindly negative—and composing three or four more newspaper odes, but the tide was running against him. His fourth volume of poems, the London book, the lectures, all lay undone and forgotten, and he was even deeper in debt to his landlady. Eighty years before, he knew, one sensational article had opened for De Quincey the pages of every journal in London, even the most respectable. If he could achieve a similar triumph, he may have felt, then he could write when and where he pleased and be infinitely better paid for it.

The "narrative" was finished by February 1901 and sent to *The Nineteenth Century* through Meynell. Until his *Confessions* struck home he was going back to the streets, and this time without visiting Meynell first. "Again I am staking all on a manuscript," he wrote to his friend, "may success come sooner than before since I am in no way to hold out long this time. The reserves of youth are gone. I have no pigheaded desire to sever communications with you—if it can be of any use, any letter will find me addressed to *Poste Restante,* Charing Cross." In a second note he reveals more of his trepidation at the step: "God help me in the struggle which now begins, for I see the conditions will be much harder than before, and I have reason to dread the worst . . . I wish I had thought to make my will before I left. You ought to have it."[14]

The article never appeared, in *The Nineteenth Century* or any other magazine, and the manuscript has long since vanished, even its existence being unsuspected until now. Such a document would have been of prime importance to his first biographer, but Everard Meynell, who began his research in 1909, nowhere shows awareness of it, nor does his sister, Viola. Again the well-meaning hands and heart of Wilfrid Meynell come under suspicion. Not much imagination is needed to gauge what would have been his reaction to Thompson's article, nor is much needed to conjure up the scene attending its probable end: Thompson sitting dejected but acquiescent in the library at the Palace Court house, while Meynell dropped his *Confessions* into the fire. If such did happen, from one point of view it was an action easy to understand; still, it was a pity that he interfered, for it is likely that the composition really would have created a sensation, gaining Thompson unlimited access to periodicals, and mitigating all his financial worries. He very probably would have begun a second career as one of the recognized writers of the day; the truth could have hurt only himself—and he was beyond that.

Twice in the space of six months he had been ready to give up, and had been kept from the step only by the patience of his friend. Now, as 1901 wore on, he somewhat abruptly acquired a steadiness and a heightened industry that were to carry him into his most productive prose period, the four-year span between 1901 and 1904. Judged on quantity alone, the change was marked: from two or three reviews a month, he began in the spring of 1901 to contribute five or six, occasionally as many as eight. It was not just a brief spurt and the pace didn't slacken. About 250 reviews and articles came from his pen during the four years, nearly all distinctive in style, incisive in thought, and lightly buoyed on a wide erudition. Though he still had to struggle with illness, loneliness, lack of money, and conscience pangs over the opium, it appears that he did not again think seriously of going back to the streets. He was resigned and his resignation gave him an unaccustomed serenity. This surprising change may have come naturally from his own overwrought heart, sprung at need out of the underlying strength that was always in him—but a coincidental fact deserves to be recorded: just about the time the change took place Katie King died. On March 26, 1901, following the birth of twins, she succumbed to puerperal fever.[15]

II

A pall of opium hung over Thompson's last years. Friends and acquaintances, all who knew him, were aware of it, and it was scarcely thought worthy of remark in London's literary and journalistic circles. "His plight," confessed Meynell, "was visible to all men." His pathetic appearance and manner only intensified the picture of him as a relic of past glory. One friend recalled him as "a shrunken figure in a long, yellow ulster, which he would wear even at midsummer, with a straggling beard, and a little red nose." Another remembered "his great brown cape, which he would wear on the hottest days, and his disastrous hat . . . a picturesque, nondescript garb that was all his own and made him resemble some weird pedlar," a likeness which was enhanced by the old basket slung over his shoulder on a strap for transporting books. His carriage was upright, but not, it seems, from any intrepidity of spirit; under the bulky cape the frail body "was so thin there didn't seem to be any weight about him to make him stoop." His face, according to Wilfrid Whitten, who saw him once or twice a week for over five years, was "worn by pain and the fierce reactions of laudanum," and Whitten also noted the perpetually neglected hair and straggling beard that capped his unkempt and slightly wild appearance. "His cheeks were so sunken," explained a fellow boarder, "as to give undue prominence to a little grey beard that was pointed at the end but otherwise untrimmed." His low voice had a peculiar quaver, a slight wobble in the tone, that emphasized its curiously measured cadence; it had "none of the quick movements of voice which suggest either animation or gaiety; it was an absence of gaiety rather than melancholy." Thus the portrait of a wasted and ineffectual personality that was generally accepted in Edwardian London. It was understood that he still dabbled in prose, but the prevailing belief was that he "misspent his powers and wasted his minutes as he wasted his matches." What few suspected was that this outlandish wreck of a man had, in reality, become one of the most competent and prolific literary critics of the day.[16]

Until T. L. Connolly published in 1948 the results of a decade of patient research, the surprising industry of Thompson's later years remained a secret.[17] Not even the Meynell family had been aware of the true extent of his work. They knew he had labored fairly steadily for the *Academy* and the *Athenaeum,* but they had no real idea of the quantity or the breadth of the subject matter. Five years after Thompson's death Wilfrid Meynell was still explaining that his friend had continued to write prose during the last decade of his life, but "a little fitfully." The reason for this ignorance lies in the fact that most of Thompson's contributions were not signed. A large portion of the journalism at the turn of the century was anonymous, and no more than forty articles, during his entire writing career, carried his name. That even the Meynells should have been unaware of the true situation is understandable. Thompson did not conceal his work from them, but the weekly flow of it was often submerged in the fuller stream of daily events, and in the Meynells' own voluminous literary endeavors. His assignments were talked of at random and only if some special reason prompted; many were considered nothing more than ephemeral journalism, to be done and forgotten.

The total of reviews and articles that scholarship has so far recovered from the bound volumes of the old periodicals has passed five hundred and may well reach six hundred. About two-thirds of the amount is devoted to literary subjects, but he handled as well science, history, biography, politics and, occasionally, cricket; the great names of English literature he treated almost as personal acquaintances. "Anyone who reads these reviews, written week after week for a period of ten years," Pierre Danchin commented after a long and careful scrutiny, "must be continually surprised and must feel a profound admiration for the writer's immense knowledge: he is not only familiar with all the important facts of English literary history but knows the works themselves."[18] French literature he knew almost as well, and in translation handled Italian, Greek, Roman, and even Indian literature with a surprising facility. His critical approach was one of appreciation and elucidation; his opinions had nothing radical or startling about them. Not profound in thought, or the search for principles, he managed to make old works seem new by showing them in a new light, and contemporary work he judged on its own merit, though in a traditional framework.

He gave warm welcome to both William Butler Yeats and G. K. Chesterton, and generally anticipated the judgment of posterity on his contemporaries (but he was not infallible: in common with all his colleagues he dismissed Emily Dickinson as beneath notice[19]). Perhaps the most striking facet of his work during the decade is the care he used in his style, having largely rid himself of his captivity to De Quincey and Browne. Suited to the subject he is handling, it is simple or elaborate, slow-moving or forward-springing, lightly casual or deeply involved.

Everard and Olivia Meynell about 1905.

It is never loose, hesitant, or haphazard. He was a conscious, conscientious artist at all times, whether at a table before the fire in his room, huddled at a desk in the British Museum, or hastily scribbling under a gas lamp in the street at night in order to catch a last post.

Another consideration raised by the work of Thompson's later years is the question of his finances. From the writings of the Meynells, it has always been assumed that Thompson never quite managed to support himself and that up to the day of his death he was continually dependent on them to make up the difference. This was implied by their customary casual approach to fact and by some offhand statements in the *Life*, such as "If Francis's rent fell sometimes in arrears, it was not because there was any falling-away in willingness, but because it had taken its place among the many liabilities of the master of a large household, and had to wait among them for its turn to be met." There is no doubt that Thompson continued to lean heavily on the Meynells' but he was not the helpless dependent generally portrayed by later writers.

His subsistence level was about £8 a month, perhaps £100 annually. It is not possible now to detail with precision his month-to-month income, but in the period 1897–1907 he earned at least £750 from periodicals, £155 from the biography of St. Ignatius, and at least another £100 from miscellaneous sources such as the newspaper odes and the monograph *Health and Holiness*. Thus, for the ten years his known income was about £1000, and he could have lived on that amount without any outside help. But that, of course, is not the whole story. This income was not available on a regular basis, and the slightest disturbance of his simple way of life immediately threw his finances into confusion. Two such factors, illness and the drugs, perpetually recurred, and both of these put sudden, extra demands on his personal economy, and temporarily robbed him, as well, of the strength to continue his necessary reviewing pace. It was at such times that Wilfrid Meynell came to his aid, perhaps on three or four occasions a year. For the rest of the time, except for his final year or so, Thompson supported himself. Meynell's role in the journalistic years was less financial, and more one of pure friendship, encouragement, and contacts with magazine editors and publishers.[20]

From time to time Thompson made strenuous efforts to augment his income and become fully independent. Such was his reason for writing the two newspaper odes, *Cecil Rhodes* and *Peace;* for taking on the uncongenial task of preparing articles for *Nelson's Encyclopedia;* for agreeing to edit a Spencer selection; for accepting an invitation to contribute regularly to *The Weekly Critical Review.*[21] Some of these tasks he performed and some he didn't, defeated by opium, illness, or both. The two odes, *Cecil Rhodes* and *Peace,* were written within a period of six weeks, and at a time when he seems to have been indulging his drug craving to an unusual extent. These verses, neither of them true poetry but both above the common level of such rhetoric, could only have been done as imposed labor, thrown off by a firm effort of will. C. L. Hind, the *Academy's* editor, had talked Thompson into trying a poem on Rhodes the day after the empire builder's death on March 26, 1902. "He brought in the Ode on press day, hours late," Hind remembered; "he fumbled in various pockets of his time-worn clothes for the bits of paper on which it was written, then thanked me profusely when I gave him half-a-crown to purchase some dinner, and promised to return at 9 P.M. to read the proofs. He arrived at ten, *exalté* with port and laudanum: he read the proof standing and swaying."[22] The piece was published on April 12, and was good enough to impress W. J. Fisher, editor of *The Daily Chronicle,* who asked Thompson on May 16 if he would like to do something similar on the peace treaty then imminent in the Boer War. When Thompson didn't immediately answer the request, it was repeated a few days later, and by the twenty-second he had sent in a manuscript of 101 lines. It was in type by the twenty-seventh, and the Boer treaty was signed on the thirty-first, but for some reason the *Chronicle* never printed the poem. For his trouble Thompson was paid the handsome sum of ten guineas, but the effort such work cost him can only be imagined. A letter written to Hind some three months later provides a glimpse into the dulling miseries that sat with him in his room while he was engaged in such work, and even dogged him in the streets: "I was taken sick on my way to the station, not having been to bed all night, and having been working a good part of today; and though I came on as soon as I could pull myself together again, I was too late. So I leave here the Dumas article which I brought with me, and will be down tomorrow morning, when I am told you will be here . . ."

When necessary and when his personal preferences were aroused, he was capable of furiously sustained effort. On the sudden death of Aubrey de Vere, in January 1902, he received a telegram from Hind asking for an article "by first post tomorrow morning." The request was made on January 22. In the January 25 issue of the *Academy* there appeared a long and incisive commentary on de Vere, with more than a hundred lines of well-chosen extracts from his work. There had been no sleep for Thompson the night of the twenty-second, but from many hints in his letters and notebooks that can have been no uncommon occurrence.

Across from his room on the fourth floor of 28 Elgin Avenue there lived a young Indian student named Sarath Kumar Ghosh, who was keenly aware of his proximity to the man he considered the leading English poet of the age. In a rambling, amateurish novel he wrote some years later, both Ghosh and Thompson figure as characters, and one passage captures the simple reality of these nocturnal vigils. Thompson retains his own name in the book; "Barath" is Ghosh himself:

> That night Barath was sleepless; the air was hot and oppressive. He arose and opened the window wide at the top. He looked at his watch and found it was past two o'clock. To let in some fresh air he also opened the door for a moment, and then stood still. Thompson's room was just opposite, across the corridor. Under the door Barath saw a thin line of light. A moment after it was obscured—just for a second, after which it was visible for seven seconds, and was again shut out. The occultation was repeated several times, almost with the same regularity. Thompson was slowly pacing up and down the room at that hour wrapped in thought.[23]

Thompson lived at No. 28 for five years, the longest he ever occupied one dwelling after leaving home, but his natural reticence prevented him from making any real friends in the building, aside perhaps from Ghosh. He was well acquainted, however, with some half-dozen of the other boarders and seems to have felt at home among them. Evenings in the parlor "he would talk of something he had seen or read; or of food, cricket, or clothes. He wished he had bought a suit in a shop window, because he had given more for those he wore . . . he would eat; then walk up and down the room talking at any ear that might be listening or at none; then he would write under the gas-jet." On occasion he would even take part in cricket outings. One such, the first in eighteen

years as he said, occurred in August 1901. "I enjoyed it," he reported to
Meynell, "though Bryant was dead on the stumps—*my* personal and
fleshly stumps—which he peppered freely; finishing with a trimmer on
the knee-cap (causing it to swell), and a beautiful ball on my left
temple, which cannoned off a yard or two behind the wicket. My hat
saved me. Bryant thought I was hurt, till I reassured him by a bad
joke."[24]

Away from his lodgings he would be found at the British Museum,
the Meynells' house, the *Academy* or *Athenaeum* offices, or at a little bar
parlor in Chancery Lane where he often sat "with a glass of port and
staring in front of him at nothing." Many evenings were spent at a pub
called the *Skiddaw* around the corner from his lodgings, and he seems
also to have frequented still another pub called *The Pillars of Hercules*,
in Greek Street near Soho Square, where he became friendly with the
proprietor, and whiled away an occasional evening over cigars, wine, and
literary talk—no doubt quite conscious of his nearness to the scene of De
Quincey's early sufferings.[25] It can be seen that he was not a recluse in
the sense of shunning contact with others, but unfortunately few of the
people who met him in these days have left descriptions. A certain J. M.
Stuart-Young, an otherwise unidentified friend, has preserved the memory of one meeting near Temple Bar, probably in 1904:

> It was a misty day in November; the pavements were iridescent with
> London's most irksome slime. Thompson wore a frowzy Inverness
> cape; and the said cape was thrown back, thrust half aside to accom-
> modate a fish basket, slung by leather straps over his shoulder . . .
> He was not handsome; and yet there was a brilliancy in his restless
> eyes that arrested attention . . . his hands were noticeably artistic—
> long and white and plastic. On this occasion I drew him aside into the
> peace of Fountain Court . . . we found a seat even while the sponge-
> soft rain soaked our faces and our knees. Soon I persuaded him to talk
> to me of his visions. The slight moodiness that had shrouded his face
> vanished as if by magic; and he rhapsodized for an hour snuggled be-
> neath my umbrella.[26]

In the flood tide of journalism, even literary journalism, poetry faded
nearly to oblivion; aside from the newspaper odes, he appears to have
written only three or four poems in a stretch of five years. But one of
these has taken its place among the approximately half-dozen on which
his fame chiefly rests: the posthumously published *The Kingdom of
God*. What fortunate event may have revived his abilities is not known,
but the poem was in existence by late 1903 and may have been started as
much as a year earlier.[27] Two separate manuscripts exist, one of which,

in January of 1904, Thompson gave to Boswell Dodd, a friend of the Meynells. Just why he did not himself publish the poem is puzzling, since he must have been aware of its excellence; it may be that he was holding it back for inclusion in the volume which he still hoped to bring out.[28] Certainly, it is a pity that it did not appear, for it would have been a revelation to the bustling throng of *littérateurs* who thought of him as an empty husk.

> O world invisible, we view thee,
> O world intangible, we touch thee,
> O world unknowable, we know thee,
> Inapprehensible, we clutch thee!
>
> Does the fish soar to find the ocean,
> The eagle plunge to find the air—
> That we ask of the stars in motion
> If they have rumour of thee there?
>
> Not where the wheeling systems darken,
> And our benumbed conceiving soars!—
> The drift of pinions, would we hearken,
> Beats at our own clay-shuttered doors.
>
> The angels keep their ancient places;—
> Turn but a stone and start a wing!
> 'Tis ye, 'tis your estrangèd faces,
> That miss the many-splendoured thing.
>
> But (when so sad thou canst not sadder)
> Cry;—and upon thy so sore loss
> Shall shine the traffic of Jacob's ladder
> Pitched betwixt Heaven and Charing Cross.
>
> Yea, in the night, my Soul, my daughter,
> Cry;—clinging Heaven by the hems;
> And lo, Christ walking on the water
> Not of Gennesareth, but Thames!

The only poem he did publish during this period, a sing-song fillip on women's fashions, merely confirmed the opinion that his powers had withered. The poem—*Dress*, printed in *T.P.'s Weekly* on February 27, 1903—earned him one guinea.

III

In October 1903, with Hind gone from the editorship of the *Academy*, and a policy of shorter articles instituted by the new editor, Thompson began to contribute regularly to the *Athenaeum*, dividing his efforts between the two journals for the next year and a half. But by the spring of 1905 the surging mental vitality that had swept him along for over three years began to subside in illness and increased addiction. He had striven to keep an account of his opium intake, as he knew De Quincey had done, in order to restrict it to a maintenance level, but with increasing tolerance the level had risen until he was often using up to forty ounces a week. A single druggist's bill, which was found among his papers, detailing eight lots of "laudanum supplied from Dec. 24th/04 to Feb. 28th/05," for a price of six shillings and fourpence, has misled many commentators into pronouncing, with transparent relief, that his addiction was "comparatively small." But a few of the careful, pathetic lists in the notebooks of the amounts consumed have survived, and they show that by 1904–5 he was taking about six ounces daily. The lone druggist's bill probably represented only one of his sources,[29] and it is likely, also, that he now first began habitually to combine drugs and liquor, in the form of wine or brandy. His final surrender had started, but it was grudgingly made. In 1903 the total of his magazine articles and reviews was over sixty, and it was in this same year that he completed his lengthy monograph *Health and Holiness,* an interesting, if rather shallow, treatment of religious asceticism; in 1904 his prose pieces still numbered close to fifty and he had begun, as well, his biography of St. Ignatius.[30] In 1905 his reviews and articles dropped to thirty, and then under twenty in 1906. For the eleven months of his final year he managed to produce ten, the last being completed less than two months before he died.

The state of his health, of course, was closely bound up with the drugs, but it will never be possible to say with certainty to what extent one was the cause of the other. By 1905 he was not only still subject at various times to dyspepsia, influenza, diarrhea, and other less definable ills, but had also developed gout. The drugs and the bodily frailty reacted on each other, twining in a spiral of misery. "I was too exhausted and shaken to see you today after a dreadful time last night," he explained to Everard Meynell in January, ". . . am not at all well tonight." Dreams, of the terrible sort that haunted De Quincey and Coleridge, invaded his

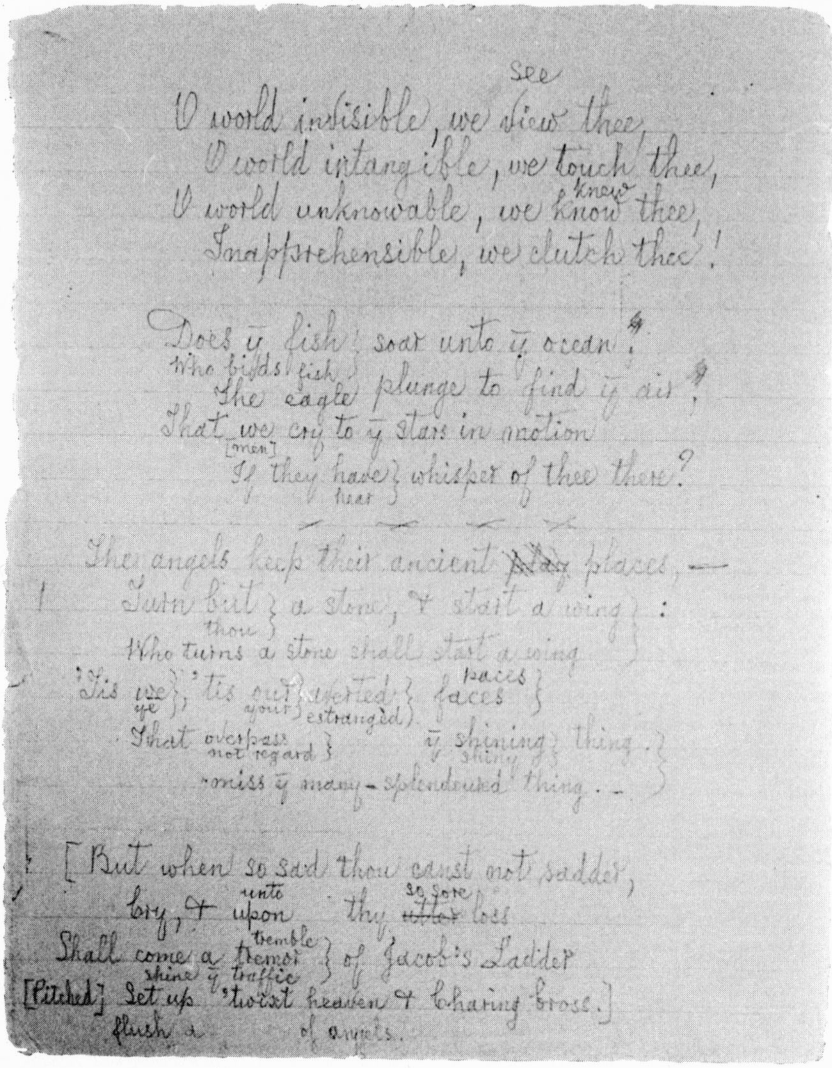
O world invisible, we view thee,
O world intangible, we touch thee,
O world unknowable, we know thee,
Inapprehensible, we clutch thee!

Does the fish soar unto the ocean?
The eagle plunge to find the air?
That we cry to the stars in motion
If they have whisper of thee there?

The angels keep their ancient places, —
Turn but a stone, & start a wing:
Who turns a stone shall start a wing
'Tis we, 'tis our averted faces
That overpass the shining thing.
miss the many-splendoured thing.

[But when so sad thou canst not sadder,
Cry, & upon thy utter loss
Shall come a tremor of Jacob's Ladder
[Pitched] Set up 'twixt heaven & Charing Cross.]

Here, and on the following two pages, appears Thompson's working draft of The Kingdom of God.

gleam)
shine } upon)

glitter)
[Cry, & shall tremble } on } thy loss
    The traffic of ȳ shining } Ladder]
              trembling }

But in ȳ night, my Soul, sad } daughter,
                  my)
[But when hope follows } hope to } slaughter]
         sickens on
    Cry, clutching ~~heaven~~ by ȳ hems;
And lo! Christ walking } on ȳ water
         coming
    Not of Genesareth, but Thames.

[And lo! where Christ walks on ȳ water)]
  And Christ shall meet thee on ȳ water)
          whirling whirling
        circling)
Not past ȳ outmost wheeling } system
  Where contemplation daunted soars;
     storm
The waves } of pinions, would we list 'em, [list them
  draft at
Beats on } our shut [↑] } fleshly doors.
      closed }   clayey }
      shuttered } earthy } - shuttered doors.

[Not where ȳ wheeling systems darken,
  And fire is frozen at ȳ cores;   to flowless
                           [cores;
            to)
  And flowless fires freeze to ȳ cores;
  And fires freeze } flowless to ȳ cores;
  And fires are frozen at ȳ cores;
              at)

{ rolling
{ hustling
Not where ∴ { whirling } systems darken,
{ rumbling

   Whereto our numbed conjecture) soars ;
                          conceiving }

     draft }
The { storm } of pinions, would we harken,
     drift }

   Beats at (our own clay)- shuttered doors.

            earthy }
        our { } earthy - shuttered doors
            clayey -

       our shut } and { earthy doors.
         closed }   { clayey }

sleep, as a random note suggests: "A most miserable fortnight of torpid despondent days and affrightful nights, dreams having been in part the worst realities of my life."[31] By summertime, in an effort to control the addiction and keep Thompson under something like regular surveillance, it was arranged that he should collect money for his daily needs at a small bookstore then recently opened by Everard, The Serendipity Shop. It was located in Westbourne Grove, about ten minutes on foot from Elgin Avenue, and nearly half the distance to the Meynell house in Palace Court.

To offset his dwindling ability to keep up the hectic pace of full-time reviewing, toward the end of 1904 Wilfrid Meynell negotiated a commission for him to write the biography of St. Ignatius Loyola. The contract was made with Burns, Oates, after the Jesuits had agreed to underwrite part of the expenses of publication. Not a mere piece of hackwork, as it is sometimes called, the task was enthusiastically undertaken by Thompson, who had long been interested in the saint, as well as in hagiography for the more cultured portion of Catholicism, "which should appeal to their scholarship and yet not minimize in the least the spiritual and miraculous aspect." He was not expected to attempt any original research, but was to use as his source the huge, 600-page biography written by Stewart Rose and published by Burns, Oates in 1891. As he progressed in the writing, he was to be paid piecemeal, at the rate of one pound for every three pages, with the Serendipity Shop serving as depository and treasury. He was thus enabled to work without leaving his room and at his own leisure, but had, in addition, a slight goal to draw him on. As he made his way into the subject, however, he did not restrict himself to the Rose biography, but consulted a half-dozen other books that he found at the British Museum.

It was after a day of such study that he was met in the street by another acquaintance, a literary agent named Daniel O'Connor, who was sufficiently struck by the encounter to preserve another of the few personal glimpses of Thompson in these last years. With two or three companions, O'Connor hailed him in a West End street late one evening in 1905. Thompson explained he had just come from the British Museum, where he had been researching Ignatius, and the books under his arm bore on the same subject. O'Connor's party was about to take supper and Thompson accepted an invitation to join them. In the restaurant, after the others had ordered conventional meals, Thompson, pampering his digestion with a diet of his own devising, requested porridge and beer. He was, remembered O'Connor, "A startling apparition . . . like a sleep-walking ghost, dazed shining eyes and scarecrow figure."[32]

This was a difficult time for the Meynells, as well as for Thompson. Wilfrid had risen to the position of Managing Director of Burns, Oates, and Alice had come into her full inheritance of fame. Their home was a rendezvous for the religious and literary elite. Thompson, with his opium-eater's shining countenance, flushed and dozing in a library chair, would have been troublesome to the kindest-hearted of friends. Even when not dulled by the drug he was a disturbing element in the lively, bustling household. Whenever he postponed one of his three or four daily doses of laudanum in order to spend a few hours with the Meynells, "he would say an easy thing once and finding it easy would say it over and over again." Harriet Monroe, with her sister, attended a supper at the Meynells' about this time and has left a picture of Thompson almost cruel in its unsparing truth. "The most pathetic little figure of ruin I have ever seen," she described him, "plain, almost repellent with his ragged sandy beard, blotched skin and watery eyes, his blurred consciousness unaware of us or of anything that was going on, but with a dignity of sorrow in his aspect . . . he scarcely said a word, but fell asleep once or twice almost on my sister's shoulder, until Mrs. Meynell rose from her seat and led him away."[33] The Meynell children, too, were growing up and finding Thompson's shabby presence disturbing in front of their friends. "We rather despised him," Madeline admitted, "because of his peculiar appearance and uncared for dress." The lack of personal hygiene was less irritating to Francis Meynell, then in his early teens, but he still found Thompson to be "something of a joke." To the children, generally, he was a waiflike creature, "whom we just accepted but certainly had no very personal feelings for."[34]

During May, June, July, and on into August, Thompson arrived at the Serendipity Shop almost every morning to receive the shillings that would buy him breakfast, lunch, and supper; each evening he would dispatch a note to the shop to assure Everard that he could be expected the next day. Occasionally he handed in some of the *Ignatius* manuscript, and often stayed to chat in the room at the back of the shop where the twenty-two-year-old Everard, seriously interested in painting, had set up an easel. The result was not only a striking oil portrait of Thompson in a drug torpor, but a life mask which still exists, and a cast of his hand which has been lost. A sensitive, perceptive youth, Everard's attitude toward his friend was a mixture of pity and awe, and Thompson was soon depending on him nearly as much as he had on his father. A note written on May 2, 1905, provides a glimpse into his hapless and restricted existence at this period, and shows the extent to which the younger Meynell had become necessary to his daily routine.

I will be at the shop tomorrow morning as early as I can, twixt ten and eleven, if possible, hoping that you will be there. I missed you to-day, unluckily. Just as I was starting I found that my coat was decorated with candle-drippings, and it cost me over half-an-hour's delay to scrape the grosser traces away, by which time I was too late. I then made a shot for half-past three, as about the time you might return; and it should seem got there just as you left. Deceived by a notice on the door, I waited till your assistant (I never recall his name) turned up about five. From his kindness I had a shilling, which enabled me to get a little to eat, and to go to the *Academy* where I had a belated article to deliver. It was unlucky; but I should have got off earlier to begin with. Of course, I could not get to Palace Court afterwards without sacrificing the last shred of a wasted day.[35]

Cricket was an interest shared between them, and Thompson's daily notes contain a number of remarks on the current games as well as a reiterated resolve to attend some particularly important matches at Lord's. For one reason or another he seems never to have gotten there, and more than once the obstacle was the gout: "The disease has too surely, I fear, come to stay; breaking out in one when it abates in the other foot . . . I must resign, I doubt, to its habitual companionship henceforth. It is a sore thing to me, whose one physical pleasure and resource against ill-health lay in my freedom and activity of foot." A month later the gout still restricted his outings to the short walk between Elgin Avenue and Westbourne Grove. "Today my heel is swollen," he complained, "and sodden like a baked apple—the skin puffed from the foot. I am giving it as much rest as I can, the base of the large toe being also painful. The persistence of the gout is discouraging. The soreness and stiffness extend up the calf of the leg, with irritation also in the other or left ankle. Cricket indeed recedes from prospect; but the worst is the general exhaustion induced by chronic pain."[36]

Despite the quiet, affectionate patience that Everard customarily used in his dealings with Thompson, no young man, busily committed to life, could bear such continuous melancholy invalidism without exasperation, and on occasion Everard understandably was short with his friend, perhaps now and then failing in some duty. Small enough failings, no doubt, but by August Thompson's miseries, and drug-induced despairs, had deepened, and even unintended slights affected him keenly:

*The Thompson life-mask, made by
Everard Meynell in 1905.*

Being better than I have been the last two days, I will be at the shop
tomorrow between twelve and one—I would be there earlier were there
any chance of seeing you. And I ask you, as an act of kindness, (I do
not pretend any claim on you) to be there before me. I have urgent
need to finish work tomorrow (it should have been done today, had I
not been so weak and exhausted to start with), and I cannot begin it
till I have had a full meal being still weak though my feet seem better.
I must seize every hour my health and strength may leave me to clear
arrears finally out of the way in this next two days. Do not refuse me
the aid you can give, which I cannot do without. All things else have
failed me: give me that at least for a time.

This is, I think, the last letter I shall write you, since they have
seemingly ceased to be of any avail. So far as I can see, it may—I am
reluctantly driven to believe—be very near the end with me altogether.
This ignominious life cannot, as I think, go on many days further. Did
it affect none but myself, I should (please God) keep patience and wait
till the end, whatever it might be; since I believe that one should always "try the last" and play out the game, not despairing of Providence.
But I have no right to involve others in loss which there are no reasonable, no foreseeable means of preventing or repairing. And those means
on which I had justifiable and sufficient cause to depend have helplessly failed me. A day or so will put a final term to my long suspense.
But virtually any expectation has already left me. In that day I must
put through my work, before the night come in which (perchance) I
can work no more. Even for this I must rest on you. Do not be wanting
to me in that which you can. Your own dark day may come, dear lad;

who think it now as little as I once thought it—though I had never your lightness of heart, was never without sad overshadowings of the hurrying calamity.[37]

The brooding elicited a concerned reaction from Everard, to which Thompson replied apologetically, but with no brightening of mood: "I am sorry I wrote you so gloomily—though there was and is cause enough. But I should not have troubled you with it." Whatever was at the bottom of this particular emergency, it was dissipated a few days later with the arrival of a check, "unexpectedly large."

It now became apparent that Thompson's physical and emotional slide was accelerating. During the latter part of June and through all of July he had done no reviewing at all, and probably had even suspended work on *Ignatius*. In the first week of August he reworked for the *Athenaeum* a review he had already contributed to the *Academy*, and managed some comments on a biography of Fitzgerald, also for the *Athenaeum*, but that was all.[38] Over a span of three months he had written only about five reviews, and now, for the third time, Wilfrid Meynell concluded that if his friend was to recover, a break with London, and seclusion under a watchful eye, was called for. Probably because of the presence of Thompson's old companion from Pantasaph, Fr. Anselm, the nearby Franciscan monastery at Crawley suggested itself. Mrs. Blackburn, still employed as a sub-editor for the monks, had also taken up residence at Crawley and it was under her close surveillance that Thompson was to be placed. Lodgings were found for him near the Friary, and by mid-August preparations for his departure were under way.

He recognized the necessity, but was uneasy at yet another effort to separate him from the drug, or at least to loosen its grip. Wearied by his uncompanioned suffering, he was still reluctant to leave the makeshift existence he had grown accustomed to in Elgin Avenue, and forebodings filled him as he felt the past receding and the future looming with doubtful change. "In my youth I sighed against monotony, and wanted romance; now I dread romance," he confided to his friend, ". . . once step aside from the ways of 'comfortable' men, you cannot regain them. You will live and die under the law of the intolerable thing they call romance . . . One person, indeed, told me that my own life was a beautiful romance. 'Beautiful' is not my standpoint." Who this "person" was is not known, but Thompson's remark was prompted by more than any single comment: the legend of his "romantic" life, its destitution and salvation, had already begun to crystallize and his remark in the letter appears very much as a subconscious protest at the distortions he perhaps envisioned following his death.[39] Everard rounded up the few things he needed for his journey ("I asked a night and a day-shirt—you sent only the night-shirt") and on August 19th he left London for the hour's train ride to the south.

A few weeks before, while finishing a late note to Everard in the candlelit quiet of his room, he had ended quickly as the diminishing wick guttered: "Love to all—candle going out!" he scribbled. To anyone aware of the circumstances of Thompson's later life the phrase starts from the paper. "Candle going out!" The flame had indeed at last begun to flicker.

When on the threshold of the green recess
The wanderer's footsteps fell, he knew that death
was on him.

Alastor

10

THE GREEN RECESS

MR. AND MRS. TED GRAVELY, RECENTLY MARRIED AND BOTH STILL IN their twenties, occupied a small attached house at No. 11 Victoria Road, Crawley. Having no children, they readily accepted Thompson as a boarder, after a recommendation from the nearby Franciscan monastery. Though he had been not quite willing to leave London, soon after his arrival Thompson was pleasantly surprised to find that Mrs. Gravely provided "better food than I ever had in lodgings since Storrington." But when the weather turned cold shortly after his arrival he thought with regret of the familiar surroundings of Elgin Avenue and complained that "I have been sitting shivering in my overcoat and wishing for fires and town."

This sojourn at Crawley, it appears, had a twofold purpose. Primarily it was to afford a closer control over the drugs, but it was also meant to

The main house at Newbuildings, the Sussex estate of W. S. Blunt.

provide leisure to complete a commission, given him by the *Dublin Review*, for an ode in honor of the English Catholic martyrs of the sixteenth and seventeenth centuries. He understood that his stay was to last about a month, time enough at least to complete the ode, but this may have been just a gentle ruse to secure his agreement to the change. When he learned, a couple of weeks afterwards, that the Meynells were about to leave on holiday he was upset and wrote in some anxiety: "I am surprised to hear you are off to Italy tomorrow, without having communicated with me. What am I to do with the poem when I have finished it? What am I to do when the month is out?" But Mrs. Blackburn, following instructions, had already broached the idea of his remaining in Crawley through the winter and, though reluctant at first, he finally agreed. He did not stop taking opium (it was mailed to him by a chemist in Harrow Road) though he may have lessened his consumption of it; but he kept to himself, and as the days passed the Gravelys came to regard their strange lodger as a shy, sickly man who took "quack medicines for his cold."[1]

Through the fall, in addition to the ode, he managed to keep busy doing a review every two weeks or so. In October he reread the *Journals* of Dorothy Wordsworth and was moved to some sensitive comment in which he shows himself wistfully envious of Wordsworth's good fortune in possessing such a sister: "She gave him freely both of her personal service and of her finest thoughts . . . She makes, bakes and mends for him, copies out his verses, tires herself to death about the house, and on a bitterly cold night is afraid to get herself more blankets for fear of waking him." What, he seems to be wondering in the silence of his solitary room, could not *he* have done with such a companion! By the end of the year, the *Ode to the English Martyrs* was finished and sent off to the Meynells. He didn't think much of the verses—"I shrink from calling them a poem"—but felt that he had adequately fulfilled his commission: "the *Dublin* might go further and fare a good deal worse. Even in my ashes, I think there lives a little more fire than in any other Catholic versifier of whom I know." Journeywork though the verses might be, they had cost him considerable effort. When Meynell, a few days later, requested some revisions he demurred, explaining that "I just put them through by a terrible dead-lift, and can do no more. The last reserve of power I could husband was discharged into them."[2]

Though addressed directly to Catholics, the poem opens with a lengthy and peculiar passage depicting the doom and destruction hanging over a sinister and corrupt world—a pathetic reflection of the drug-induced paranoid tendencies that he had exhibited more than once in the previous months. It was largely through the laudanum haze of his last years that he glimpsed such visions as this:

> Our world is venomed at the flaming heart,
> That from its burning systole
> Spurts a poisoned life-blood. See
> The gathering contagion thence
> Such influence
> Shed on the seasons, and on men
> Madness of nations, plague, and famine stern,
> Earthquake, and flood, and all disastrous birth,
> Change, war, and steaming pestilence . . .

Meynell deleted the entire passage, some forty-seven lines, and the poem appeared in the April 1906 *Dublin Review.*[3]

By mid-November his energies failed him altogether and for some eight or nine weeks he did no writing at all. Then, in January 1906, domestic trouble flared when his habit of sleeping late in the morning and calling for a late breakfast, and of staying in his room for days at a time, often in a dazed condition, began to tell on Mrs. Gravely's nerves. Mrs. Blackburn had spoken to him more than once, of course to no avail, but when she approached him again about January 15 he indignantly denied her charges: "This is the second time you have used toward me a manner against which I have, I think, a right to remonstrate . . . My conscience acquits me of having done anything to bring on my illness, or altered my habits for the worse in any way since I came here. I wish my illness were attributable to the cause you allege; for then I should have the remedy in my own hands, and could readily apply it. As it is, it is not . . ."[4] With that, he took to his room, and did not emerge, except for meals and to allow Mrs. Gravely to clean, for two weeks. On January 30 Mrs. Blackburn reported to Meynell: "He is more than ever a nightmare to me . . . he is worse than ever, and his landlady called last

The cottage at Rascall's Corners, where Thompson stayed for a month or so shortly before his death.

night to ask how long he intended to stay . . . No one can do anything with him, not even Fr. Anselm. I will ask his landlady to keep him till Saturday four weeks, that is March 4th, but I don't know if she will. The change to town may rouse him, and to tell the truth I shall be very glad when he is gone . . . If he is ill really (I don't think he is) he ought to go to a hospital." Still insisting that his difficulties were physical illness and a constitutional apathy—"the bother is just that I answer automatically to the call at my door, without really waking"—Thompson a few days later informed Meynell that Mrs. Gravely had agreed to keep him another month, so long as he rose for breakfast when called.

By mid-February Mrs. Blackburn could report that "for nearly a fortnight he has come down to his breakfast between 10 and 10:30, a wonderful improvement. He also goes out. So his landlady has consented to keep him." When she saw him in the village shortly after, she noted with satisfaction that he was not shuffling as he had done since he first came to Crawley, but was "striding along in the old sevenleagued boots style."[5] A letter written early in March reveals his satisfaction in his slight improvement, which, however, was to prove all too temporary.

Dear Wilfrid,

Draw the tooth; this is your hour and the power of darkness—or of the D.R. As an article of commerce, do with it what seemeth good unto you. Shouldn't dream of publishing it (in book, I mean). If any poetry *has* got into it, it is a pity; I intended best silver-gilt, and *that* is wasteful—brass is much cheaper, and preferred for commercial purposes.

Sorry I can't tell you I am rioting in health—no use hoping it till winter ends and sun comes—if there's any left. But have certainly been better last three weeks or four—I can't calculate time here. Been well enough for work anyway. Not so well last 2 or 3 days, but think mainly stomach. While cramp still knocks now and again at door, though doesn't come in, and noises in ears at times—not often, must keep in wholesome fear. But certainly much more capable of work, and on the whole been certainly better. *Athen* work done: had 2 proofs, but none since, which makes me anxious. Still, only 2 weeks delay, and others may yet come.

The new scheme has answered, and I have got up and downstairs regularly of a morning. So I think all troubles at my lodgings has blown over. The only thing which might give trouble is if we should not be able to pay them regularly; since I am afraid they are not in a position to purchase supplies for me, or get them on credit, if they should have to wait for their money. It is the money-question that—as ever—puts me in fear for the future.

I cannot offer you a lively Crawley if you come down, though it would be good to see you again. Anselm is away, and will only return to leave altogether in about a week after his return. The other friars mostly know us not: Cuthbert seems seldom here. And Crawley in winter is not lovely; I myself am as I say. I have not yet reached the ideal depicted in the enclosed remarkable drawing, which Ev's jealousy will probably exclude from exhibition at his studio.[6]

He remained through the spring, wrote four or five reviews but did little else, and by May it was decided he should return to London. The reasons for his leaving Crawley may have been nothing more than a desire on his part to be again in touch with city bustle, but just possibly it could have been due to one of the simpler facts of life. Mrs. Gravely was expecting her first child and was in her fourth month of pregnancy by May, a state ill-suited to accommodating the behavior of erratic poets.[7]

II

Mrs. Blackburn's notion that the change to town might rouse him proved correct. Back at Elgin Avenue, he resumed work on *Ignatius,* and did reviews at the rate of one a week. The unlooked-for access of energy also swept him into a new project, a collection of his prose. He had long considered such a move, but shrank from the labor involved. The bulk of his writing during the decade had been in the form of brief book reviews and short articles, and to give these substance and permanent value, he knew, would require careful and lengthy overhauling, a task almost beyond his strength. In a long and rambling notebook entry, made toward the end of 1906, he tried to convince himself otherwise.

Consult back *Academies* when and if possible . . . especially my article on Agnes Clerke's *Astrophysics,* with *Milton's prose, De Quincey, Macaulay, Pope, Serpent* article etc. etc. . . . and have I Emerson? Nay, that on Milton's poetry is also lost—two of the finest prose bits I ever did in the *Academy* with that on M's first *Napoleon Ode*—lost, too, and who can reckon how many more, thanks to my carelessness and Mrs. R's incorrigible animosity towards unbound literature—Rouse myself to face unpleasant task of renewing *Museum* ticket *at once* (see if it be in my possession, and where, ere too late—perhaps in drawer); recover these and other references, if possible, from Newspaper Room, copy all missing articles, and compile a volume of revised essays. Copy from W's M.E.'s *Moest. Encomium:* find *D.* as a *Modern Man* (where is it, that it is missing from my prose collection?); copy from *M.E.* also *Paganism;* get my boxes *now,* see if missing *Academy* papers be therein, and likewise my back *M.E.*'s with Mme de Krudener— besides Fr. R. Clark and other things—if not copy it too from W's if he have it, as we alack! in this day of neglect of all my past work. And so get ready a book for C's refusal. If refused try others. There may be money in it; there must be posterity, if I close up the rivets. And there, at any rate, is a congenial yet practical labour for me—at last; if not on too late a day. It should have been done, at least provided against, when I mooted it to Andrews, and back numbers were mine for only the asking, and strength still mine for worthy revision. Now all is un-certainty and labour immense, with failure, too, too possible! On every side, in every way, failure threatens. Yet try, ere the night close utterly in and my prose be lost to posterity after a lifetime of toil not less than set De Quincey at the front of English prose. Pull yourself together at this last, and try it. See if the *Academy* yet exist. If so, when you have learned dates and titles from the B.M., it might be possible to buy some of the back numbers, and so abridge your drudgery. Or failing this, Brown's, supplied with needed data, might manage to keep a look out for and pick up some of the numbers. Yourself *gave away* a hecatomb of such to them years and years ago. They must have drifted some-whither, and might be caught by a net let down into third-hand seas . . . Here is work to train your disused muscles.[8]

He did actually begin such a compilation: into a thick, new notebook he copied some titles and parts of articles, but the work demanded a vitality he no longer possessed. It never seems to have occurred to him that a publisher could have been found who would do all the gathering

Chalk sketch of Thompson made in August, 1907, by Neville Lytton at Newbuildings.

of materials, leaving his part to entail no more than a shifting of segments, some editing and rewriting. That was the arrangement that had allowed the ailing and elderly De Quincey to carry through the prodigious task of rescuing over a hundred of his magazine contributions. Thus Thompson neglected to imitate the one action of De Quincey's life which would perhaps have benefited him most.

In the late months of 1906 he moved his lodgings, for the last time, to 128 Brondesbury Road, Kilburn, where he took a small room at the top floor, reached by a steep flight of narrow steps. Its small dormer window overlooked a railway at the back, which his landlady thought should be company for him, though she admitted that "the trains, when all's said, aren't the same as the company he could get downstairs."[9] The place was a good distance north of Elgin Avenue, adding perhaps a half hour to the walking time to the Meynell apartment in Granville Place (the Meynells gave up the Palace Court house in mid-1905 and took a flat over the offices of Burns and Oates), but it had the charm of being close to an old haunt, Queen's Park, where he had spent much of his leisure time on first coming to London from Storrington twenty years before.

Soon after leaving Crawley he told Meynell that he was "too ill and exhausted to get to see you. My journey exhausted me very much, and walking tires me after being shut in the house all winter; while a cold and pain in the chest, which I have had for several days, became worse, and—conjoined with my general seediness—troubled me a good deal."[10] As the days lengthened into 1907 and the wintry cold deepened, his exhaustion became more pronounced and the colds turned to influenza. The daily dosage of laudanum was increased to about seven ounces and the effects were plainly visible: "He was thinner, even less punctual, more langorous when he fell into fits of abstraction . . . He had grown listless and slow."[11] By this time, however, he knew how to live with continual distress and when he somehow injured his foot he could write lightly of it to Everard:

> Unto thy sire revered relate how I to-morrow to his hospiteous tent cannot my pledgèd and preparèd foot duly direct, for that I housel me (great thing by me forgot!) if forth I go; and doubtful is it if I forth can go, whereas in my already swollen foot, out of mere weakened and enfeebled strength, I, from his tent hospiteous homeward bound, the thongèd tendon brake. Yea, in the instep where, some summers past, in like wise feebled, I the sinew string brake, I re-brake it; that, more swollen by thrice, it doth my painèd loveliness immure, and I keep forcèd house. In plain words, I am very weak, and my foot so swollen and painful in walking that I cannot much more than limp . . .[12]

His visits to the Meynell house had fallen off to one or two a week, although, aware of his condition, the Meynells were careful to keep him in sight through his landlady; there was also *Ignatius* to be discussed, of course, and manuscript to be handed in. His personal eccentricities had now become more pronounced than ever, and his talk usually ran almost wholly to the repetition of trivialities; his evenings at the Meynells' would be "divided between silences and explanations." Alone in the street, however, as Everard observed one evening, "he would find himself face to face again with the realities of life that he chose to keep private, and be loudly talking to himself . . . past puzzled policemen he would stride away in fierce agitation." The realities of life for him at this point were the realities of literature, and only when in contact with its great names did his spirit retain its force and clarity. His body was wasting by degrees, disintegrating, but his mind, against all odds, kept its power. When he did manage to complete the reading of a book his review was as honest, complete, and painstaking as each of the many hundreds that had preceded it.

Dear Wilfrid,
It has been a miserable debacle with me, and I don't know whether I'm on my head or my heels. I couldn't get my Henry James done for the *Athenaeum* at the beginning of last week, as I should have done, and they were waiting urgently for it, while another book came in. I specially engaged myself to do the *James* at once. Yet I have been so com-

No. 128 Brondesbury Road, Kilburn, Thompson's last lodging.

pletely upset by aggravated renewal of diarrhoea and dyspepsia which seemed for a day or so to have cleared off, that with every attempt I have only been able finally to get the *James* through this very moment —at four o'clock on Friday morning (for the Thursday at top of this is misleading, I discover). It has been a wretched time and my legs are so weak I fear to cross street in front of a vehicle, lest they drop me before it . . . The remaining *Athenaeum* work doesn't tie me up; since I have not bound myself to instant execution, I can use some latitude. But the James has been a series of perpetual abortive efforts, frustrated and dragging it forward but a little way, to be resumed same fashion next day. I just jump if the note-paper slips, my nerves are so unstrung. The James was a beast of a book to get through—I didn't know what I was undertaking so lightheartedly.[13]

The James review—a 2000-word commentary on Henry James's *The American Scene,* printed in the *Athenaeum* for March 9, 1907—displays no sign of the agitation under which it was written. The style and purpose of James's 450-page book are coolly analyzed and in a single sentence its mainspring is bared. James, said Thompson, is continually "seeking psychological problems as a dislodged limpet seeks a rock or stone to fasten on." After writing all night, at four o'clock in the morning a weary Thompson concluded succinctly that James's book was a "tantalising, endlessly clever, engaging, perverse, compelling and repelling by-product of the most fastidiously probing mind in present literature."

He had always been frail, but his excessive thinness began to prompt real concern. Father H. K. Mann of Ushaw, bearing a commission for an ode in celebration of the school's centenary, met him in early April 1907 at the Meynells' house and was appalled at "how woefully emaciated he had become." Thompson accepted the commission and quietly expressed a hope that he would be spared to take part in the celebration. Father Mann, glancing at the "wasted appearance of his body," abruptly realized that the remark had come from the heart; Thompson *did* feel that he was dying and might not be alive for the Ushaw Jubilee of July 1908.[14]

Through the spring and into the summer, though he complained of no dangerous illness, his condition worsened. He seemed merely to be the prey of general debility, a gradual breakdown of body chemistry and organ function, complicated by bad habits of eating and sleeping. When he showed no improvement in the comparative warmth of July and August, Meynell suggested a month or so of complete rest in country air, and Wilfrid Blunt agreed to provide quarters on his Newbuildings estate in Sussex. Departure was fixed for August 24, but when the Meynells arrived at his Brondesbury Road lodgings at eleven o'clock that morning they found he had gone out; "When at last he came, he carried a paper bag with food purchased at a shop far distant. No gourmet could have been at greater pains to secure the particular pork-pie, and no other, that he wanted." Thus in his wry manner, Everard Meynell related the incident, entirely overlooking more obvious probabilities. Thompson's surprising activity that morning was not solely an eccentric quest for the pork-pie, but the deadly serious business of arranging for some chemist to mail regular supplies of laudanum to Newbuildings.[15]

The trip to Newbuildings was made by automobile, sparing Thompson the hated ordeal of train travel. Blunt, who had not seen him in ten years, was shocked at the sight that met him and that night wrote in his diary: "He is emaciated beyond credibility, his poor little figure a mere skeleton, with clothes lent him for the occasion by the Meynells. He has the smallest head and face of any grown man I ever saw, colourless, except for his sharp nose, where all light is concentrated, and his bright eyes." Everard Meynell was to be Thompson's companion for the week and the two were lodged in a guest cottage near the main house. "I used to see him in his room," wrote Everard, "propped against the pillows, with candles burning and his prayer-book in his hand far into the night; and his light would still be bright when the stars had begun to grow pale." The worldly, self-assertive Blunt, so unlike his fragile guest, was fascinated, and when Thompson seemed rested he questioned him about his early life, curiously endeavoring to trace the spiritual sources of his poetic power. Uncomfortable under the scrutiny, Thompson spent much time "twisting his mustache and pulling down his cuffs" at his host's approach, but his talk was candid and Blunt concluded that the vitality of his work came from the tragedy of his life. But he saw nothing

Thompson entry (No. 315) in the hospital register, specifying "Morphomania" as the illness. (Names of other entries have been obscured at the request of the hospital.)

supernatural in it, "nothing above the nature of many other good people who are without his talent for speaking what he feels," he added in his diary, and seemed to be questioning whether it had all been worth it. Still impressed by Thompson's appearance, which he felt was like some sixteenth-century Spanish saint, he summoned his son-in-law, Neville Lytton, to do a portrait. The picture, never quite finished, was a profile in colored chalk. Blunt thought it was wonderfully exact, and noted that Thompson himself was pleased.[16]

The seven weeks spent at Newbuildings were given over almost entirely to rest, but it couldn't halt Thompson's decline. Everard had lingered for only a week or so, long enough to see that his friend felt at ease, and after he left Thompson was moved to a room in another cottage, called Rascall's Corner, to be under the care of a former servant of Blunt's, David Roberts. Feeling slightly lost, but enjoying the unaccustomed companionship, he spent much time in desultory conversation with Roberts' wife. When he was able, he would "walk from his room to the kitchen and as Mrs. Roberts prepared the meals, he would sit and talk to her quietly but steadily."[17] These were idle moments, but not empty; they were undoubtedly full of the nostalgia of his mother's kitchen in Ashton-under-Lyne where he and his friends had often spent hours in aimless chatter with Mrs. Thompson. His main meals he took at the mansion with Blunt and spent the afternoons reading or dozing on a large wicker sofa. The drug-taking was not furtive, and he seems to have been supplied with something besides laudanum: Blunt noticed that every day after lunch, "he would retire to the New Room, carrying with him a glass of wine with which he mixed some white powder." The combination of the drug with wine had put him in the grip, as he himself had earlier expressed it, of "the most fearfully destructive power conceivable."

He was still bothered by assorted ills, and his condition varied; he was better and brighter one day but alarmingly weak the next. Early in September, a doctor was called to treat him for a violent diarrhea, but he found no indication of any further illness, and did nothing more than place him on a milk diet.[18] A second examination was planned but somehow Thompson avoided it. By mid-September Blunt was convinced that his guest had begun a slide into semiconsciousness, and was intellectually defunct. In his diary he noted that "Thompson goes on in a half-alive state at David's, apparently content with his existence purely negative. He takes laudanum, David reports, daily, and sleeps at night with a stertorous sound . . . He seems incapable of bringing his mind to bear on any complex thought."[19] But the amazing mental drive that had brought Thompson unscathed through his life on the streets had not, even yet, diminished, and while Blunt was pitying him he was engaged in writing a review of the recently republished works of Sir Thomas Browne. It was his last review and it shows that, to the end, his faculties were not only clear, but precise, and that his memory was still unimpaired.

The Browne review was completed by the end of September, and thereafter he gave himself up entirely to drugs. He remained shut in the cottage at Rascall's Corner, windows tightly closed, fire blazing and a bottle of laudanum conspicuously beside him on the table. After two weeks of this, Roberts and Blunt, helpless before the unnerving spectacle, became very worried. "I am not satisfied about Thompson," Blunt informed Meynell, "and should be glad to get him safe back to London. So don't put off sending Everard for him. He seems quite given up to laudanum now, and I feel anxious lest he should have some sudden break-down or break-up." On October 16 Everard called for him at Newbuildings. He was so weak he had to be helped into the carriage.

Within a day or two of his return to Brondesbury Road, Wilfrid Meynell went to see him. Unable any longer to hide the truth, all pretense melted and Thompson admitted what everyone already knew: his life now was a continuous torpor. Moreover, the accumulation of toxic drugs was killing him, or so he thought. "I am more ill than you think," was his frank answer to inquiries, "I am dying from laudanum poisoning." Then, as he had done twenty years before, he turned helplessly to his friend: "I place myself in your hands."[20]

The question facing Meynell was the same as it had been the first time: was it safe or sensible or even worth while to attempt a cure? And once more the answer was the same, though both Thompson and Meynell were aware that this time the risk was much greater. Choice of a hospital was not difficult. Madeline Meynell, married in April of 1906, had been threatened with appendicitis while pregnant with her first child, and in October she had entered the Hospital of St. John and St. Elizabeth in St. John's Wood. With Madeline nearby, Thompson was more easily persuaded that he would not be abandoned, and he consented to enter.

On November 2, he arrived at the hospital, escorted by Percival Lucas, Madeline's husband. Sitting huddled on a bench outside the admissions office, he presented such a picture of physical destitution that the memory of it still remains; the matron had "never seen anything so pathetic." While he was being undressed for examination, little packets of white powder, not surprisingly, were found tucked in his shoes. His soiled and ragged clothes off, a nurse attempted to remove a medal that hung round his neck, but he weakly raised a hand in protest. His weight was only half what it should have been—an incredible seventy pounds. To the medical officer he admitted that his daily dosage of laudanum amounted to more than seven ounces, and in the hospital register his illness was entered as "morphomania." He was put to bed in an isolated corner of Ward 5, on the second floor.[21]

The laudanum was terminated, being replaced by various medicines to alleviate the agonies of withdrawal, none of which, probably, had any great effect. He seems not to have suffered much initial distress, but remained calm, and, after a visit on November 5, Everard could report that he had "entered into the spirit of his cure admirably." Rather surprisingly, he showed an immediate marked improvement, and by the eighth or ninth day Wilfrid Meynell informed Mrs. Randle, the landlady at Brondesbury Road, that her lodger would be returning shortly, and asked her to hold his room. "I am very pleased to hear that Mr. Thompson is better," she replied on November 11, "and that he will be spared to reflect on his past that his future may have a brighter aspect. With regard to the room I would keep same for 3/-per week . . . I will take great care of all Mr. Thompson's papers, books and memoranda."[22]

The turn for the worse was sudden and complete. By the eleventh or early on the twelfth, it was realized that he was dying; the hospital chaplain, Father Edward Smith, administered the last rites, in his hurry not even knowing the identity of the man he blessed. The drug cure was given up, and he was allowed medicinal doses of laudanum. All day long on the twelfth, various of the Meynells and their friends drifted in and out of the ward where Thompson was still able to recognize and smile fleetingly at his visitors. By mid-afternoon he was failing badly, his chest barely moving with the feeble breath. Caleb Saleeby, husband of Monica, alone kept some presence of mind. Taking a small piece of paper, he wrote:

Nov. 12th, 1907

I leave absolutely my literary copyrights and papers, including my manuscripts of published and unpublished poems, to Wilfrid Meynell, of 4 Granville Place Mans. W.

Needing an unconnected witness, Saleeby asked the help of another patient in the ward, a young man named Joseph Fevre. Together they watched as the paper was held before Thompson. Scarcely able to grip

Nov. 12th, 1907

I leave absolutely my literary copyrights and papers, including my manuscripts of published or unpublished poems, to Wilfred Meynell, of 47 Granville Place Mans. W.

Francis Thompson

Witnessed by:
C.W. Saleeby
13 Greville Place — N.W.
J. Arnold Gore(?)
15 Eric Road(?)
N.W.   Affidavit

Thompson's will, made about twelve hours before he died. The body of the document was written by Caleb Saleeby, husband of Monica Meynell.

FRANCIS THOMPSON

Death-sketch made by Everard Meynell on the day Thompson died.

the pen, the dying poet traced his name in shivering letters at the bottom of the statement; underneath, Saleeby and Fevre signed.[23]

The hours passed slowly. There was little talk, but at least once the dying man was heard to murmur a phrase from *The Poppy:* "my withered dreams, my withered dreams."[24] By the bed sat Wilfrid Meynell, his hand in Thompson's bony fingers. A young nun, Sister Cecelia, entered the ward on an errand; warned that a famous poet was near death in the room, she moved noiselessly, but on the way out she glanced for a moment at the bearded face on the white pillow. It was excessively gaunt, almost like a skeleton, and the impression stayed with her the rest of her life.[25] At nightfall, with Thompson seemingly able to last another day, Meynell and the other visitors went home. "He got rapidly weaker after your departure that night," Dr. Williams explained later, "When I saw him again at midnight he was practically unconscious, and remained so till the end. When I asked him if he was in any pain, or wanted anything, he could just rouse up enough to shake his head, and then relapse in a semi-comatose state again."[26]

His final moments are almost clinically described in the lines from
Alastor in which Shelley depicts the passing of his Poet:

> thus he lay,
> Surrendering to their final impulses
> The hovering powers of life. Hope and despair,
> The torturers, slept; no mortal pain or fear
> Marred his repose, the influxes of sense,
> And his own being unalloyed by pain,
> Yet feebler and more feeble, calmly fed
> The stream of thought, till he lay breathing there
> At peace, and faintly smiling:—his last sight
> Was the great moon, which o'er the western line
> Of the wide world her mighty horn suspended

He survived through the night, but as November 13 dawned, with only
the night nurse in attendance, his breathing ceased.[27]

A few weeks later an anonymous obituary writer commented: "Now
that this poet has passed beyond the confines of things mortal, more than
ever does his earthly wandering seem the straying of an alien spirit who
lost his way into this world, stared at it briefly . . . and passed again to
his rightful heritage."[28] Despite the part that drugs played in making
Thompson an alien spirit, that observation remains essentially true.

EPILOGUE

WHAT WAS THE CAUSE OF THOMPSON'S DEATH? WAS IT CONSUMPTION, AS it is invariably stated, or could it have been connected with the drugs, as Thompson himself believed? Unfortunately, there exist no clear-cut hospital records relating to the course of the illness, and in order to find some answer to that question it is necessary to take a more critical look at the available facts, both published and unpublished.

At first glance the theory of death by consumption seems well established. The official death certificate, signed on November 14 by Dr. E. U. Williams, the hospital medical officer, specified "pulmonary tuberculosis." Dr. John Harold, a specialist who assisted in Thompson's treatment, said in a note of November 18 that Thompson had suffered from "extensive pulmonary mischief which medicine could not cure,"[1] and Wilfrid Meynell in his lengthy obituary notice in *The Nation* for November 23, identified the fatal disease as tuberculosis. In the 1913 biography the consumption theory is put forward firmly, with the additional information that Thompson for some years before his death "had but one lung, and that diseased."[2] Thompson, it was explained, had not known the extent of his trouble. In the face of all this, there hardly seems room for doubt; yet there is strong indication that, despite his consumptive condition, opium was at least equally to blame.

Worthy of note is the fact that he showed none of the usual signs of terminal consumption: coughing, hemorrhage, and respiratory unease. This was reported incidentally by Viola Meynell, who commented that he was thus "saved from some of the worst manifestations of his disease."[3] Her brother, Everard, confirmed that "only when in the acutest need [of laudanum] were the last days distressing for him." In conjunction with this must be placed the evident fact that on the day of Thompson's death, it was believed that the attempt to effect a drug cure had proved fatal—that the vaguely understood miseries of withdrawal had reacted suddenly on his frail constitution. So much is clear from an unpublished letter of Caleb Saleeby (himself a doctor) to Wilfrid Meynell, written only a few hours after the poet had passed away. The letter also affords a personal glimpse into Thompson's last hours, and is here given in its entirety:[4]

13, Greville Place
St. John's Wood

Wed.

My Dear Mr. Meynell,

I must go to Scotland tonight: and write now to tell you how I really sympathize with you in our loss of a true poet. Poor fellow, he suffered very little indeed. As for me, I have only the consolation that by interfering yesterday afternoon when he was moribund—at 3:30—I enabled you to obtain the power to see justice done to his unpublished work. You know I wish I could have done more. Though he undoubtedly died from the drastic deprivation of his necessary drug the tuberculosis would shortly have killed him and his life would have been worth nothing to him or the world. There is therefore no cause to regret that you put him into the hospital. Not otherwise would his last days have been so peaceful and free from distress. That nurse is a beautiful being: the poor poet will meet nothing better where he has gone. I know better than anyone else how devoted she was, how she loved him from the first and made him love her, and cheered and comforted his last days. She is a poem and not unworthy of some memento of the poor fellow for whom she did her best—a precious best, the end notwithstanding. I am very glad to remember the smile with which he used to greet and say goodbye to me when I visited him. It was a rare spirit never more beautiful than at the last and it will not die out from the life of man. That we know who know what genius true to itself is worth to the world. You have the precious and lasting consolation of knowing that you were the instrument without which he could not have sung and that you were his best and indispensable friend for so long. After Life's fitful fever he sleeps well and we sorrow for ourselves only. Read Adonais and the end of Wordsworth's lines on death.

Yours affectionately and in real sympathy,

Caleb

It is uncertain whether a post-mortem was performed, but Everard Meynell's reference to Thompson's having only one lung seems to point to it (the first successful lung removal was not accomplished until many years later, so Everard's statement must mean that the lung had been rendered useless, and this could only have been determined by an autopsy). It is not difficult to surmise what would have happened once the full truth of his extensive tubercular condition became apparent. The consumption could be held at least equally responsible with the opium as the cause of death—with the tuberculosis presenting itself rather more starkly—and it was thus entered, with perfect legality, on the death certificate. The fact that Dr. Williams, in signing the death certificate, made a choice between two causes is clear from a letter he wrote to Wilfrid Meynell on November 22. "I am quite convinced that the lung trouble had more to do with his death, than any opium excesses," Dr. Williams declared. "He told me once that he was in the habit of taking 7 ounces of *Tr. Opii* daily, but I am sure this was an exaggeration, because the small amounts he had administered in the hospital, had an effect far in excess of what they would have, had he been accustomed to such large doses. However this may have been, the pulmonary disease was so far advanced, that he could not have lived 6 months at the outside, whether he was an opium drinker or not." Thompson, of course, was not exaggerating, and Dr. Williams was perhaps too eager to console the dead man's friends. In another remark in the same letter he says, "It is some consolation to know that his death was mainly due to natural and entirely unpreventable causes rather than to any acts of his own."[5] The word "mainly" in that sentence is pertinent.

It was at this stage that Meynell performed his last service to the saga of his dead friend's life. He quickly recruited acquaintances to write sympathetic notices in which tuberculosis was prominently specified, and all word of the poet's passing was kept from the press until these were

Wilfrid Meynell in the library at Greatham, about 1927.

ready. They were released simultaneously, and on November 19th most London papers carried obituary paragraphs. The fact that they largely emanated from the same source is evident in a similarity of phrasing, but there is some more direct evidence for Meynell's attempt to control matters. Wilfrid Blunt, one of those who agreed to do an obituary, noted in his diary at the time: "It was so arranged that nothing was known of Thompson's death till mine and a number more articles about him were ready to print."[6] Thus Wilfrid Meynell, because of his position and his extensive connections, was able effectively to push into the background all question of an opium-connected death. By the time the public learned that Thompson was dead, he had already been three days in the grave. He was buried on the morning of November 16, in Kensal Green, only a few blocks from the house in which he finished *The Hound of Heaven*. At the graveside stood perhaps a dozen people, including Wilfrid and Alice Meynell, Everard and his wife, Grazia, and Mrs. Randle.[7]

The proper ending to the story of Thompson's life, however, is not concerned with his pathetic death, but with the circumstance that he was able eventually to make full recompense to the Meynell family for the help which they had extended to him during the twenty years of his working life. Through the sales of his works he conferred on them a large portion of financial ease: his three original volumes of poetry, a

Selected Poems issued in 1908, his biography of St. Ignatius, finished just before his death and published in 1909, separate publication of the Shelley essay and *The Hound of Heaven,* and a three-volume *Works* brought out in 1913, all enjoyed prodigious sales in the decade before World War I when his reputation was at its height. From this, the Meynells benefited both through royalties and through Wilfrid's stock interest in the publisher, Burns and Oates. In 1941, with the sale of the original manuscript of *The Hound of Heaven* for £1000, the manuscripts, notebooks, and letters began to yield substantial revenue, and to date these have realized a small fortune. Francis Meynell did not exaggerate in saying that the money spent on Thompson had been repaid "many, many times over," or when he labeled his parents' spontaneous act of benevolence as, in strange reality, "the richest of investments."[8]

More than is usually true of poets, Thompson's artistic life did not end with his death. Verse salvaged from his papers continued steadily to find its way into print for a period of five years, after which there was a hiatus until 1957, when a slim volume of "new poems and plays" appeared in America, though not in England. The fact of his posthumous publication has some real importance, for it means that of the approximately 250 poems presently in print under Thompson's name, only about half appeared in his lifetime, and perhaps as much as a third of the total existed in only a rough state and was edited to completion by others. Thus, in a good deal of his poetry, there are unsuspected traces of a half-dozen other minds—a situation that has never received a proper amount of critical attention.

Wilfrid Meynell came into possession of all Thompson's literary remains, and also inherited the rights to his published work. The material found in the room at Brondesbury Road, piled in a large metal box, included some 150 penny exercise books in which Thompson had, for twenty years, mixed autobiographical jottings, book-review notes, grocery lists, opium accounts, and snippets and drafts of poems, both published and unpublished. Also found were separate manuscripts, apparently final, of about fifty additional unpublished poems, and fragments of perhaps a hundred others in scattered drafts. Meynell and his wife prepared this material for publication, editing where necessary—that is, they chose among many line and word variations (which often were not variants at all, but a mechanical groping towards something only half realized) and also canceled or rearranged parts and stanzas. Between 1908 and 1913 about forty-five "new" poems were added to the Thompson canon in this way, and perhaps half of these, to one degree or another, had been subjected to the editing process, without indication as to how much or by whom.

Subsequently, the bulk of Thompson's papers, with American publication rights, passed to Boston College, where the late Father Terence Connolly had begun a Thompson Collection. In 1957, after years of editorial gleaning, Father Connolly issued *The Man Has Wings*, containing no less than seventy-three "New Poems," and of that number fully forty had been put together from rough drafts. The operation was performed by Father Connolly and an assistant, who later explained that many of the poems had been pieced together from meaning and repetition, with Father Connolly choosing a final version from among the varied readings.[9] Regarding this singular procedure, Father Connolly in his Preface says merely: "From rough drafts and corrected copy, the version selected appears to be the one of Thompson's choice."[10] Both Wilfrid Meynell and Father Connolly loved Thompson's work and devoted themselves to his memory; but neither was a man of much detachment, and perhaps it was inevitable that their zeal should have somewhat distorted the truth of his life and work.

Wilfrid Meynell's career, after his friend's death, was long and active, and in time he became a patriarch of English Catholic letters. His wife's death in 1922 put an end to an era, but as the center of a bustling clan, and as one of London's best-known personalities, he continued to write, work, and dispense encouragement to young hopefuls. He lived until December 1948, and died in his country house at Greatham, Sussex, which Thompson's legacy had largely helped to provide. His daughter, Viola, described him in his last year sitting outside the library door, his hands still busy, "breaking up thin branches into useful small kindling wood." Francis Thompson's poetry, Viola said, had been a "transforming thing" to her father; without it he would have been a different man, and still vividly alive in the family's memory is the way he would tilt back his head, close his eyes, and recite *The Hound of Heaven* without a pause. He lived for ninety-six years, and for twenty of them, as he well knew, he had touched and helped to shape a high immortality. The tie between Thompson and the Meynells had been a unique one, and it was Thompson himself who best summed up its inspiring and lasting nature:

> More than friends, second father, second mother,
> To all succeeding days we live in one another;
> No selfish ray can any of us shed,
> But all must crown with light each other's head.[11]

APPENDIX: THOMPSON'S SPACE RAPTURE

NOTES AND SOURCES

SELECTED BIBLIOGRAPHY

INDEX

THOMPSON'S SPACE RAPTURE

This brief exposition is included here because the topic has so far received little attention, yet it is essential to an understanding of Thompson and his poetry. It has particular importance in showing that the cosmic elements in his verse are not basically drug-connected, but derive naturally from the broad stream of English literary tradition. The drugs did not induce, in De Quincey's phrase, the "tyrannous expansion of space and time;" the tendency was inborn and was brought to vivid life by Thompson's immersion in the work of earlier writers.

IF IMAGERY WAS THE SOUL OF FRANCIS THOMPSON'S POETRY, THEN THAT SOUL had a soul of its own, for at the very center of his imagination there pulsed a radiant core that spread its kindling, iridescent influence over the greater part of his work. Even cursory analysis of his imagery shows that he was preoccupied to the point of rapture with the sublimity of transtellar space, with the heavenly bodies, and with all manner of celestial phenomena. *Rapture* is the correct word, for Thompson's feeling about the universe suggests a psychological involvement, bordering on the hypnotic, and resembling the strange intoxication experienced by divers in the ocean's depths. As the diver who is struck by "the rapture of the deep" wanders the watery world oblivious of the life he left behind him at the surface, so Thompson wandered in vision the depths of space.

The cosmic content of his work has been looked at before, but what has not been realized is the degree to which it is fundamental. Nor has its true nature hitherto been recognized, for this cosmic rapture was in reality the culmination of a tradition that began in the late sixteenth century as a portion of what has been called "the aesthetics of the infinite."

Of course, not all readers or critics of Thompson's day were attracted by this unique note. "Let him not use the universe quite so irresponsibly for a playground," one commentator chided in 1894, and the opinion has been echoed right up to the present by such remarks as "large cosmic forces are handled with a sometimes too easy assurance." Not everyone, it seems, is comfortable swinging on a star, and the split in opinion has hampered closer analysis. Too often the mistake is made, moreover, of treating Thompson's space imagery as a part of his attitude toward nature in general. It is true that nature includes all of the physical universe, but in practice the terms *nature* and *cosmic* are divergent, and the distinction is particularly apt with regard to Thompson. He sings of the sun and the stars because he is awed by the cosmos itself. The rapture is induced by contemplation of illimitable distances, unimaginable sizes, inconceivable immensities—by the sheer, staggering mystery of it all. This, to speak simple truth, is not the nature of every day.

The difference, perhaps, resides in the vantage point. Thompson's cosmic imagery is concerned with universal space and the various phenomena therein, and includes the earth only when it is treated as a planet, that is, in its relation to the other heavenly bodies. When he descends to earthly existence—to life on the surface—he is cosmic only in the usual sense. Now and again, however, he will throw off an image essentially natural, but which swells with such sudden exaltation that it looms to cosmic proportions. Thus

> The wind that sings to himself as he makes stride
> Lonely and terrible on the Andean height

though an earthly and very natural wind, still inclines toward the cosmic because of the quick grandeur of its conception. The point is especially pertinent with regard to his sunset images. Sunsets exist only in relation to the watcher, of course, and so properly belong to the category of nature. But Thompson's sunsets were never seen by any mortal except himself and the poet at those times must surely have been treading other soil than earth's.

Some part of his space rapture is perhaps traceable to the events of the times in which he lived. The present heady experience of living in an age when the fantastic, dreamlike pageantry visible from space capsules awakens a pristine wonder, naturally arouses speculation as to how much of Thompson's own interest in the heavens might have been stimulated by the feverish interest in powered flight that prevailed throughout his lifetime. That he was aware of such things and showed a keen appreciation of them can be seen from a review he wrote in September 1902—nearly a year before the Wrights' initial success—of a book called *Travels in Space: A History of Aerial Navigation*. In his review he says that one of the most interesting things in the book is "the description of Mr. Langley's aerodrome, with the exceedingly picturesque and striking frontispiece showing its flight." Viewed thus, against the background of his Victorian contemporaries, Thompson seems curiously modern. How he would have boggled to know that, less than sixty years after his death, man has not only conquered the air, but has smitten the moon on the cheek, taken the temperature of Venus, and peered at last into the face of old Mars!

Some forty of Thompson's poems contain space imagery, but since the total number of his poems is nearly 250, this might not seem impressive. However, if attention is restricted to the poems published in his lifetime, excluding those edited to completion after his death, the proportion exceeds one third. Even this sort of statistical approach is a distortion, and it is more to the point to say that *all* of his best-known and most characteristic work, the work for which he will be remembered, is dominated by space imagery. *Ode to the Setting Sun, Sister Songs, A Corymbus for Autumn, To My Godchild, An Anthem of Earth, Orient Ode,* and *The Hound of Heaven* all possess extensive cosmic coloring, and intermittent gleams of it flash through many of the lesser pieces.

He includes in his celestial grab bag more than a dozen categories. Most frequently treated are the sun, the earth, the moon and the stars, but he turns his gaze now and again to the winds, clouds, rainbows, nightfall, moonrise, thunder and lightning. A final, most significant heading is flight through space—an exuberant soaring among the planets and galaxies.

The only way to appreciate his sustained originality in all this is to isolate a sufficient number of examples, but some idea of his range and inventiveness may be gained by glancing at a few of the different attitudes in which he casts the heavens. Among the images involving earth, for instance, are a woman bathing, a bracelet ornament, and King David. The moon, while usually represented as a girl or woman, is also seen as a bird and a stranded fish. Stars become scattered pebbles, gold nuggets, candles, banners, bells, marbles, and egg yolks. For thunder and lightning he conjures up, now a celestial debauch, and now a pack of hounds in pursuit of game. The sun is put through an absolute riot of change: it is a bee, a lion, a dragon, and a pawing horse; a bunch of grapes, a bowl of flowers, a drunkard, a glowing coal, a censer, and flowing wine—to mention only ten of fifty. And so it continues through a total of over 125 separate images.

The sun is lord of Thompson's universe, though he seems to love it best at setting. Of the fifty-one poems in which there is reference to the sun, twenty contain extended images inspired by sunset.

> O thou down-stricken Day,
> That draw'st thy splendours round thee in thy fall

Color and light, though not specifically alluded to, seem to flash between the very words of those two deceptively simple lines and somehow to sparkle on the face of them. Here, in three lines he conjures up the serenity of a cathedral service, with the sun serving as a gong:

> The calm hour strikes on yon golden gong
> In tones of floating and yellow light
> A spreading summons to even-song

But from such scenes of airy architecture he can startle his reader into half-reluctant admiration, as he sees the setting sun

> Like a golden bee
> Sting the West to angry red

Or, equally audacious and quite as unexpectedly, engage the senses of taste and touch:

> If Even burst yon globèd yellow grape
> (Which is the sun to mortal's sealèd sight)
> Against her stainèd mouth

with its undoubtedly deliberate reminiscence of Keats. Or flash on the skies a merry willfulness:

> Round the nodding sun, flush-faced and sunken,
> His wild bacchantes drunken,
> Reel, with rent woofs a-flaunt, their westering rout

Or a mutely fascinating still-life:

> Ere all the intertangled West
> Be one magnificence
> Of multitudinous blossoms that o'errun
> The flaming brazen bowl o' the burnished sun
> Which they do flower from

Probably the most stirring sunset image in his whole gallery is the marvelously sustained choral note, often referred to as a nearly perfect instance of synaesthesia, in *Ode to the Setting Sun*:

> High was thine Eastern pomp inaugural;
> But thou dost set in statelier pageantry
> Lauded with tumults of a firmament:
> Thy visible music-blasts make deaf the sky,
> Thy cymbals clang to fire the Occident,
> Thou dost thy dying so triumphally:
> I *see* the crimson blaring of thy shawms!

But such long-dying grandeur frequently gave way to a bracing violence:

> Too soon fails the light, and the swart boar, Night,
> Gores to death the bleeding day;

And the dusk has no more a calm at its core,
But is turbid with obscene array

Less often, the *rising* sun called forth a response from the poet, and the reason may have been nothing more complicated than Thompson's slug-a-bed habits. But he must have risen with the dawn, now and again, for he produced a dozen sunrise images of high quality. Two of them, curiously enough, relate to wine:

The bowed East lifteth a dripping sun
A golden cup to the lips of Night
Over whose cheeks in flushes run
The heats of the liquid light.

If young day tread, a glorious vintager,
The wine-press of the purple-foamèd East

The sun at its meridian received proper attention, too, and this delineation of an autumn sun seems exactly right:

The sopped sun—toper as ever drank hard—
Stares foolish, hazed,
Rubicund, dazed,
Totty with thine October tankard

Thompson's affinity for the sun, in a physical as well as an imaginative way, is too well known to call for comment, but it might not be amiss to point out that he also had an active interest in the concretely scientific aspects of solar phenomena. In an unusually long review he wrote in 1903 of a book entitled *Problems in Astrophysics,* he discusses knowingly and with evident relish the leading features of solar study. He concludes his review with the opinion that the problems connected with the subject have "the remoteness and fascination of the stars themselves."

In Thompson's personal universe the stars, for some reason, possess not only a fascination, but an idiosyncrasy all their own: they are nearly always small enough to be held in the hand, no matter in what guise they otherwise appear. It may be that there is some meaning in this that has not yet become apparent; what *is* apparent, however, is the differing reactions to it on the part of readers. The little angels, for example, who

Looked up from disport at the passing comer
As they pelted
Each other with handfuls of stars

have pleased and annoyed critics in about equal proportions. The idea is echoed, rather more acceptably, in

> From nightly towers
> He dogs the secret footsteps of the heavens,
> Sifts in his hands the stars, weighs them
> as gold-dust

and is heard most touchingly in the child's questioning of the baby Jesus:

> And didst Thou play in Heaven with all
> The angels who were not too tall,
> With stars for marbles?

When he sees the stars as candles he is, to be sure, following custom, yet he manages to impart something of his own to the vision:

> Round the earth, still and stark,
> Heaven's death-lights kindle, yellow spark by spark,
> Beneath the dreadful catafalque of the dark

Still thinking of candles, in six simple words he succeeds in conveying a tremendous and chilling picture, of Apocalyptic dimensions:

> When doom puffed out the stars . . .

There is one star image, written soon after the days of his terrible London destitution, which has always seemed too painfully a child of memory:

> The stars, forlornly fair, shiver keenly
> through the air,
> All an-aching till their watch be ceased

Is this not the ragged Thompson of the streets huddled in some West End doorway gazing in hopeless patience through the dark at a winter sky?

Thompson's universe, it can be seen, was not a static one and animals very often came to violent birth in it; twice, at least, he let loose celestial predators. Here is a ravening sun in the morning of creation:

> When thou didst, bursting from the great void's husk,
> Leap like a lion on the throat o' the dusk

which is an arresting enough picture, but which he later developed even more fully in portraying both sunrise and sunset in one image:

> As, fore-announced by threat of flame and smoke,
> Out of the night's lair broke
> The sun among the startled stars, whose blood
> Looses its slow bright flood
> Beneath the radiant onset of the sun;
> So crouches he anon,
> And, nostrils breathing threat of smoke and flame,
> Back to the lairing night wherefrom he came.

Two "action" scenes were derived from thunder and lightning:

> Desires that hunt down Beauty through the Heaven
> With unslackenable bounds, as the deep-mouthed
>   thunder-hounds
>   Bay at heel the fleeing levin

The second, more unconventional yet, has a Frans Hals touch:

> When that drunken Titan, the Thunder,
>   Stumbles through staggered Heaven,
> And spills on the scorched earth under
>   The fiery wine of the levin

But for sheer abrupt originality in this category, a five-line passage in *Sister Songs* is probably unsurpassed:

> Thou wert to me that earnest of day's light,
> When, like the back of a gold-mailed saurian
>   Heaving its slow length from Nilotic slime,
> The first long gleaming fissure runs Aurorian
>   Athwart the yet dun firmament of prime

It was in his treatment of earth that some of Thompson's most memorable images leaped to life. Possibly the best known is the bracelet figure in which he makes direct reference to the cosmic preoccupation of his poetry:

> The linkèd fantasies in whose blossomy twist
> I swung the earth a trinket at my wrist

But two of his foremost poems commence with extended images in which earth is seen as a sailing vessel, cleaving its lordly way through the seas of space. The first, incidentally, makes oblique reference to a very late spring in 1891; the second, written some three years later, was very probably inspired by the first. *To My Godchild* opens with:

> This laboring, vast, Tellurian galleon,
> Riding at anchor off the Orient sun,
> Had broken its cable and stood out to space
> Down some frore arctic of the aerial ways;
> And now, back-warping from the inclement main,
> Its vaporous shroudage drenched with icy rain,
> It swung into its azure roads again

And *An Anthem of Earth* with:

> Immeasurable Earth!
> Through the loud vast and populacy of Heaven,
> Tempested with gold schools of ponderous orbs,
> That cleav'st with deep-revolving harmonies
> Passage perpetual, and behind thee drawest
> A furrow sweet, a cometary wake
> Of trailing music!

But Thompson can turn from such impressive journeyings and, with admirable dexterity, set the earth dancing. Here he is addressing the sun:

> God whom none may live and mark!
> Borne within thy radiant ark
> While the earth, a joyous David,
> Dances before thee from dawn to dark

His seminary training shows itself in liturgical imagery, and while he was not unique in this, it can be doubted whether any other poet ever achieved quite the same, or even nearly the same, effects as he did. None other, at least, has constructed and filled such cosmic houses of worship. The first fifteen lines of the *Orient Ode* are widely known in this regard, but there is in *A Corymbus for Autumn* an even longer, and equally impressive passage of such ceremonial imagery:

> All Nature sacerdotal seems . . .
>   See how there
>   The cowlèd Night
> Kneels on the Eastern Sanctuary stair.
> What is this feel of incense everywhere?
> Clings it round the folds of the blanch-amiced clouds,
> Upwafted by the solemn thurifer,

The mighty Spirit unknown,
That swingeth the slow earth before the embannered throne.

Unquestionably the most characteristic and striking aspect of Thompson's cosmic rapture is his soaring tendency—his, so to speak, travels in space (and under this heading are included those passages describing a species of enlarged spatial existence, as well as actual, if metaphysical, flight). The best-known instances occur in *The Hound of Heaven,* but there are a number of others of equal interest in the other works. The *Orient Ode,* for instance, contains:

> I with wingèd feet had run
>   Through all the windy earth about,
>   Quested its secret of the sun,
> And heard what thing the stars together shout

Retrospect, one of his lesser efforts, affords one of the most arresting examples:

> . . . though the cry of stars
> Give tongue before His way
> Goldenly, as I say,
> And each from wide Saturnus to hot Mars
> He calleth by its name,
> Lest that its bright feet stray . . .

Interestingly enough, his headiest and most sustained extraterrestrial romp occurs in his prose—the great passage in his essay on Shelley which seems to acquire another dimension and a more precise significance when read in the light of his own response. He is describing, it will be remembered, Shelley's childlike quality:

> His play is such as manhood stops to watch, and his playthings are those which the gods give their children. The universe is his box of toys. He dabbles his fingers in the day-fall. He is gold-dusty with tumbling amidst the stars. He makes bright mischief with the moon. The meteors nuzzle their noses in his hand. He teases into growling the kennelled thunder, and laughs at the shaking of its fiery chain. He dances in and out of the gates of Heaven; its floor is littered with his broken fancies. He runs wild over the fields of ether. He chases the rolling world. He gets between the feet of the horses of the sun. He stands in the lap of patient Nature, and twines her loosened tresses after a hundred wilful fashions to see how she will look nicest in his song.

An echo of this can be found in *An Anthem of Earth,* where Thompson alludes to his own youthful poetic aspirations:

Then, O Earth, thou rang'st beneath me,
Rocked to Eastward, rocked to Westward,
Even with the shifted
Poise and footing of my thought!
I brake through the doors of sunset,
Ran before the hooves of sunrise,
Shook thy matron tresses down in fancies
Wild and wilful
As a poet's hand could twine them;
Caught in my fancy's crystal chalice
The Bow, as its cataract of colours
Plashed to thee downward:
Then when thy circuit swung to nightward,
Night the abhorrèd, night was a new dawning,
Celestial dawning
Over the ultimate marges of the soul;
Dusk grew turbulent with fire before me,
And like a windy arras waved with dreams.

The passage demonstrates that Thompson was well aware of the unique quality of his personal response to the heavens. And he was not only aware of it, but now and again reflected on it with something of wonder:

I, a wingless mortal, sporting
With the tresses of the sun?
I, that dare my hand to lay
On the thunder in its snorting?

The fact that there are only two *specific* pictures of metaphysical flight in *The Hound of Heaven* may come as something of a surprise to those who have not tried to discover the source of that poem's magnificent movement, but such is the case:

Across the margent of the world I fled,
And troubled the gold gateways of the stars;
Smiting for shelter on their clangèd bars;
Fretted to dulcet jars
And silvern chatter the pale ports o' the moon

and

To all swift things for swiftness did I sue;
Clung to the whistling mane of every wind.
But whether they swept, smoothly fleet,
The long savannahs of the blue;

> Or whether, thunder-driven,
> They clanged his chariot thwart a heaven.
> Plashy with flying lightnings round the spurn o'
> > their feet . . .

These passages, however, are reinforced throughout the poem by others in which movement above the earth and a species of cosmic enlargement is assumed or implied; for instance:

> I laughed in the morning's eyes
> I triumphed and saddened with all weather,
> > Heaven and I wept together,
> And its sweet tears were salt with mortal mine;
> Against the red throb of its sunset-heart
> > I laid my own to beat,
> > And share commingling heat;

In truth, the entire poem was generated out of Thompson's cosmic awareness, was written at the very top of some sustained rapturous involvement with his vision of celestial harmonies.

There is a passage in *Sister Songs* in which he expressed a wish about his poetry, which concludes with one of the loveliest of his space images. Both in expression and idea it is the perfect embodiment of his use of the cosmic tradition.

> Oh! may this treasure-galleon of my verse
> Fraught with its golden passion, oared with cadent rhyme,
> Set with a towering press of fantasies,
> > Drop safely down the time,
> > Leaving mine islèd self behind it far
> Soon to be sunken in the abysm of seas
> (As down the years the splendour voyages
> > From some long ruined and night-submergèd star)

The cosmic tradition, stretching back more than three hundred years, has so far eluded any detailed scrutiny, though Marjorie Hope Nicholson, in *The Breaking of the Circle*, has touched on its beginnings. She professed, however, to see little essential difference between the inspiration that blossomed from Copernican theories and that which had flowered from the old Ptolemaic universe. She viewed pre-Copernican interest in space as continuous with the excitement generated afterward: "In trance, in ecstasy, in vision the soul had long travelled to the spheres; on Pegasean steeds poets had always mounted into space." It is true, of course, that poets have never quite managed to ignore the heavens, but it can be shown that pre-Copernican awareness was much less ecstatic, was in fact of a decidedly inferior brand to the joyous enthusiasms that followed. True space rapture is relatively modern.

In ancient times men regarded the heavens with a different sort of awe, and the difference can clearly be seen in their tamer allusions to things celestial. Poetic imagery in Greece and Rome never, or very seldom, rose above nature; always, even in its highest flight, remained within sight of the earth. Virgil's wish to learn

> The paths of heaven, the stars, the sun's eclipse,
> The labors of the moon

was no more than the desire of an earthling, and one who would contemplate the heavens only while his feet safely trod mundane soil. The nearest approach to actual space rapture in ancient writings probably is to be found in the *Apocalypse:*

> And a great sign appeared in heaven: a woman clothed with the sun, and the moon under her feet, and on her head a crown of twelve stars . . .

But here again, the first concern is not with the universe itself: space and the heavenly bodies appear in St. John's vision merely as background. A millennium later, authentic cosmic enthrallment still had not visited the mind of man. The Middle Ages took delight in Latin tales involving aerial excursions, such as the *Anticlaudianus*—tales which Chaucer himself enjoyed and which lent to his *Parliament of Fowls* and *The House of Fame* a cosmic fillip—but not even here did the talk of space take on rapturous proportions. The heavens, curving overhead since the dawn of time, were simply too well known for awe (or too little known?).

Very striking and altogether conclusive evidence of this contained and rather cool attitude toward the cosmos can be found in Dante's *Paradiso.* The entire action is concerned with the travels of Dante and Beatrice through space, with stops at various planets, on their journey to Paradise. They pass through the entire solar system, penetrate beyond the realm of the "fixed stars," and continue on into "Empyrean." But there is absolutely no sense of spaciousness, no impression of speed or movement, nothing exotic or strange in their surroundings, no attempt at description of any kind—when they arrive at a planet they are merely *there,* and so far as the reader is concerned it is an earthly stage on which the story unfolds. Of the mechanics of the whole trip from Earth to Paradise, and of the scenery along the way, Dante says only that the experience "may not be told in words," and he confesses somewhat weakly "I am in amaze how I transcend these lightsome bodies." Thus, though the sun, moon, stars, planets, and all the rest of the celestial machinery appear fairly regularly in literature from ancient times through the Middle Ages, the spirit remained earthbound, weighted down, by the fantastic complications of the Ptolemaic patchwork universe.

Only when Copernicus began the unscrambling of the solar system did men first gaze upward in unsuperstitious awe and benumbed understanding. Copernicus' work, *De Revolutionibus Orbium Coelestium,* was published in 1543 and by the early seventeenth century, following the work of Brahe, Kepler, and Galileo, the new astronomy had become the great topic of inquiry and almost simultaneously the most alluring subject among poets, especially the metaphysicals—it was the true morning of space rapture. Donne and Drummond, Crashaw and Cowley, Traherne and Henry More, among many others, responded with delighted enthusiasm. Strange to say, however, no really memorable cosmic verse came from them; for too much of the time, it seemed, they were busy with mere metrical discussion of the astronomical controversy and its implications in philosophy. Henry Vaughan, perhaps, was the first to sing unforgettably of the expanded firmament:

> I saw Eternity the other night,
> Like a great Ring of pure and endless light,
>   All calm as it was bright
> And round beneath it, Time in hours, days, years,
>   Driv'n by the spheres
> Like a vast shadow mov'd, in which the world
>   And all her train were hurled.

Some seventeen years after Vaughan, *Paradise Lost* was published and the true supernova of celestial rapture burst into being. Directly and decisively influenced by the new astronomy, and especially by the dramatic discoveries of Galileo's telescope, Milton (in the phrase of Douglas Bush) "accepts the universe as his scene and his imagination triumphantly expands to fill it." In the lines from Adam's speech to Raphael, he even seems to confess something of a personal feeling:

> . . . I behold this goodly Frame, this World
> Of Heaven and Earth consisting, and compute
> Their magnitudes, this Earth a spot, a graine,
> An atom with the firmament compared
> And all her numbered starres, that seem to rowle
> Spaces incomprehensible . . .

After Milton the deluge. During the ensuing hundred years, many imitations, gargantuan and uninspired, attempted to reproduce the Miltonic tone, and in so doing automatically perpetuated in some degree the cosmic freshness of the seventeenth century. Edward Young's *Night Thoughts,* which attracted a good deal of attention in the mid-1700's, is a good example of the class. Its cosmic moments, however, are sometimes effective:

> How swift I mount! Diminished earth recedes;
> I pass the moon; and from her farther side,
> Pierce heaven's blue curtain . . .
> I pause at every planet on my road,
> And ask for Him who gives their orbs to roll,
> Their foreheads fair to shine. From Saturn's ring,
> In which, of earth's, an army might be lost,
> With the bold comet take my bolder flight
> Amid those sovereign glories of the skies . . .

Throughout the eighteenth century there were at least a half-dozen elephantine epics similar to *Night Thoughts* that achieved some celebrity, yet it is something worth noting that the most enduring cosmic utterance of the period occurs in a poem of only twenty-four lines—Blake's *The Tyger*. Following Blake, Robert Southey indulged in aerial meanderings in *The Curse of Kehama,* and to a lesser extent in *Thalaba,* but he never quite succeeded in kindling a rapturous spark. His chief importance, in this line, lies in his influence on Shelley, who counted *Kehama* as one of his favorite poems, and it is in Shelley that Milton had his greatest, because most original, disciple before Thompson. It is in Shelley, in fact, that space rapture takes on a sudden new appeal, because of the flexibility of tone and the daring concepts that he brought to it. Carl Grabo has shown the extent to which science affected Shelley, especially the astronomical studies of Sir John Herschel, as they were filtered through the mind of Erasmus Darwin. Shelley, in fact, occupied the same chronological position in relation to Herschel as Milton did to Galileo—the impact was very nearly identical. At some time in his youth, into the space-oriented mental mélange that drifted across his mind, there came the vision of Volney's *Ruins,* which is expressed largely in a framework of aerial wandering. The immediate result was *Queen Mab:*

> The Fairy and the Spirit
> Approached the overhanging battlement—
> Below lay stretched the universe!
> There, far as the remotest line
> That bounds imagination's flight,
> Countless and unending orbs
> In mazy motion intermingled,
> Yet fulfilled immutably
> Eternal nature's law.
> Above, below, around,
> The circling systems formed

A wilderness of harmony;
Each with undeviating aim,
In eloquent silence through the depths of space
Pursued its wondrous way.

If there is little doubt that Shelley took Milton as a point of departure, it must also be admitted that he visited tracts of the universe undreamed of by the older writer. Shelley, of all poets in history, made the upper regions his natural element, but it was not just in the area of unfettered flight that he carried the cosmic tradition along: by his daring personifications and more lyrical vision he added a new dimension to Milton's sublimity. The moon had sat to poets for at least three thousand years yet it was Shelley who first saw that it might reflect something other than the fair and the beautiful:

Like a dying lady, lean and pale,
Who totters forth wrapped in a gauzy veil,
Out of her chamber, led by the insane
And feeble wanderings of her fading brain,
The moon arose up out of the murky East,
A white and shapeless mass . . .

And from the moon he could leap to the very center of a wildly populated universe:

As the sun rules, even with a tyrant's gaze,
The unquiet republic of the maze
Of planets, struggling fierce towards heaven's free
                                                    wilderness

And whether Carl Grabo was right or not in calling Shelley "a Newton among poets," Shelley supplied his own description of the wonder with which he viewed the astronomer:

The lightning is his slave; heaven's utmost deep
Gives up her stars, and like a flock of sheep,
They pass before his eye, are numbered and roll on!
The tempest is his steed, he strides the air . . .

But to attempt to show Shelley's cosmic attitude by quoting him only distorts the truth, for the greater part of his verse, like Thompson's, glows with aerial beauty.

Between Shelley and Thompson there occur two poets who contributed importantly to the cosmic tradition, and even more directly to Thompson's own development. The first, Phillip James Bailley, in the matter of poetic imagination, was little more than a belated Miltonic imitator; his interminable 40,000-line poem, *Festus,* seldom rises much above Young's *Night Thoughts.* In its space imagery, however, it does give evidence of something like real power, and the following examples bear a particularly interesting relation to some of Thompson's images.

Man,
Whose soul-star inly burns with living light,
Who holds the constellations in his hand

His arm
The Almighty then uplift and smote the worlds,
Once, and they fell in fragments like to spray,
And vanished in their native void. He shook
The stars from heaven like rain-drops from a bough

All things are calm and fair and passive. Earth
Looks as if lulled upon an angel's lap
  Into a breathless, dewy sleep

But terror hath a beauty even as mildness;
And I have felt more pleasure far on earth
When, like a lion on a day of battle,
The storm arose, roared, shook out his shaggy mane,
And leaped abroad on the world, and lay down red,
Licking himself to sleep as it got bright

Rossetti enters the tradition with only one poem, *The Blessed Damozel.* First published in 1850, it was revised and republished in 1856 and 1870, showing improvements each time. Thompson probably came into meaningful contact with it by 1883, at the latest, which is the most likely date for his initial encounter with Rossetti's work. He was twenty-two years old at the time, deeply immersed in literature and in that raw kind of poetic awareness that only youth knows. He was involved, as well, in a massive neglect of his medical studies and was slowly surrendering to opium. Only a couple of years before, his mother had died of a lingering illness. In such a tangled emotional situation Rossetti's lines must have struck deeply:

The Blessed Damozel leaned out
  From the gold bar of heaven;
Her eyes were deeper than the depth
  Of waters stilled at even;

It was the rampart of God's house
   That she was standing on;
By God built over the sheer depth
   The which is space begun;
So high that looking downward thence,
   She scarce could see the sun.

. . .

The sun was gone now; the curled moon
   Was like a little feather
Fluttering far down the gulf; and now
   She spoke through the still weather.
Her voice was like the voice the stars had
   when they sang together . . .

Rossetti never again wrote in this fashion, but these lines contain some of the most strikingly phrased space imagery in the language. It was ultimately through them, perhaps, that Thompson's own rapture was sealed on him—through them that he first, as he wrote in *An Anthem of Earth,* heard a sunset

   Break like a clash of cymbals and my heart
   Clang through my shaken body like a gong.

NOTES AND SOURCES

STATEMENTS OF FACT AND QUOTATIONS THAT HAVE BECOME FAMILIAR IN Thompson biography I have not always felt it necessary to document. With new material I have invariably done so, supplying, where it seemed worth while, additional information. I have attempted to give the manuscript source of all direct Thompson quotations (aside from his published writings) as well as their present location; thus much that is usually quoted as from the writings of the Meynells is herein restored to its primary existence in Thompson's notebooks and letters. The same holds true, in general, for quotations from others. Thompson seldom dated his letters, but a careful study of a group of nearly two hundred of them (nearly all that have survived), gathered from various points, has enabled me to date them with a fair amount of accuracy. Except for two or three instances, all extracts from these are from photostats in my possession. Occasionally, when the notes came too thick and fast, I have grouped them by paragraph, repeating in the note the pertinent matter from the text. The following abbreviations have been used:

EM—*The Life of Francis Thompson,* by Everard Meynell, Burns & Oates, Ltd., London, 1913. All references are to this first edition.

VM I—*Alice Meynell, A Memoir,* by Viola Meynell, Burns & Oates, Ltd., London, 1929.

VM II—*Francis Thompson and Wilfrid Meynell,* by Viola Meynell, Hollis & Carter, London, 1952.

Danchin—*Francis Thompson: La Vie et L'Oeuvre d'un Poète,* by Pierre Danchin (Doctor of Letters at the University of Nancy), A. G. Nizet, Paris, 1959. Available in French only.

Essays I—*Literary Criticism* by Francis Thompson, edited by Rev. T. L. Connolly, E. P. Dutton, New York, 1948.

Essays II—*The Real Robert Louis Stevenson and Other Critical Essays,* by Francis Thompson, edited by Rev. T. L. Connolly, University Publishers, Inc., New York, 1959.

(S)—Manuscript in possession of the Sowerby family, Greatham, Sussex. Mrs. Sowerby is the former Olivia Meynell, daughter of Wilfrid and Alice. Indicates personal inspection.

(H)—Manuscript in possession of the Harriss family, Chichester, Hampshire. Mrs. Harriss is the former Joan Meynell, daughter of Everard Meynell. Indicates personal inspection.

(BC)—Manuscript in the Thompson Collection, Boston College. Thompson notebooks in this collection all bear a number, some preceded by the letters BC. Indicates personal inspection.

MHW—*The Man Has Wings, New Poems and Plays by Francis Thompson,* edited by Rev. T. L. Connolly, Hanover House, New York, 1957.

Journal-letter—A very long (some ten thousand words) chatty letter written by Thompson to Father John Carroll (to be passed on to the Thompson family) in May-August 1890. The original has been lost, but a copy prepared in 1909 is in my possession.

Prologue: ALASTOR

1. Letter from Mary Thompson to T. L. Connolly, November 27, 1937 (BC). In the same letter she comments further: "I may say that his eyes were full of intelligence and light; he had good, well-formed eyebrows, and eyelashes also very dark, almost black." His hair she describes as "very dark brown, so dark as to appear almost black at first sight," and his complexion as "also dark (not brown though) and not much color in his face."

2. Letter from W. B. Yeats to Wilfrid Meynell, undated but probably November 1907; quoted in EM, p. 140.

3. Wilfrid Meynell in conversation; quoted in Connolly, T. L., *In His Paths,* p. 150.

4. *Epilogue* to *A Judgment in Heaven.*

Chapter One: THE BRIGHT SILVER DREAM

1. Thompson's birthday has been given as both December 16 and December 18, 1859. He himself noted it as December 18 in the school register for 1877 when he enrolled at Owens College.

2. That Thompson's mother was turned out of her home for embracing Catholicism is generally stated (cf. EM, p. 4); overlooked is the fact that her father, at his death, was living with her, indicating an earlier reconciliation. (See Note 8.)

3. Edward Healy Thompson (1838–1891), originally an Anglican clergyman, became a Catholic and served briefly at Dublin University as an English instructor. He edited, compiled, and translated a number of religious works, notably the writings of the mystic Marie Lataste, and a life of St. Joseph.

He also published a volume of sonnets, a sample of which can be found in *Merry England*, September 1887. John Costall Thompson (1822–1889) was a clerk in the Bank of England and a convert to Catholicism. In 1848 he privately printed *A Vision of Judgment and Other Poems*. In later years (after 1908) some members of his family received financial assistance from Wilfrid Meynell.

4. The present owner of 226 Stamford Street, Mr. Fred Kenworthy, has checked the records and says that Dr. Thompson did not own the property. The flight of stone steps at the rear has been taken down, but Mr. Kenworthy remembers them. May Richardson, niece of the second Mrs. Thompson, at an interview in 1964, gave some details of Dr. Thompson's practice: "The house in Stamford Street had an entrance front and back, and the poor people used to come in at the back and if the doctor thought they needed food they were sent into the kitchen premises to have food in preference to medicine. He was terribly good to the poor, you know, and they followed him in hundreds, when he died, to the grave."

5. EM, p. 10, quotes from a Thompson notebook, unlocated.

6. Letter from Thompson to William Archer, May 31, 1897; quoted in *William Archer*, by C. Archer (Yale 1931), pp. 221–223.

7. Quotations in this paragraph, in order: "Insurgent darkness . . .," Thompson, Francis, "Books That Have Influenced Me," *Weekly Register*, January 26, 1900; reprinted *Essays* I, pp. 542–544. "The crinolined and chignoned girls . . .," Thompson notebook BC 29 (BC).

8. The record of the three deaths is in *Pedigree Register*, March 1913, pp. 354–357; it was compiled by Percival Lucas, husband of Madeline Meynell. The quotation "World-wide desolation . . ." is in Thompson notebook, unnumbered, (H). These words are usually misapplied as referring to the death of Mrs. Thompson. The confusion was caused by Everard Meynell's neglecting to note the opening sentence of the passage: "Mother missed in street."

9. Quotations and details in this paragraph, in order: Thompson's early interest in military matters, cards, painting, and microscopy is from two letters of Mary Thompson to Wilfrid Meynell, June 19, 1908, and January 27, 1911, (S). "My sport was solitary sport . . .," Thompson notebook 21, (BC). "Up in the moon again!" Mary Thompson in a 1946 conversation, quoted in Danchin, p. 19.

10. Byrne, E., "Boyhood Days in Ashton: Francis Thompson," *The Ashton Reporter*, December 1930 (clipping seen at [BC]; exact date not available).

11. *Ibid.* Byrne says Thompson was for a time a member of the St. Ann's group, which included professional actors. He comments: "It was so obvious that Thompson was too stiff and jerky ever to be a success as an actor." Thompson's interest in acting receives no mention in biographies but it is clear that it had an abiding attraction for him. The Meynells occasionally performed amateur theatricals in their home, leading Thompson in later years to confide in a notebook: "I should like to try private acting before I

am quite too old. I could do it still, I believe, more intelligently if with less fire than I might have done twelve or so odd years back. I specially long to try three characters—Hamlet, Shylock and Richard III . . . The difficulty is to get . . . the most moderately efficient amateur support." Notebook, unnumbered, (H). The entry probably dates to 1897–99.

12. In an EM manuscript fragment (S) "Lucidè" is equated with Lucy Keogh. She was the daughter of a local judge and a school friend of one of his sisters.

13. Letter from L. C. Casartelli (later Bishop of Salford) to Wilfrid Meynell, November 28, 1907, (S).

14. Mary Thompson in a 1946 conversation; quoted in Danchin, p. 36.

15. The records of the Convent of the Holy Child, St. Leonard's-on-Sea, contain only one reference to Thompson's mother: "Miss Moreton [sic] came and went into Retreat with V.M.J." The entry is dated May 16, 1855. It was just a little over two years later that Mary Morton and Charles Thompson were married, on September 24, 1857, in Manchester. She had earlier been engaged to a young man who died, and it was after his death that she had entered the Holy Child Order.

16. Thompson's *Ushaw College Notebook* (BC), pp. 19–20. His father appears also to have been very much in favor of his entering the seminary. According to Dr. C. S. Spencer, who succeeded to Dr. Thompson's practice in 1896, the poet's father "seemed to account it one of the greatest privileges to devote his son to the priesthood." *Ashton Reporter,* March 27, 1926.

17. Thompson notebook, unnumbered, (H).

18. Quotations in this paragraph, in order: "A capacious whin-bush . . .," *Ushaw Magazine,* March 1908. "The malignity of my tormentors . . .," Thompson manuscript fragment (BC) entitled "Personal Data." The three personal descriptions are from *Ushaw Magazine,* March 1908.

19. Father Adam Wilkinson in a letter to *The Tablet* (London) December 13, 1913. The point was still a sore one with Wilkinson and his classmates a year later. On October 29, 1914, he said in an unpublished letter to Everard Meynell: "About three weeks ago a few old school-fellows of Francis Thompson met, as is their wont once each year. They expressed a hope that in your next edition of the Poet's life, you would delete the objectionable passage which I pointed out to you last November. Like me they resent it for its want of truth. One of his masters was also with us and he pointed out that Thompson was dealt with more leniently than others in his class . . ." It is clear that Thompson's introduction to Ushaw was marred by the initiation he received, and that the effects lingered. The real reason for the misunderstanding about the Ushaw years was Everard Meynell's undiscerning use of the isolated scribblings Thompson left behind. Most of these were parts of, or notes for, an autobiographical article written in 1901 (see Note 13, Chap. 9) and which should be regarded more as an artistic rendering than strict fact. One detached leaf, for example, contains the following unpublished De Quinceyish strain: "My childhood! oh, my childhood! Shall I ever forget it?

The one time of golden joys I have ever known! For it ended with my departure to college in the last (closing) months of my tenth year. After that I was still a child, I still—when I was at home—remained capable of fervid (excited) delight over simple and seldom pleasures up to my eighteenth (or nineteenth) year. But I had learned the taste (savour) of tears, of agony, of sick dread—yes even of despair. From that time I date my boyhood—the childhood suppressed and latent for its vacations of home and solitude—and boyhood is to me a harsh and cruel (sinister hard) memory. I am thankful to be delivered from it; but look back with longing regret to the fairy-tale (dream) of childhood, sundered by the sharp demarcation of my setting forth for the savage world of college life." (Manuscript S.). Meynell took this as relating to the entire Ushaw period where it probably refers only to the first year or so and is an attempt on Thompson's part to delineate his growth as a poet. In fact in a similar fragment he specifically refers all this to his first year; see Danchin, p. 36.

20. Letter from an Ushaw teacher to Dr. Thompson, dated Easter 1872; quoted in EM, p. 26. The essay mentioned in this paragraph, entitled "The Storming of the Bridge of Lodi," is printed in *Ushaw Magazine*, March 1908.

21. *Ushaw Magazine*, March 1908.

22. Thompson in conversation with Wilfrid Blunt, quoted in Blunt's *My Diaries*, II, p. 594.

23. *Ushaw Magazine*, March 1908.

24. This Notebook was purchased from one of Thompson's classmates by Everard Meynell about 1910. It is now at (BC).

25. From an anonymous article in *Ushaw Magazine*, March 1910.

26. Unpublished letter from Ushaw authorities to Thompson's family, quoted in the draft of the EM manuscript, (S).

27. The "Thompson relative" was the same Agnes Martin mentioned in EM, p. 3. She was the daughter of John Costall Thompson. Her opinion can be given little weight since contact between these branches of the family was almost nonexistent. It is doubtful, in fact, whether Agnes Martin ever met her cousin Francis.

28. Unpublished fragments in a draft of the EM manuscript, (S).

29. *Academy,* December 4, 1897.

30. EM, p. 32.

Chapter Two: TOWERS OF BABYLON

1. An Owens register shows him in the fall of 1877 entered for a class in mathematics; his name first appears in the register of the Manchester Royal Infirmary, where the Owens students did their laboratory work, for the fall session of 1878. The list of students in the *Owens College Callendars* for 1878–81 shows him entered for both summer and winter sessions. The

Calendar for 1882–83 does not list his name, indicating a possibility that he may have dropped out of school between May 1882 and October 1883. His name reappears in 1883–84.

2. The neighbor was J. Saxon Mills, who contributed some reminiscences to *Cassell's Weekly*, May 26, 1923. Mills had charge of the church theatricals in which Thompson took part.

3. See, for instance, *Owens College Calendar* for 1883, pp. 111–112: "The attendance of all students on lectures is registered . . . habitual neglect of work in any class without good reason assigned will be regarded as a breach of discipline, and may subject a student to suspension from class." Warning is also given that such unexplained absences will be reported to the student's parents. The same announcement was repeated from year to year in the *Callendar,* and each student was expected to possess a copy, and be familiar with it.

4. EM, pp. 46, 49.

5. Interview with the author, London, April 1964.

6. Connolly, T. L., *In His Paths,* p. 190.

7. Letter from Norbert Thompson to the author, July 2, 1964.

8. Letter from Edward Healy Thompson to Wilfrid Meynell, October 14, 1889, (S).

9. *Academy,* April 29, 1899; reprinted *Essays* II, pp. 111–112.

10. The house was standing as late as 1909; see Chancellor, E., *The Romance of Soho,* p. 119.

11. In a letter to Wilfrid Meynell, January 1891, Thompson explains the source of *Amphicypellon:* "Many years ago, when Schliemann's things from Troy were first exhibited at South Kensington, I remember seeing among them a drinking-cup labelled 'Perhaps the Amphicypellon of Homer.' It was a boat-shaped cup of plain gold, open at the top and with a crescentic aperture at either extremity of the rim, through which the wine could either be poured or drunk. So that you could pour from either end, and (if the cup were brimmed with wine) two people could have drunk from it at the same time, one at either extremity. In a certain sense, therefore, it was a double cup. And it also had two handles, one at either of its boat-shaped sides, so that it was a two-handled cup. You will see at once why I have applied the name to my double poem." He could only have seen this cup in 1879. Gold vessels from Troy were lent to the South Kensington Museum (now the Victoria and Albert) by Schliemann during 1877–79 only; Thompson could not have been in London for his examinations till 1879. For Schliemann's loans to the museum see *List of Art Objects in the South Kensington Museum Lent during 1877–1883.* The name *Amphicypellon,* of course, Thompson later dropped in favor of *Sister Songs.*

12. The official death certificate for Mrs. Thompson specifies "Hypertrophy of liver six months."

13. Thompson called these lines *This Is My Beloved Son;* they were first printed by Wilfrid Meynell in *Who Goes There?* (1916) with lines 13–14

deleted. The manuscript is now at (BC). For "Second Death" see *Apocalypse,* 20:6.

14. Letter from Mary Thompson to Wilfrid Meynell, November 15, 1907, (S).

15. From the original manuscript of Thompson's article, *Our Literary Life,* written in spring 1890, but not published until 1948, when it appeared in *Essays* I. The passage quoted, however, was deleted by the book's editor, T. L. Connolly.

16. The sentence occurs in the rough manuscript of the Shelley essay (BC). The opening paragraphs of the published essay, in fact, constitute a more reasoned and subtle argument along the same lines, and there is an admonition very similar to this canceled sentence: "Eye her [poetry] not askance if she seldom sing directly of religion: the bird gives glory to God though it sings only of its innocent loves."

17. This notebook was almost certainly compiled by Thompson at the request of Wilfrid Meynell after their first meeting in 1888, as is suggested in Chapter 4.

18. At least three books on Rossetti and his work appeared in the year following his death: *Recollections of Rossetti* by Hall Caine; *D. G. Rossetti* by William Sharp; *Introduction to Rossetti's Poems* by Walter Pater. Rossetti's close friend, Theodore Watts-Dunton, also attracted attention with an article, "The Truth About Rossetti," in *Nineteenth Century,* March 1883.

19. There is no indication as to how Thompson might have eliminated the extra line in the sestet of the fourth sonnet. Regarding Lucy Keogh, his friendship with her could not have been very intimate, since she later claimed to have been unaware of any special feeling on his part; see EM, p. 14.

20. The three quotations in this paragraph, in order: *Weekly Register,* April 22, 1893; *Academy,* December 20, 1902; manuscript fragment, "Things Seen," (BC).

21. "The Fourth Order of Humanity," *Merry England,* December 1891; reprinted in Thompson's *Works,* III, pp. 66–70.

22. *Academy,* November 30, 1901.

23. The description of Thompson's frail figure is by J. Saxon Mills, in *Cassell's Weekly,* May 26, 1923; the nickname, "Elasticlegs," is mentioned in a letter from Mary Thompson to Wilfrid Meynell, January 17, 1911, (S). The only personal description of Thompson as a student at Owens occurs in a 1932 book of essays by Robert Mackenna, *As Shadows Lengthen.* Mackenna gives it as coming from a fellow-student of Thompson's, who is unnamed, and it must be remembered that the informant was drawing on a memory of fifty years, at a time when Thompson's fame had become worldwide. It is a rather brutal description and no doubt exaggerated, but it may contain a seed of truth in its picture of a withdrawn young student suffering in the tightening grip of drug-addiction. "I have had a description of him," Mackenna wrote, "from one who daily travelled in the same train. My informant tells me that Thompson was at this time a loose-limbed, untidy-

looking boy, with a vacant stare, weak lips, and a usually half-open mouth, the saliva often trickling over his chin. He was the butt and jest of the many schoolboys who used to travel by the same train, and who tormented him unmercifully." Whatever element of truth the words contain must refer to the later Owens years, perhaps 1883–84, when he had been taking laudanum for about five years, and was prevented by his attendance in school from satisfying any early morning cravings.

24. Thompson notebook (purple cover), (H).

25. Letter from Norbert Thompson to the author, July 2, 1964; also Danchin, pp. 32–33, impliedly from a conversation with Mary Thompson.

26. Letter from Mary Thompson to Wilfrid Meynell, November 25, 1907, (S).

27. Letter from Mary Thompson to Wilfrid Meynell, May 21, 1908, (S).

28. Letter from Mary Thompson to Wilfrid Meynell, November 24, 1913, (S).

29. Interview with Sister DiSalle at the Presentation Convent, Manchester, April 1964.

30. Letter from Mary Thompson to Wilfrid Meynell, May 21, 1908, (S).

31. Letter from Mary Thompson to Wilfrid Meynell, November 25, 1907, (S).

32. Letter from Thompson to Wilfrid Meynell, July 1900, (S).

33. Persistent early references to Thompson's "walking to London" from Ashton suggest that he probably walked into Manchester after leaving home. His trip to London was made by train.

Chapter Three: THE LONE CHORASMIAN SHORE

1. Both plays were well advertised; see London *Times*, November 16, 1885.

2. EM, p. 68, identifies the reading-room as the Clarendon, but there was no reading-room by that name in the Strand in 1885–86. Gillig's, in the Strand, was one of the best-known reading-rooms and mail depositories then in the city.

3. Dent's *Encyclopedia of London*, (1951), p. 358. In a Guildhall Library register (destroyed when the library was hit by bombs in the war) Thompson in 1886 gave his address as "Dane's Inn Coffee House, Strand." The street known as Dane's Inn during Thompson's day abutted on the present Aldwych —ironically, just across the Strand from Meynell's office at 43 Essex Street. Dane's Inn was a narrow, hidden backstreet, little more than an alley, and the Directories list four or five artists as living there. It is possible that it was a sort of diminutive Bohemian cul-de-sac. Thompson's connection with it was preserved accidentally in *The Evening News*, October 8, 1923, in a story on the Guildhall.

4. This incident was related in a lecture by Agnes Tobin, a friend of the Meynells, who gives it as coming from Thompson himself during a

conversation in London; manuscript of the lecture at BC. She does not specify the Ghirlandaio picture, but that was the only painting in the National Gallery in 1886 that fits the case.

5. Rossetti's *Ecce Ancilla Domini* was acquired by the National Gallery in 1886; it has since gone elsewhere.

6. From *Notebook of Early Poems;* printed in MHW, p. 39.

7. McMaster, John, *A Short History of the Royal Parish of St. Martin in the Fields,* (1916), p. 116. The book contains only a brief reference to Thompson. In later years, it appears, McMaster gave up bootmaking and opened a print shop, still in Panton Street. About 1927 he was visited there by R. Thurston Hopkins, whose record of their conversation shows that McMaster had, as usually happens, embellished the legend. "That chair you are sitting on," he told his visitor, "was the one which Thompson used when he was in my employ, and, as I think of him this evening, I can see him on the first night he came in the shop. He was the very personification of ruin, a tumble-down, dilapidated opium-haunted wreck. He gave me the impression of having been dropped in the chair—all in a heap. I confess that my first impulse, and a strong one, was to give him a few shillings and get rid of him . . . And then suddenly I had a counter impulse. What was I that I should set myself up to pronounce sentence after a first careless impression? Perhaps after all here was a messenger . . . one who carried some secret treasure. So I gave him a job in the shop." The "secret treasure," inevitably, turned out to be a draft of *The Hound of Heaven* stuffed in the bedraggled poet's pocket. Hopkins, R. T., *This London,* p. 197.

8. Everard Meynell quotes McMaster in a canceled passage of the rough manuscript of the 1913 biography, (S).

9. McMaster, *op. cit.,* p. 117.

10. EM, p. 74.

11. EM, p. 75.

12. Thompson manuscript fragment, (BC); it is filed under *First Letters to Meynell,* but it is probably a part of the autobiographical article Thompson wrote in 1901, referred to in Chapter 9.

13. From *Notebook of Early Poems,* (BC).

14. The first quotation in this paragraph is from Thompson's article, "Catholics in Darkest England," *Merry England,* January 1891; the second and third quotations are from Thompson Notebook BC 29, (BC).

15. *Academy,* December 6, 1902.

16. Thompson Notebook 10 (BC); the lines, unpublished, have been edited from a fragment.

17. "Catholics in Darkest England," *Merry England,* 1891; this portion of the article was dropped when it was reprinted in *Works,* III, pp. 52–65.

18. Thompson Notebook, unnumbered (green cover), containing a draft of *Sister Songs,* (H). "Reuben May" was probably a cousin, perhaps encountered in the street; "My two ladies" may refer to the incident with Ghirlandaio's picture in the National Gallery.

19. *Athenaeum*, November 23, 1907; reprinted as Introduction to *Selected Poems*, 1908.

20. Thompson Notebook BC 23, (BC).

21. Hutton, John, *Guidance From Francis Thompson in Matters of Faith* (1926), pp. 15–16.

22. Thompson manuscript fragment, (H).

23. Separate Thompson manuscript, (BC).

24. Interview with the author, Manchester, April 1964.

25. McMaster, J., *op. cit.*, p. 117.

26. It has always been believed that Thompson and his father never met after the son left home, but it can be shown that Thompson visited his father in the fall of 1894, subsequent to the publication of his first volume and during the first flush of the fame that resulted. See Note 24, Chapter 7.

27. Los Angeles *Times*; undated clipping preserved at (BC).

28. Letter from Dorothy Richardson (Sister Mary St. Felicien) to the author, December 6, 1964.

29. Copy of Dr. Thompson's will in author's possession; the value of the estate was made up of property at Preston, insurance policies, and cash. Francis Thompson is named after his stepmother, his brother Norbert, and Norbert's heirs. Mary Thompson, then a nun in Manchester, is not named. Probate was admitted on May 8, 1896; copy in author's possession.

30. There is one bit of actual evidence to support the conjecture: Wilfrid Meynell told Wilfrid Blunt in September 1907 that Dr. Thompson had "cast off" his son because "he had failed to retain any permanent employment," and because he believed that "he would never come to any good." Blunt's *My Diaries*, II, p. 184. As with most of Meynell's testimony relative to hard fact, this may be taken as an approximation of the truth; the important element in it is not the reason assigned, but the indication of a rejection by the elder Thompson.

31. Thompson Notebook 45, (BC). This also contains drafts of some poems later copied into the *Notebook of Early Poems;* most of the writing is in pencil and very faded; it was almost certainly kept while Thompson was on the streets.

32. Occasional doubts have been expressed over the reality of Thompson's suicide attempt. Doyle Hennessy, for example, in *The Catholic World*, February 1950, attempted to show that the story depended entirely on the diaries of Wilfrid Blunt, who could have misinterpreted a conversation with Wilfrid Meynell. Doyle surmised that Thompson might only have dreamed the incident and that in subsequent retellings it had been elevated to reality. The basis of this theory was the fact that, in the 1913 biography, Everard Meynell had no mention of suicide. But while it is true that the published book contains no reference to suicide, the rough manuscript, (S), does. In a penciled note Everard wrote: "On posting this Francis found himself without a penny, and he could not wait even for a day without being thrown into desperate straits. For the sake of a 'curtain' in his drama we will here place

the incident of his contemplated suicide." There is also a scribbled fragment regarding Chatterton's part: "What kept him alive, what stirred the shade of Chatterton—shade of Francis' shadowed mind—to help him?" For some reason, obviously, there had been second thoughts about including the incident. There are two other early printed references to a suicide attempt, in John Thomson's *Francis Thompson: The Preston-Born Poet* (1912), and Kingsley Rooker's *Francis Thompson* (1913), a critical study published in French by Herbert and Daniel. Both of these writers obtained their information from Meynell himself.

33. Wilfrid Meynell in conversation with Wilfrid Blunt; quoted in Blunt's *My Diaries*, II, p. 183. Regarding the role played by Chatterton's ghost in the incident, it is interesting to recall that Rossetti had made a well-known painting of the young poet's unfortunate but famous death scene; note that Thompson says he recognized Chatterton "from the pictures of him."

Chapter Four: UPON RESPLENDENT CLOUDS

1. The building was pulled down in 1896.

2. Letter from Thompson to Katharine Tynan (Hinkson), July 15, 1892; original at Harriss Library, Preston; printed in Katherine Hinkson's *The Middle Years*, pp. 14–15. He says he bought the issue because it contained her poem "Poppies" (*Merry England*, April 1885), "and the twopence I gave for it was a truer gage [sic] of admiration than many a sovereign. For at that time I was struggling for mere existence and a penny spent on aught but the necessaries of life was a plank withdrawn between me and starvation."

3. Meynell mentions the fact in "A New Poet," *Merry England*, November 1893.

4. Oldcastle, J. (pseud.), *Journal and Journalism*, p. 32.

5. Original at (BC), the paper bears a watermark of "Hawtin, Son and Cook," a London firm of papermakers, printers, and engravers; its uneven edges show that it was cut from a larger sheet.

6. Quotations in this paragraph, in order: "When I am angry . . . ," *At a Station*, an essay; "It would be a pity . . . ," *Laughter*, an essay; "Had never seen her unfinished or unprepared," VM I, p. 346; "There was the charm of a beautiful abbess about her . . . ," Le Gallienne, *Romantic '90s*, p. 75; John Drinkwater's comments can be found in his *The Muse in Council*, pp. 153–154.

7. Hinkson, K. T., *Memories*, p. 42.

8. VM I, p. 137.

9. Rossetti commented favorably on *The Pen*, but it does not appear that the Meynells ever met him.

10. These connections, of course, would have been tremendously impressive to Thompson, especially that with Shelley's family. After his long period of intellectual isolation, he would have felt at last in touch with the reality of English literature.

11. Hind, C. L., *Napthali*, p. 60.

12. A copy of EM's 1913 life of Thompson at (BC) contains a marginal note by the elder Meynell correcting the period to "Six *weeks*, My Son!" Earlier, in *Merry England*, November 1893, he specified "two or three months."

13. Thompson, in the journal-letter 1890, quotes the incident as told to him by Meynell.

14. Everard Meynell notebook (purple cover), (S).

15. Hind, C. L., *Napthali*, p. 61.

16. There is also a clear link to Rossetti's *Ave*.

17. Mary Thompson in conversation; reported in Connolly, T. L., *In His Paths*, p. 140; also Danchin, p. 47. Just how contact was re-established is not clear; probably Thompson had written home for money sometime in the spring of 1888, shortly after his suicide attempt.

18. Original at (BC).

19. EM, p. 89. The only chemist in Drury Lane in 1888 was Edward Thomas, at no. 44, in a building which no longer exists.

20. Interview with Francis Meynell, London, April 1964.

21. *Sister Songs*, II, ll.169–177. Though the lines certainly describe Thompson's first visit to Meynell's office, the resemblance between this passage and the opening of Crashaw's *To the Countess of Denbigh* is more than a little interesting:

> What Heaven-entreated heart is this,
> Stands trembling at the gate of bliss?
> Holds fast the door, yet dares not venture
> Fairly to open it, and enter;
> Whose definition is a doubt
> Twixt life and death, twixt in and out.

22. Original at (S). Thompson's uncle informed Meynell, "He has been a great trouble and sorrow to his father from his utter want of ballast. He started with every advantage, but has stuck to nothing. He was supposed to be studying for the medical profession, while he was doing nothing of the kind, having, it appeared, an ambition to distinguish himself as a literary man. At last, he went off from Ashton-under-Lyne, where my brother lives, to London, and there seems to have lived a sort of Bohemian life . . . I have not seen him for thirteen years. He used to write to me until I gave him some advice, which I suppose he resented, for he never wrote to me again. His letters were all of a literary cast, and showed I thought, no small amount of self-conceit in the way of habitual criticism and fault-finding . . ." This contact between Meynell and Edward Healy Thompson led to the latter's contributing some memories of the poet William Lisle Bowles to the Septem-

ber 1888 *Merry England*. As a young Anglican curate he had served under Bowles.

23. EM, p. 83; Everard Meynell's use of a direct quotation from this girl indicates that Thompson must have earlier told the story to Wilfrid. A second quotation from this girl, two paragraphs farther on, is from the same source.

24. Everard Meynell notebook, (S).

25. The compilation was done in a small account book, now known as the *Notebook of Early Poems*. Sufficient evidence that this notebook was made up for Meynell's perusal is the fact that it does not contain *The Passion of Mary*, which had already been printed in the April *Merry England*, and contains only the title of *Dream Tryst* with the notation "Sent in to Merry England." There is also a notation in Thompson's hand on the first page: "Verses you wished to see are on page 52; it may save you search."

26. First published in *The Man Has Wings* (1957). And De Quincey again intrudes: in his reminiscences of Wordsworth he has a reference to Semele.

27. At this time occurred the most bizarre coincidence in Thompson's life. During the very weeks he was searching for his prostitute friend, London was in an uproar over the ghastly deaths of five such women at the hands of Jack the Ripper. In these circumstances his concern for his friend's welfare would naturally have been heightened. The police threw a wide net over the city, investigating thousands of drifters, and known consorters with the city's lower elements, and it is not beyond possibility that Thompson himself may have been questioned. He was, after all, a drug addict, acquainted with prostitutes, and, most alarming, a former medical student! A young man with a similar background and living only a block from McMaster's shop, was one who early came under suspicion; see Cullen, T., *When London Walked in Terror*.

28. Thompson manuscript fragment, (S). The note was probably a part of the "narrative" referred to in Note 13, Chapter 9.

29. Thompson Notebook BC 22, (BC).

30. *Observer* (London), March 5, 1933.

31. It has never been made quite clear whether he was also being treated for tuberculosis at this time. It would appear, however, that he was not. Brompton Hospital was the only institution in South Kensington, and for quite a large portion of the surrounding area, that cared for tuberculosis patients at that time, and the hospital's records, complete as far back as 1841, do not include Thompson's name. Many hospitals, on the other hand, could have been found to admit a drug addict. Information courtesy of K. Miles, Governor of Brompton Hospital.

32. My view of the sequence of these events is derived from a study of all available evidence. It is possible, however, that the girl did not disappear until *after* Thompson had gone into the hospital. In a conversation with Wilfrid Blunt in August 1894, Meynell said that "the girl insisted that he should go

to the hospital, and when he came out of it cured she had disappeared."
(Blunt's *My Diaries*, I, p. 148). But another conversation between these two,
a dozen years later, makes everything less clear again (Blunt's *My Diaries*, II,
p. 184).

33. Hinkson, K. T., *Memories*, pp. 24–25.

34. Thompson wrote steadily for *Merry England* from 1888 until its
demise some seven years later. In that time he contributed nearly thirty prose
pieces, all of some distinction, as well as thirty-seven poems, a good portion
of which still stand among the best poetry of the late nineteenth century.
If Thompson owed his life and his chance for fame to Wilfrid Meynell, then
it must be said that Meynell owed to Thompson some part of the success of
Merry England—a success which later played an important role in his rise
to the Directorship of the firm of Burns and Oates.

35. There is no direct evidence that Thompson relapsed at this time, but
since three months or so intervened between his leaving the hospital and his
going to Storrington, it does not seem likely that his departure to the country
could have been connected with his initial withdrawal period. His letters
from Storrington, in fact, show that he was just then (February 1889)
undergoing the pains of withdrawal.

36. Thompson to Wilfrid Meynell, February 1889; original at (S). Mrs.
Blackburn was a friend of the Meynells, and a sometime editorial assistant.

37. From *Health and Holiness,* a monograph published separately in 1905;
see *Works,* III, p. 263. In a notation in the *Works* Meynell explained that
"the poet was Francis Thompson himself."

38. "The Macbeth Controversy," *Dublin Review,* July 1889, was the
article done at the invitation of Bishop Vaughan, not *Shelley,* as Everard
Meynell stated. A letter of Bishop Vaughan to Lady Herbert, April 12, 1889,
refers to the article as overdue; see *Letters of Cardinal Vaughan to Lady
Herbert* (1942), p. 391. The article is basically a review of a book by
Comyns Carr.

39. Thompson to Wilfrid Meynell, May 1889; quoted in part in VM II,
p. 31. Another portion appears in EM, pp. 100–102. The original has been
lost.

40. References by Thompson to his beginning the poem at sunset while
beside the cross, and completing it on Kithurst Hill, appear in Notebooks 3
and 23-A, (BC).

41. That he interrupted the Ode to write *Non Pax—Expectatio* is indicated
by the contents of Notebook 25, (BC). This is a small pad made by folding
together several pieces of paper, probably for tucking in a pocket on his
rambles. The sonnet occurs between two fragments of the Ode. It gives the
impression of having been scrawled out suddenly, almost breathlessly, without his usual heed to the confining lines on the paper, and seems to have
been written at one swoop. Several word changes were made before publication (*Merry England,* July 1889), such as "gap" for "pause" and "white"
for "space."

42. No. 47 Palace Court was built at this time, with funds inherited by Alice Meynell.

43. The words are Medieval English and mean "vitality in her tillage." Thompson could have found them in *The Tempest*, II, 1, lines 152, 163. He had just finished his article on *Macbeth* and had a volume of Shakespeare in his possession.

44. Edward Healy Thompson was one who received the booklet, and on October 14, 1889, he replied: "I have followed F's literary course with much interest, and I have read his Ode more than once, and on perusal have found it more intelligible—for I confess that some passages were beyond my comprehension, but probably from not understanding the allusions. He has great command of diction, and no doubt the composition is overloaded with imagery, but then how gorgeous was the subject. There are lines that live in one's memory and have a wonderful music of their own . . . My brother sent me a letter of F's written to Canon Carroll, which was very consolatory. I hope he has now absolutely [illegible] renounced the use of that fatal drug . . . There was nothing in his home life to lead him to divulge himself, no encouragement and no sympathy with his ambitions. His sisters, who might have been of use in expounding him—if I may use such a phrase—have so little of the poetic element in them that they seem on principle to have eschewed all poetry as if it were a temptation and a snare. No wonder he shut himself up in himself, as he literally did in his room. This I believe to be the key to, and so far an excuse for, his deceitful proceedings, and his apparent callousness and ingratitude. No doubt the opium had the effect on his mental and moral perceptions which he now laments." The fact that he lays the blame so squarely on Dr. Thompson's shoulders, without any awareness of far more complicated factors, seems to reveal something less than family closeness. At the end of the letter he makes a casually cruel remark concerning still another brother, John Costall Thompson: "A younger brother of mine showed some promise of being a poet, and was taken up by Gladstone and Sir H. Taylor, years ago, but he proved an utter failure, as indeed, his life may be said to have been." When the words were written the younger brother had been dead six months. Original at (S).

45. Original in possession of Francis Meynell.

Chapter Five: THE BREATH OF HEAVEN

1. Thompson to Wilfrid Meynell, January 1890. The periodic loneliness and despondency he experienced in his rural retreat he expressed strikingly in a previously unknown sonnet written at Storrington (one final manuscript is contained in a Storrington notebook H). It is entitled *Cor Meum:*

> Unpriced of chafferers in any mart;
> Most valueless and precious; What thou art
> Dearly despised! I know not, and would know!

Which God has built without so poor and low
Love's crowned head cannot stoop to pass thy gate,
Yet within ample for thy purple state;
Too mean a cup for Midas-love to hold
Although his lips would turn thee into gold.
Tent of the arab tale! That I can pitch
Over what rustling multitudes! yet which
I bear in so strait compass thou art hid.
Too great for merchandise, though kings should bid;
Too little for the beggar in the street
To heed, if thou lay naked at his naked feet.

2. The assertion that *Finis Coronat Opus* was begun in late summer 1889 and not spring 1890 is based on the fact that finished portions of it appear on the reverse of sundry leaves of the *Shelley* manuscript, (BC). This manuscript was out of Thompson's hands, at the *Dublin Review*, from January to August 1890. *Finis* appeared in the June 1890 *Merry England*, indicating that it was completed no later than April 1890. It must have been started well before January, and since Thompson was engaged on the Shelley essay and *The Hound of Heaven* between October and January, he must have begun *Finis* as early as August or September. An added bit of evidence is the scrawled draft of a verse for *Daisy* on the back of one of the sheets.

3. Letter from Daisy Reid (née Stanford) to Everard Meynell, October 17, 1913, (S). She was married and living in Montreal at the time she wrote to Meynell.

4. The journal-letter.

5. *Ibid.*

6. "Nature's Immortality," *Merry England*, February 1890; the whole passage from which the quotation is taken was dropped when the essay was reprinted in the *Works*, 1913.

7. *Ibid.*

8. For instance: in *The Sere of the Leaf* there are "saddened thoughts" that fall from "the mind's autumnal tree," presaging the *Hound's*

> dank thoughts that shiver
> Upon the sighful branches of my mind

In *Daphne* there are "feet less fleet than the feet that follow," anticipating the *Hound's* "strong feet" of "majestic instancy." *The Song of the Hours* has an eleven-line passage that is almost a miniature sketch for the *Hound*:

> Our transcience is only a mortal seeming;
> Fond men, we are fixed as a still despair,
>   And we fleet but in your dreaming.
>   We are columns in Time's hall, mortals,

> Wherethrough Life hurrieth;
> You pass in at birth's wide portals
> And out at the postern of death.
> As you chase down the vista your dream or your love,
>   The swift pillars race you by,
> And you think it is we who move, who move—
>   It is you who die, who die!

There are a number of especially interesting examples in the Shelley essay. Wondering why so many lyric poets lived unfortunate lives, Thompson comments: "Such a poet, it may be, mists with sighs the windows of his life until the tears run down it," and in *The Hound* the hunted one hides from God "in the mist of tears." Treating Shelley's imagery he remarks "to sport with the tangles of Neaera's hair may be trivial idleness or caressing tenderness . . ." which in *The Hound* becomes "Wantoning with our Lady-Mother's vagrant tresses." It appears that two of the best-known lines he ever wrote are also linked to each other in this way. Of the young Shelley he commented: "The child fled into the tower of his own soul and raised the drawbridge," which leads naturally to "I fled Him down the labyrinthine ways of my own mind."

9. Irving Buchen, in *Victorian Poetry,* II, 2 (1964), pp. 111–115, points out passages in St. Gregory, St. Augustine, and St. Paul which refer to dogs as symbolic defenders of the faith and the faithful. But his presentation, while interesting, is misleading since in his commentary he uses the word "hound," which appears nowhere in these early writings. It has long been customary, of course, to picture Christ as a lamb, a dove, or an eagle, etc., but the only complementary use of "hound" as a title seems to occur in Irish legend, where Cuchulain is referred to as "The Hound of Ulster." The word also seems to have been used during the Inquisition, when the inquisitors were sometimes named "The Hounds of God," and ancient Greek poetry occasionally has "the hounds of Zeus."

10. Thompson manuscript fragment, (S).

11. Here, and subsequently, is treated specific literary influence; the general influence from Scripture and religious tradition has been mentioned in the preceding chapter. No attempt is made, of course, to present all the sources for the poem. One or two of the examples have been noted before; most are here presented for the first time.

12. In "Stray Thoughts on Shelley," *Merry England,* September 1892. The article was written in 1889, at the same time as the Shelley essay itself. He asks: "Could he have waxed inebriate with the heady choruses of 'Prometheus Unbound' . . . if for the Baths of Caracalla with their 'flowering ruins' . . . had been substituted the blear streets of London . . . ?" Shelley's letter would have been available to Thompson in the Dowden biography. The "arches of the years" perhaps also owes something to Tennyson's *Ulysses:*

Yet all experience is an arch wherethro'
Gleams that untravell'd world whose magic fades
For ever and for ever when I move.

13. Shelley's *Prometheus Unbound* (I, 805) has "labyrinthine soul," and his fragment: *Love the Universe* has the phrase, "Life's labyrinthine way." Thompson was also undoubtedly familiar with the seventeenth-century lines of Henry King:

Life is a crooked Labyrinth, and we
Are daily lost in that Obliquity.

14. William Sharp's *Browning*, p. 210, has this: "The hand of Destiny . . . putting out the lights of Heaven one by one, like candles after a feast," which certainly is related to the lines in *The Hound*:

I was heavy with the even,
When she lit her glimmering tapers
round the day's dead sanctities

And, lest that be thought a coincidence, a second instance of borrowing from Sharp's book can be cited. On page 208 Sharp wrote of Browning: "He is, among poets, what Wagner is among musicians; as Shakespeare may be likened to Beethoven, or Shelley to Chopin." In his essay on Shelley, Thompson wrote: "Here we have that absolute virgin-gold of song which is the scarcest among human products, and for which we can go to but three poets—Coleridge, Shelley, Chopin." In a footnote to that statement he adds: "Such analogies between masters in the sister-arts are often interesting. In some respects, is not Brahms the Browning of music?" It is a moot point whether he improved Sharp's comparison. His review of Sharp's book appeared in *Merry England*, July 1890, but his letters show he was reading it the previous fall at Storrington.

15. When the phrase "deliberate speed" turned up in the United States Supreme Court's 1954 desegregation decision, there quickly followed speculation as to its origin. *The Hound of Heaven* was immediately cited, but a claim was also quickly put in for Justice Holmes, who used the words in his opinion on *Virginia vs. West Virginia*, 1911, giving them as "the language of the English chancery." In a 1909 letter to an English friend, Holmes mentioned "Your chancery's delightful phrase, with all deliberate speed." Both men probably got the phrase from the English court; where the Supreme Court found it remains unsettled.

16. The passage in *Epipsychidion* in which these lines occur is usually pointed out as a prime source of *The Hound*, but, more likely, it was the inspiration for the cosmic sections of the *Shelley* essay, and is related to *The Hound* at one remove, so to speak.

17. The idea of heavenly "battlements" is an old convention. They were usually described as "crystal," as in *Paradise Lost*, though Shelley describes them as "pearly" in *Queen Mab*. De Quincey, at the end of the *Confessions*, quotes a passage from Wordsworth in which the idea occurs strikingly.

18. *Apocalypse*, 10:7; 11:15,19.

19. No drafts or fragments of *The Hound of Heaven* appeared to have survived, which was seen as something of a puzzle since drafts of most of the other poems from the period existed. All that was available in Thompson's hand were the two fair copies of the final manuscript, the first sent to *Merry England* and the second made later for Sir Sidney Cockerell. The mystery was explained when the author, in October 1964, discovered what appeared to be a near-final draft in the Thompson notebook owned by the Harriss family. Written in pencil, it had been erased by Thompson and the pages reused to draft *Sister Songs*. Barely visible here and there, around and under the words of *Sister Songs*, are phrases and words such as "trumpet," "wild sea-snortings," "mine own moods," "contentst not me." The word "turrets" in line 147 of the finished poem was "walls" in this draft.

20. Thompson manuscript fragment, (S).

Chapter Six: A TREACHEROUS CALM

1. The cost of Thompson's stay at Storrington has been calculated from a number of bills, submitted to Meynell by the monastery, (S). The charge for food, lodging, laundry, and "breakage" was something over a pound a week.

2. Thompson to Wilfrid Meynell, September 1889, (S), quoted in EM, p. 96. The remark was made when the idea of returning to London was first broached.

3. The address occurs in the journal-letter and in the records of the British Museum Reading Room for 1890, where Thompson obtained a reader's ticket shortly after reaching London.

4. The journal-letter.

5. *Ibid.*

6. Alice Meynell to Wilfrid Meynell, undated but probably early 1891, (S).

7. This biography of de La Salle was not intended entirely as original, but was based on a French work published in 1891. Thompson's efforts consisted largely of condensation, paraphrase, and adaptation, and he was careful to acknowledge his dependence. The operation was much the same as his uncle, E. H. Thompson, customarily performed on religious works.

8. The journal-letter. The verses are less than outstanding, but they show how Thompson's mind seemed almost automatically to reach back to former ages for inspiration, and since they have been lost sight of, it might be appropriate to record them here. They are entitled simply "John Henry Newman."

When our high church's builders planned
To re-erect within the land
    The ruined edifice,
    What was the builder's price?

Stern was the toil, the profit slow,
The struggling wall could scantly grow:
    What way to expedite?
    Men had of old a rite!

Into the wall that would not thrive
He gave him to be built alive,
    A human sacrifice.
    And lo! the walls uprise.

The same idea and some of the phrases in this he later employed in *From The Night of Forebeing,* ll. 253–259.

9. Thompson to Wilfrid Meynell, January 1892, (S).

10. Thompson to Alice Meynell, August 1892, (S).

11. Thompson's article on Catholic literature, *Our Literary Life,* (manuscript at BC) when compared with the piece that did appear in *The Tablet* (May 17, 1890), is seen to be too rambling, essayish, and critical to answer the purposes of a survey. His treatment of both Alice Meynell and Coventry Patmore is disproportionate and rather excessive. However, it was not the fulsome praise of Patmore, as T. L. Connolly suggested (*Essays* I, p. 545), that led to the article's rejection. The one that did appear praised Patmore as a poet ahead of his time. *Our Literary Life,* as well as the other two essays mentioned in the paragraph, were first published in 1948 in *Essays* I.

12. The journal-letter. The editor of *The Dublin Review* at this time was Bishop Hedley.

13. *Ibid.*

14. Thompson to Wilfrid Meynell, fall 1890. His abstracted stroll on this occasion took him about four miles past his destination. The Burns and Oates Office was at 28 Orchard Street, just off Oxford. Instead of turning in at Orchard Street, he must have continued along Oxford, New Oxford, and the High Holborn to Smithfield Market at the junction of Holborn Viaduct and Farringdon Road. It was in this same region, seven years later, that he was knocked down by a hansom cab (see Chapter 8).

15. According to the journal-letter, both *To a Poet Breaking Silence* and *Before Her Portrait in Youth* were written during August-September 1890.

16. Thompson to Alice Meynell, December 31, 1890, (S).

17. Interview with the author, Greatham, April 1964.

18. Thompson to Wilfrid Meynell, September 1890, (S). He does not specify Queen's Park as the locale of his meeting with the little girl, but this was the only park close to his lodging at 25 Third Avenue. Queen's Park today is still the neighborhood resort of children and mothers. The portion

of the letter quoted here was erroneously applied, in VM II, p. 92, to Thompson's meeting with Maggie Brien.

19. Thompson Notebook 15, (BC).

20. Both quotations in this paragraph are from interviews with the author, Greatham and London, April 1964.

21. Thompson to Wilfrid Meynell, May (after the 12th) 1891, (S).

22. Alice Meynell to John Lane, undated but probably 1891, (BC).

23. The two Katherine Tynan quotations in this paragraph, in order, are from *The Fortnightly Review,* February 1, 1910, and *The Bookman,* June 1918. The remark about "the inexhaustible well of literary allusion . . ." occurs in a letter from Alfred Hayes to Wilfrid Meynell, October 30, 1911, (BC). Strangely enough, the Meynells themselves always describe Thompson's conversation as banal, ineffective, and uninteresting, and the possible reasons for the divergence of opinion afford another small insight into the relations between them. Evidently Thompson's day-to-day association with the Meynells did not rouse him to verbal self-expression and this may well have been because of his position of "older child" in the family. Alice Meynell customarily referred to him as "my child," and Wilfrid's influence over him was almost that of a father. Such an atmosphere, obviously, would have lacked the needed encouragement to inspired conversation. Still, there must have been moments when they heard him discourse with some fascination, and perhaps the real explanation is that the Meynells remembered him most vividly in his last years, when he had indeed retreated into a loose and hesitant, opium-dominated strain of talk. In 1895–96, however, when he was in the fittest mental and physical condition of his career, he was often a different man. Harriet Patmore remembered him at that time: "One has many pleasant recollections of his evenings with my husband in his study at the Lodge. How Mr. Thompson's face would become transformed with light and beauty and his conversation was a delight to the listener." (Harriet Patmore to Wilfrid Meynell, November 25, 1907, S).

24. Hind, C. L., *Napthali,* p. 97. Thus, fleetingly, came together two of the saddest literary lives of the nineties, each remembered, popularly, for one poem, but poems at opposite ends of the scale of human aspiration. Out of his tragedy Thompson trumpeted the everlasting supremacy of the spiritual. Dowson found only the pointless, pale regret of *Cynara.*

25. Thompson to Alice Meynell, fall 1890, (BC). The play was the incomplete and unpublished *Venus' Fly-Trap* (manuscript at BC). intended as a satire on contemporary literature, including his own writing. "To finish with even-handed justice," he adds in the letter, "I have in the verse of *Johnson* satirised the more conspicuous defects of my own earlier poetry. And faith! I think I have hit myself hardest." The remark reveals the beginnings of an attitude that was to result in a profound reversal of his approach to his art; see Chapter 7. Among Everard Meynell's rough notes occurs the following: "W. B. Yeats and the Rhymers' Club. Francis once attended with some scorn." (S)

26. See, for instance, Mégroz, R. L., *Francis Thompson, the Poet of Earth in Heaven*, p. 28; Reid, J. C., *Francis Thompson, Man and Poet*, p. 37; and Rooker, K., *Francis Thompson* (in French), p. 136.

27. Thompson to Alice Meynell, October 1890, (S).

28. The quotations in this paragraph, in order: "The first among all poetry . . .," *Essays* II, p. 341 (Sappho, he adds, may be the exception, but her case is "injudicable"); "I hope it was the result . . ." and "Her youthful portraits . . ." are both from the journal-letter; "It is to me as if the moon . . .," Thompson to Alice Meynell, December 31, 1890, (S).

29. But one of its most effective images came from the Romantics. The much-quoted lines

> Upon the heavy blossom of her lips
> Hangs the bee Musing

he almost certainly improved from Wordsworth's description of Coleridge:

> Heavy his low-hung lip did oft appear,
> Deprest by weight of musing Phantasy

30. The question of whether Thompson was "in love" with Mrs. Meynell is much commented upon, but his response toward her has been greatly distorted by viewing it in isolation. He loved her, as did almost everyone else in the Meynell circle, as the distant and unapproachable perfection of womanhood, both in person and in mind. This adulatory attitude pervaded the group that gathered at Palace Court house, and it is clear that Alice Meynell did her best to fill the part cast for her. Praise amounting to homage was showered on her especially by the younger writers, both male and female, such as Bernard Whelan, Vernon Blackburn, Richard Le Gallienne, Katherine Tynan, and Winifred Lucas, and even by such ecclesiastics as Fathers Anselm and Cuthbert. The novelist George Meredith and Coventry Patmore both responded to her with a surprising fervor, and indeed Patmore's insistence on the closeness of his friendship with her led Wilfrid Meynell to request a severance of contact between them. Everything Thompson says about his feelings for Alice Meynell, and his poetry to her, must be viewed in this context. There still exists a letter (H) from Thompson to Wilfrid Meynell, sent with the first poems written to Alice, in which Thompson is careful to explain that his love is literary and not personal.

31. Wilfrid Meynell, at Greatham in 1938, related the incident to T. L. Connolly, who recorded the conversation in a manuscript diary, now at BC.

32. Thompson to Wilfrid Meynell, January 1891, (BC).

33. Thompson's request for prayers at this time is mentioned in a note by Wilfrid Meynell to the posthumous publication of *Orison-Tryst, Dublin Review*, April 18, 1910.

34. *The Observer*, (London) November 3, 1932. De Quincey at one time appears to have made a habit of sleeping off his morning drug torpors lying in front of the fireplace. See Eaton, H., *De Quincey*, p. 325.

35. Blunt, W., *My Diaries,* II, p. 183.

36. Originals are at (S).

37. This detail is evident in unquoted portions of the letters.

38. Letter from Father Mariannus, at Pantasaph, to Wilfrid Meynell, October 14, 1892. The original has been lost, but it is partially quoted in Danchin, p. 70.

Chapter Seven: WIND FROM THE WEST

1. Hinkson, H. A., "Francis Thompson—A Reminiscence," *Pall Mall Gazette,* October 15, 1908.

2. From a penciled draft in Thompson Notebook BC 10, (BC). (The same notebook contains jottings for a review of a book by Arthur Symonds which appeared in *Weekly Register,* April 22, 1893.) He mentions Maggie again in another early letter, this time to Mrs. Blackburn, December 29, 1892: "I am in a very cosy little cottage with good kindly Welsh people . . . I have a very pretty and refined girl to wait on me, to whom I speak two and a half words per diem, and a fire all day." (Quoted by Mrs. Blackburn in a letter to Wilfrid Meynell, January 9, 1908, S).

3. Thompson to Wilfrid Meynell, January 4, 1893, (S). He also mentions a "wish to tell you I was safely out of the opium." The Welsh snow, he says, "is not like London snow, which I cannot face; it is virgin, dry and pleasant for walking on."

4. Thompson to Mrs. Blackburn, February 1893, quoted by Mrs. Blackburn in a letter to Wilfrid Meynell, January 9, 1908, (S). The quotation that ends the paragraph is also from this letter.

5. Father Anselm's memories of Thompson were contributed to the Franciscan periodical, *Carmina,* for May 1931. He also wrote a similar article for *The Capuchin Annual,* 1933.

6. A remark of his in a letter to Mrs. Blackburn, December 29, 1892, probably refers to *Little Jesus:* "Spent Xmas eve in writing verses—a poor thing but mine own." Quoted by Mrs. Blackburn in a letter to Wilfrid Meynell, January 9, 1908, (S). The verses were, indeed, as he said, his own, but they owe a debt to Rossetti's *Ave,* as well as Patmore's *Regina Coeli.*

7. Thompson Notebook 101, (BC). He adds: "Two things in this world *are* poetry, and luckily do not know it:—the child and the Franciscan."

8. Thompson to Monica Meynell, February 16, 1894. The original is missing; the quotation is from a notebook containing copies of Thompson's letters to Monica Meynell, (S).

9. From the original manuscript, (BC).

10. Interview with Agnes Brien (Mrs. McIvor), London, April 1964.

11. From *Beginning of End.* The concluding line of the extract seems to show that his disturbed feelings kept him awake that night.

12. From an unpublished fragment, separate manuscript, (BC).

13. *Academy,* October 2, 1897.

14. The first quotation in this paragraph, by Agnes Brien (Mrs. McIvor),

is from an interview in London, April 1964. Mrs. Blackburn's comment occurs in a letter to Wilfrid Meynell, November 10, 1911, (S). Elizabeth Holmes, daughter of Emily Brien, remembered her mother saying that Thompson "was interested in Maggie, he liked Maggie, but mother didn't think that Maggie was very interested in him . . . Maybe she did like him and sort of hid the fact by saying she didn't. Could be, couldn't it?" (Interview with the author, Chester, April 1964.) Miss Holmes claimed no knowledge of Thompson biography, and her remark fits well with the probabilities.

15. Personal inspection of the cottage, with permission of the present occupant, William Barret, March 1964.

16. Agnes Brien (Mrs. McIvor) recalled the sudden horror of her sister's death: "She was on the bed fighting for her breath . . . we were all kneeling down . . . I could tell she was dying . . . it was all over that morning." (Interview, London, April 1964) The Thompson portrait found afterwards in Maggie's room was probably the proof Thompson mentions in his letter of February 16, 1894, as having been appropriated by "a girl at my lodgings." It is now in the author's possession.

17. It is usually stated that Thompson began preparation of *Poems* immediately on arriving at Pantasaph, but Le Gallienne's report to John Lane, (BC), is clearly dated May 6, and can only refer to the year 1893.

18. Thompson to Wilfrid Meynell, October 1893, (S). His decrying of the attempt to depict the "purely literary image" of the "hearted casement" passage in *The Hound of Heaven* should be noted by those who insist on identifying it with some supposed heart-shaped window in the village of Storrington.

19. The amount has been calculated from the publication agreements and the royalty statements, (S), which show that up to September 1894 Lane paid him a total of £95.

20. *Athenaeum*, February 3, 1894.

21. It is this fact that makes highly pertinent to any study of Thompson the "source-hunting" deprecated by some critics. It is not enough to admit that all poets show dependence on previous writers. As a rummager in the literary storehouse, Thompson stands alone among poets of importance, and cannot be fully evaluated without both a knowledge of his sources and the process through which they entered his work. Nor, of course, is it simply a matter of pointing out similarities. Take, for example, his line in *A Captain of Song*: "Where God wipes not the tears from any eyes." This can be immediately identified with St. John's "And God shall wipe away all tears from their eyes" (*Apocalypse* 21:4). But Thompson was also undoubtedly familiar with Milton's "And wipe the tears forever from their eyes" (*Lycidas*), and probably also with P. J. Bailley's "Where God shall dry all tears as sun the dew" (*Festus*). While all three poets obviously derived the image from St. John, it was only Thompson who gave it a new dimension by making it a negative statement. His action, in this case, may even have been deliberate: the reader who is familiar with the *Apocalypse* finds his understanding of Thompson's line profoundly deepened. Another example, whether conscious

or unconscious it is hard to say, shows the way in which a rather bold image picked up from another writer stayed in his mind, working itself into three different poems. In *To a Poet Breaking Silence,* likening Alice Meynell's poetry to wine, he says, "Thy wine is flavorous of God." About three years later he describes the coming of spring in *From the Night of Forebeing:* "From sky to Sod / The World's unfolded blossom smells of God." Then, a year following that, in *Field-Flower* he finally developed the thought to its fullest in a pure Thompsonian strain:

> It came up redolent of God,
> Garrulous of the eyes of God
> To all the breezes near it;
> Musical of the mouth of God
> To all had ears to hear it;
> Mystical with the mirth of God,
> That glow-like did ensphere it.

The basic image was caught, almost certainly, from a single line by Robert Hawker, a poet with whom Thompson was familiar: "The air is eloquent of God." Clearly, any critical approach to the processes of Thompson's art must be grounded in a knowledge of his sources, perhaps to a greater extent than is true for any other poet.

22. *The Dispatch* (London), April 22, 1894. Quoted here from a clipping preserved at the Guildhall Library, London.

23. From an undated Thompson letter partially quoted in an EM manuscript fragment, (S). The fragment appears to be connected with the letter given in EM, p. 139.

24. The fact that Thompson visited his father in Ashton late in 1894, perhaps in October, is recorded in a letter of Father George Richardson, brother of Dr. Thompson's second wife, to Wilfrid Meynell, November 5, 1894: "Frank has been over lately to see his father." (S) According to Mrs. Blackburn, the visit was contemplated as early as February; in a letter (S) written on the twenty-eighth of that month to Wilfrid Meynell she says: "Bishop Carroll was here last week and saw Francis a good deal at the Monastery. He told me he would ask him to come and stay a short while at Stalybridge and take him to see his father. Francis wants so much to see his own people again."

25. Thompson notebook 16A, (BC).

26. The quotations in this paragraph, in order: "Stirring of something more . . .," *Catholic World,* January 1908, an article by Father Cuthbert, a Pantasaph friend. "For what am I a poet . . .," Thompson to Alice Meynell, August 1892, (S). "We are still grateful enough . . .," *Academy,* July 15, 1899. "He came, even to the point of silence . . .," EM, p. 202.

27. Hind, C. L., *Napthali,* p. 118.

28. A reference to Patmore in the Shelley essay shows that Thompson had read Patmore's essay on the same poet in the volume *Principle in Art,* which

was published in 1889. Thompson certainly was familiar with all of Patmore's work, both prose and poetry, by early 1890, as the rejected article, *Our Literary Life,* makes clear. The Thompson comments on Patmore quoted in this paragraph are from the manuscript of this article, (BC). They do not appear in the published version, *Essays* I.

29. Thompson to Alice Meynell, January 1894, (S).

30. *Merry England,* September 1893.

31. Thompson Notebook BC 20, (BC). The description of Patmore preceding this extract is from *Academy,* November 3, 1900.

32. Thompson Notebook 5, (BC).

33. *From the Night of Forebeing,* ll. 239–247.

34. *Weekly Register,* April 22, 1893. The title *Love in Dian's Lap,* chosen by Thompson in June–July 1893, is also derived from *Timon.*

35. Thompson to William Archer, May 31, 1897, quoted in *William Archer,* by C. Archer, pp. 221–223.

36. The duration of his stay in London at this time was about two months. A letter of Wilfrid Meynell to a Mr. Day, (BC), says that "Francis Thompson has been staying with us for a couple of months, and left us yesterday on his return to the monastery in Wales." The letter is dated February 9, 1895.

37. Thompson's remark that only 349 copies of *Sister Songs* had been sold in the first year of publication (EM, p. 150) came from a misreading of the royalty statements, (S). Actually 349 copies were sold in England in the first six months, and an additional 250 in the United States.

38. John Lane to Thompson, June 20, 1895, (S).

39. Thompson to Wilfrid Meynell, February 1896, (S).

40. An anonymous article about a number of Pantasaph ghosts was published in *Franciscan Annals,* April 1897; the author was probably Father Anselm. Most of the incidents reported seem to belong to late 1895, early 1896. The Thompson quotation that ends the paragraph occurs in a letter to Patmore, November 1895, printed in VM, II, p. 112.

41. Details of the death of Dr. Thompson are from an obituary in the Ashton *Herald,* April 11, 1896. Mrs. Thompson's bitterness is mentioned by Thompson in a letter to Wilfrid Meynell, May 21, 1896, (S); see also Ashton *Reporter,* March 27, 1926, for the fact that he did not visit his home on Stamford Street. His sister's recollection of the visit to her in the convent is in Mary Thompson to Wilfrid Meynell, November 18, 1907, (S). Norbert Thompson's memory of his brother at the funeral is from a letter to the author, July 2, 1964.

Chapter Eight: HE DREAMED A VEILÈD MAID

1. Quotations in this paragraph, in order: "Greatly lost in fire and glow . . . ," Thompson to Wilfrid Meynell, May 1896, (S). "Though my aims are unfulfilled . . . ," rejected Preface for *New Poems,* printed in EM, p. 301. Of the twenty-four poems to Katie left unpublished, eighteen appeared posthumously, most shorn of their connection with her. *Works* (1913)

contained five sonnets entitled *Ad Amicam. The Man Has Wings* (1957) contained seven additional sonnets: *Elijah, Forgoing, So Now Give O'er, A Bitter Friend, Alack My Deep Offense, What Have I Left,* and *My Song's Young Virgin Date,* as well as six fugitive pieces: *Waiting, To a Wind, The Solemn Voice, Wake Not, As Morning Eyes,* and *Valete.* The remaining six of the twenty-four are in manuscript at (BC) and (S). Portions of the unpublished *Nocturns of My Friend* and *Wake Not* appeared in the biography by Everard Meynell, and two stanzas of *Nocturns* were printed in *Works.*

2. Katie King's novels were: *The Scripture Reader of St. Mark's* (1895), *Father Hilarion* (1897), *A Bitter Vintage* (1899), and *Ursula* (1900). In 1898 she also published a collection of short stories called *The Child Who Will Never Grow Old,* with a motto from Thompson's *Sister Songs:* "The heart of childhood, so divine for me."

3. The first meeting between the two is related in a note by Wilfrid Meynell in the *Ad Amicam* notebook, (BC).

4. Mrs. King to Wilfrid Meynell, June 22, 1896, (S).

5. Separate manuscript fragment, unpublished, (BC).

6. Thompson to Coventry Patmore, August (12–15) 1896, (S). Thompson sent a card (BC) from Pantasaph announcing his safe arrival, on the twenty-eighth, so he probably left London on the twenty-seventh.

7. The original letter is at (S).

8. Thompson to Coventry Patmore, August (12–15) 1896, (S). He says he accepted Katie's invitation for a visit "only two days before my final departure."

9. The original manuscript of the poem, unpublished, is in the *Ad Amicam* notebook, (BC). The poem, entitled *A Lost Friend,* consists of ten quatrains and a six-line epilogue. It may actually have been written on the train going north, since a second manuscript (BC) carries a notation "July 27th."

10. Letter of Alfred Hayes to Wilfrid Meynell, probably 1909, quoted in EM, p. 249. An earlier letter of Hayes, dated October 13, 1896, gives some details of this visit: "I am very sorry that, as all turned out well, I wrote you in some apprehension as to Thompson. He turned up at the wrong railway station and performed some other singular feats, but those were mere details, and we enjoyed his visit very much. I hope it did him good in spite of the fact that, owing to its happening to be a very busy week for me at the office, I was obliged to leave him a good deal to his own devices, which consisted mainly in smoking innumerable pipes over the books that he found in my study. The weather was so forbidding that we were only able to make two excursions afield. I hope he will come again in the summer when no infant daughter must again bar the way." (S) The visit to Stratford, by Hayes and his guest, is not specifically mentioned, except for the implication in the words "we were only able to make two excursions afield," but Hayes's Edgbaston home (Birmingham) was only a few miles from Stratford. It appears that Thompson tried to commemorate the visit in verse. In a letter to Wilfrid Meynell, May 27, 1912, Hayes writes: "Francis Thomp-

son need not have been ashamed of the literary quality of the treasured lines
he wrote in commemoration of his visit to me. In this little metrical letter the
great poet drops his robes of state and appears in mufti; and there is an un-
studied freshness in the sweet music which is a new note of that mighty
lyrist. There is nothing at all like it in all his work unless *you* have in your
possession other unpublished poems of similar informal expression. To any
observant lover of wild-flowers who has surprised the dog-violet's tiny con-
clave in some secret nook, as we did that day, or the butterwort peeping
through the dripping moss in a chink of some secluded crag . . . to such an
observer there is magic in the line 'and caught the wild-flower in its *lair.*'
There are other lines in the poem equally notable to those who know." (S)
This unknown poem has been lost, but a rough fragment of it is preserved
in Notebook BC 20, (BC):

> Do you remember how we walked
> A year ago through S-land,
> And   of W-shire,
> Where still the reverend homesteads stand,
> The undreamed fulfilment of a dream,
> And breathed about with antique airs,
> Sweet with all childishness and first desire,
> So near our young days and those old days sum?
> Do you remember how we walked,
> Remote a while from modern cares,
> Do you remember how we talked,
> And drew the wild-flowers from their lairs?

11. Separate manuscript, (BC). MHW, p. 28, prints a portion of it and
EM, p. 293, has other bits. The *Alastor* echo occurs in ll. 16–26 of that poem
where Shelley describes the river-bank flowers that "forever gaze on their
own drooping eyes/Reflected in the crystal calm." The Poet, says Shelley,

> longed
> To deck with their bright hues his withered hair
> But on his heart its solitude returned
> And he forebore.

12. The original letter, consulted at (S) in April 1964, is now at (BC).
13. "Recent Poetry," *Edinburgh Review,* April 1896, pp. 493–503.
14. MHW, p. 61, mistakenly prints the poem from which this couplet is
taken as a ten-line fragment. It is actually a sonnet, the remaining four lines
appearing on a previous page; see Notebook 43A, (BC). The rough draft in
this notebook contains many variants; one possible version, edited by Francis
Meynell, was printed in Danchin, p. 240.
15. The verses were not used in *New Poems,* and remained unpublished

until they appeared in MHW. The rough draft (BC) has a total of forty lines.

16. The lines are from one of the three fragments on Patmore's death in MHW, p. 63.

17. Thompson's emotional misery in November–December 1896 led him later into an attempt to explain *Hamlet* in terms of his own experience, in an article published in the *Academy* for October 8, 1898. He believed that Katie King after encouraging his romantic interest had rejected him. Then a few weeks later Coventry Patmore, a father-figure to Thompson, died very suddenly (and his real father had died seven months before). In his article, though he does not of course refer to his own troubles, Thompson shows Hamlet as suffering in exactly the same way: he lost his father and the girl he loved almost simultaneously, and, Thompson asserted, his feigned madness had in it the fundamental truth of a real bitterness against Ophelia. The article was written shortly after resumption of his friendship with Katie, at a time when he could reflect coolly on the emotional upheaval through which he had passed. It is a striking instance of the way in which he saw his own life as continually blended with literature.

18. A letter of Father Anselm to Thompson, March 1897, assures him that all his papers will be sent on, especially "the very particular mss. you desire viz—the poems to K. K. the letters of C. P. and the two unopened letters of Mrs. H. K." (S)

19. Mary Thompson to Francis Thompson, February 18, 1898, (S).

20. The individual items of Thompson's activity following his return to London have been a matter of record, but they are here for the first time brought together to reveal a pattern of effort striking in comparison to the unencumbered existence of the Pantasaph years. His contributions to the *Academy* had begun at Pantasaph with a "portrait" of Ben Jonson in mid-November, and that was followed in mid-December by a review of the works of Byron. Writing in London during the first six months of 1897 he produced no less than fifteen articles and reviews for the magazine, ten more for the rest of the year, and continued that pace. The London book was under contract by March 1897 and announced in the *Academy* the following month. The *Jubilee Ode* was commissioned in June 1897 and published that same month in the *Daily Chronicle*. The play, *Napoleon Judges*, was written at 16 Elgin Avenue in 1897–98, and was followed by the writing of *Man Proposes But Woman Disposes*. (Neither was published until they appeared in MHW in 1957.) Another play, *Saul*, which exists only in a very rough manuscript (BC) was next. The Boer War ode, consisting of ninety lines and entitled *To England*, was written probably in January–February 1898 and published in the *Academy* on March 19, 1898. Thompson contemplated lecturing as early as the summer of 1897, an undertaking perhaps suggested by Mrs. Meynell when she became President of the Society of Women Journalists in July 1897. In announcing her appointment, the *Academy* on July 10, 1897, noted: "Among the lectures which are a feature

of the Society's programs, one is likely to be delivered this winter by a dis-
tinguished poet who has never before appeared upon a platform." There are
notes for at least two lectures in Thompson notebooks BC 20 and 46A, (BC).

21. Originals of all the surviving letters of Katie King to Thompson are
now at (BC).

22. He may at first, because of her mother's conversion, have taken Katie's
being a Catholic for granted. His request to his sister that she pray for Katie's
conversion was made about February 1898, as is implied in his sister's answer
on February 18: "I have not forgotten your request for prayers for the conversion of your friend, and I trust she will not only be convinced of the truth
of our Faith, but will also have the courage of her convictions and become a
Catholic." (S)

23. The quotations in this paragraph, in order: "I am anxious every number of the Academy . . .," C. L. Hind to Thompson, April 22, 1897, (S).
"I am sorry that after careful consideration . . .," Thompson to C. L. Hind,
April 1897, (BC). The Tennyson, Browning, and Shelley articles appeared
in the *Academy* for April 17, May 8, and May 22, respectively.

24. The present rather distorted view of the critical reception of *New
Poems* stems from Everard Meynell's unbalanced presentation. Though he
briefly recorded some favorable comment, he makes it seem that the reaction
was one of hostile rejection. Nor is it true, as T. L. Connolly has suggested,
that Thompson was dismissed out of hand for being a Catholic. What did
happen is that non-Catholic reviewers refused to accept the use of specifically
Catholic symbolism in poetry claiming a general appeal. They pointed to this
as a defect.

25. Thompson to Arthur Doubleday, January 10, 1898, (BC). The accident occurred on the evening of November 25. It didn't cure him of his jay-
walking habits, however. The son of a later landlady recalled how he had
more than once trailed after Thompson just to see him thread his abstracted
way through a stream of carriages, horses, bicycles, and carts: "I often saw
him walking toward Westbourne Grove, and just had to follow him, because
he would cross the road amongst traffic as in a dream, it was a marvel he
wasn't killed." VM II, pp. 115–116.

26. The poem *House of Sorrows,* exists in near-final form (manuscript at
BC) but for some reason Thompson never published it, and it did not see
print until January 1911 in *The Dublin Review.*

27. He set it down first as prose: "The wandering flock of the night have
trodden down (under-foot) the little white blossom of the moon. It is dark
and none sees. Soon will the maid of the dawn stray gathering stars. Come
to me, light of my eyes, blood of my heart, before the maid of the dawn has
(have) gathered the stars, have (has) bared of stars the field of heaven.
Leave thy father, thy mother, thy brethren, the tents of thy tribe, and come:
am I not thy father, thy mother and thy brethren; is not my heart to thee
(as) the tent(s) of thy tribe? There will I shelter thee forever, in the red
tent (pavilion) of my heart." Thompson Notebook 23A, (BC).

28. *Academy,* September 3, 1898.

29. EM, p. 295, prints two stanzas of *Nocturns,* erroneously stating it was written to his mother. A third stanza appeared in *Works.* The manuscript is preserved at Lilly Library, Indiana University, as part of the sequence to Katie King that Thompson entitled *De Amicitia.*

30. Both letters mentioned in this paragraph are at (BC). Thompson's visit to the King house in 1899, mentioned in Mrs. King's letter, is corroborated in a jotting among EM's notes: "Summer of 1899 was at Epping." Hale End is in Epping.

31. From *Ursula,* published in 1900, p. 119. The name of the suitor, Nicolai, may reflect Thompson's belief that he bore a facial resemblance to Czar Nicholas, see EM, p. 328.

32. In a letter to his sister, Mary, probably of February 1898, he tells of the fire: "I have been burned out of my former lodgings. The curtain caught fire after I had got into bed, and I upset the lamp in trying to extinguish it. My hands were badly blistered, and I sustained a dreadful shock, besides having to walk the streets all night. The room was quite burned out." Quoted in VM II, p. 115.

33. Quotations and facts in this paragraph, in order: "Mr. Thompson's room was on a level . . . ," VM II, p. 116; the recollection is contained in a letter written in 1951 by L. Frey, whose mother owned the building at 39 Goldney Road. "Compelled to wound thy heart . . . ," manuscript verses, (S). Katie King's meeting her husband on a cruise is from a letter of Filumena Burr to the author, July 29, 1964. Katie's cruise on the *Heartsease* is mentioned in a letter of Katie to Thompson, September 6, 1899, and on September 13, 1899, she wrote to him from the yacht in Middelburgh, Holland; both of these letters are now at (BC). None of Thompson's letters to Katie have survived, but in one of his notebooks there exists a penciled draft of what may have been an intended letter to her. It seems to fit the period just after her return from the cruise: "I do not suppose we shall meet much in the future—we have not in the past; and not altogether, I think, through the crossing of circumstances. I loved, and love, and shall love you. You on your part have always done justice to such gifts as God has given me, while you recognized their inequalities . . . We do each other intellectual justice, and I (at least) do not wait on poor justice where yourself, not your mind, is concerned. Yet we do not draw together—shall we, perhaps, one day?" Another passage may indicate that there may have been some difficulty between them because of a difference of religion: "My ideals are not your ideals; your beliefs and my knowledge (I should credit myself with too much if I called it *belief*—to my sore responsibility it is more than that) are widths apart. You cannot breathe comfortably and humanly in the atmosphere of my intense convictions, even while you respect me for holding to them . . . Therefore we have drifted, and shall drift apart, for we have given ourselves to different currents. I should bore you if I spoke the things that are in my heart and mind—and you know it." Detached manuscript pages, (S).

34. MHW, p. 28. The rough manuscript is at (BC).

35. Thompson's two comments on marriage in this paragraph are from Notebook 30, (BC). The notebook, on internal evidence, dates to April–May 1900.

36. Thompson Notebook 23, (BC).

Chapter Nine: SOME DIM CHAMBER

1. Some later Thompson notebooks contain simple lists of the quantities of opium consumed daily over brief periods. The earliest of these is Notebook 30, which also has jottings for a book review that appeared in the *Academy* on May 12, 1900. While juxtaposition of notebook entries does not always indicate that they were made in the same period of time, the fourteen intact pages of Notebook 30 appear to belong together. Very probably, of course, Thompson began his relapse some months before May 1900, that is, before he found it necessary to keep a written record of his opium intake.

2. That he actually prepared the manuscript of a fourth volume of poetry, and submitted it to a publisher, is nowhere stated by the Meynells or any other biographer, but all the evidence points to it. In a letter of July 1900 he refers to a time just previous "when I was preparing a fresh volume" (Danchin, p. 124). That it was in the fall of 1899 that he was engaged in this task is indicated by the fact that Katie King then sent him the originals of the poems he had written to her, "first because of the corrections in them which you may care to have, and then because I do not like to think of you having to coy them all out again from my copies." (Letter dated September 6, 1899, BC) It appears, in fact, that part of the manuscript he then prepared still exists, though it has been lost sight of: the notebook entitled *Ad Amicam*, (BC), is probably not a notebook at all, but a portion of the final manuscript of his fourth volume. As it stands it contains thirteen of the poems to Katie and five other lyrics. Many other separate poems were available by the end of 1899 which might have been intended for a book, such as *Buona Notte, To Daisies, Tom O'Bedlam, A Hollow Wood, A Double Need, All Flesh*, the *Jubilee Ode, Cor Meum* (unpublished manuscript at S), etc. A scribbled note on the inside of a detached notebook cover, (H), has the following: "*Poems*. to be published. 1. Pastoral 2. Canticum Novum [an unpublished ecclesiastical ballad, manuscript at (H)] 3. Song of Hours 4. Sere of Leaf 5. Sonnets to K.K. and 2 Lyrics 6. Miscellaneous gleanings (many) 7. If needful political and other poems for a purpose." It is probable that this fourth volume was to have been called *First Fruits and Aftermath*, a title that occurs in a separate manuscript at (BC).

3. Detached notebook cover, (H).

4. Soon after Thompson's death Mrs. Blackburn wrote to Wilfrid Meynell: "I am glad the Katie King poems will ultimately be published. He told me *you* did not care for them and was greatly disappointed that you did not approve of their publication—but his timidity prevented him from insisting

or indeed expostulating." Letter dated January 9, 1908, (S). If Katie did withdraw the permission to use the poems to her, it was probably done in late January or early February 1900: her engagement to Godfrey Burr, it appears, did not take place until after mid-January 1900, since in a letter to Thompson of January 12, 1900, she tells of her hopes of being appointed an Army or Red Cross nurse with the British forces then fighting in South Africa.

5. Thompson to Wilfrid Meynell, quoted in Danchin, p. 124. The original is missing.

6. EM, p. 303. That Thompson made the statement in 1900 is evident from a letter of Whitten's (EM, p. 280) in which he says, "Some seven years since we dined at the Vienna Cafe;" Whitten wrote the letter shortly after Thompson's death in 1907. Thompson broke his resolve to forego poetry in order to write *The Nineteenth Century* (*Academy,* December 1900). He may also have written *To Monica: After Nine Years* in September of that year; the manuscript of the poem with a covering letter is contained in an envelope dated September 27, 1900, (BC). And nine years after he wrote *The Poppy* to Monica (1891) would be 1900.

7. Detached Thompson notebook page, (S).

8. Thompson to Wilfrid Meynell, July 19, 1900, (S).

9. *Ibid.*

10. Gates, L., *Studies in Appreciation* (1900), p. 182.

11. VM II, pp. 188–189.

12. VM I, p. 262.

13. Several writers (cf. Danchin, p. 122) have guessed that he intended to write the story of his life on the streets, but that he did actually write and submit such an article is a fact. His covering letter to the editor of *The Nineteenth Century* still survives: "The enclosed is a narrative of personal experiences as an outcast in the London streets. I submit it to you in the hope you may think it of interest to *Nineteenth Century* readers. Perhaps you may know my name, since the late Mr. Traill had an article on my poems in the *Nineteenth Century* during 1893 or '94. Will you kindly return to the above address in case of non-acceptance?" That he sent the article to Meynell for transmission to the magazine is shown by another letter: "Dear Wilfrid, Here is the 19 Century article. Will you please forward it, and also the accompanying letter to the Editor, for which I have no envelope. And would you enclose stamps to him for return. I have had to write the last part in pencil—I hope that will not prevent its acceptance?" Both letters are at (S).

14. The first quotation in this paragraph is from a separate Thompson manuscript, (BC), filed with "first letters." The second is from Thompson to Wilfrid Meynell, February 12, 1901, (S).

15. Information from death certificate of Katie King.

16. Quotations in this paragraph, in order: "His plight was visible . . .," *Athenaeum,* November 23, 1907. "A shrunken figure . . .," Lucas, E., *Reading, Writing and Remembering,* p. 117. "His great brown cape . . .,"

Wilfrid Whitten in *John O'London's Weekly*, July 10, 1926. "So thin there didn't seem to be any weight . . . ," Interview with Olivia Sowerby. "Worn by pain . . . ," Whitten, *op. cit.* "His cheeks were so sunken . . . ," Ghosh, S., *The Prince of Destiny*, p. 181. "None of the quick movements of voice . . . ," Interview with Francis Meynell. "Misspent his powers . . . ," EM, p. 327.

17. Connolly's first list of Thompson book reviews (*Essays* I, 1948) included 291 entries. A second list (*Essays* II, 1959), raised the total to 484. Working largely independently, Danchin (p. 450) identified or corroborated a total of 475, with another 120 "probables."

18. Danchin, p. 429.

19. By 1894 two volumes of Emily Dickinson's work had appeared in both the United States and England. Writing in *Merry England* in December 1894, Thompson says, "In spite of Boston and culture we have ceased to look much toward the West for poetry, since Longfellow was joined to Poe and Emerson." He again entirely overlooks her in a brief discussion of American culture in *Academy*, October 20, 1906. English critics generally, in those early years, turned from the Amherst recluse with only a slight smile of tolerance.

20. From occasional references to his finances in letters, as well as various bills and receipts, it is possible to state with certainty that his London board and lodging cost £5–6 per month, thus with additional meals and other expenses his yearly needs were cared for by something like £100. The estimate of his ten-year income is derived as follows. Though the pay he received for his contributions to periodicals was not constant, on the basis of various references in his letters and those of the Meynells, in addition to receipts and pay statements, a fair average would be thirty shillings per article. (Pay statements [S] show that he received as much as £3 for some of the lengthier reviews.) At the low estimate of 500 certain articles, this gives a base of £750. The £155 income from his writing of the Ignatius biography can be arrived at precisely: EM, p. 336, says he was paid for this at the rate of £1 for every three pages of manuscript, and the original manuscript (BC) consists of 466 handwritten pages. (The actual numbering reaches 666 pages, but Thompson through some oversight jumped from 379 to 580.) Allowing £100 to cover his miscellaneous efforts is conservative: for *Health and Holiness* he received an outright payment of £10; for the *Peace* ode he was given ten guineas, and probably got similar amounts for the other four newspaper odes; *Poems* and *Sister Songs* brought him nearly £10 from Lane in May 1897, and there must have been another fifteen or so from *New Poems*, despite its poor sale. Seven miscellaneous poems during the period probably earned him about £10, and he contributed eight articles to *Nelson's Encyclopedia* which realized perhaps £8. For an Introduction to Patmore's translation of a treatise by St. Bernard he was given two guineas. Meynell's role as sometime supporter is well illustrated by a note (S) he sent to Thompson on February 5, 1902: "I leave the enclosed for Mrs. Maries. Can you favor her with the amount, or shall I forward it? To save time, I enclose a cheque, but do not

use it unless you need to do, as my balance at the bank is at its dregs." Perhaps it should be made clear that, in this matter, there is no question of a deliberate distortion by the Meynells. Rather it was the commentators who followed them who clouded the picture by an uncritical and particularized acceptance of what was obviously intended as a generalization. The Meynells kept no account of their dealings with Thompson, but responded at need. Their later retelling of this aspect of the friendship arose casually out of a vague and much-crowded memory.

21. Correspondence (S) indicates that in January–March 1902 the Edinburgh publisher, T. C. Jack, offered Thompson commissions to edit selections of both Shelley and Spenser, with Introductions; £30 each was the agreed payment. A letter from Jack, March 19, 1902, shows Thompson had agreed on the Spenser, at least, but neither volume was ever produced. Further correspondence, (S), reveals that in June 1903 Thompson agreed to contribute regularly to *The Weekly Critical Review,* but nothing of his ever appeared in the magazine.

22. Hind, C. L., *Napthali,* p. 110.

23. Ghosh, S., *The Prince of Destiny* (1909), pp. 191–192. Ghosh was also an acquaintance of the Meynells. Ghosh's observations were corroborated by the landlady who showed Everard Meynell the carpet in Thompson's room "worn in a circle round his table."

24. Quotations in this paragraph, in order: "He would talk of something he had seen . . . ," letter of a fellow lodger, quoted in EM, p. 280. "I enjoyed it though Bryant was . . . ," Thompson to Everard Meynell, August 14, 1901, (S).

25. Chancellor, E. B., *The Romance of Soho* (1931), p. 250. The Pillars of Hercules still stands at 7 Greek Street; the claim that Thompson frequented the place, even occasionally working on his reviews there, was made by the proprietor and there seems no reason to doubt him.

26. *Catholic World,* August 1927, pp. 650–651.

27. The last two stanzas bear an obvious relation to Blake's *Jerusalem,* which Thompson quoted in the *Academy* on December 7, 1901.

28. One near-final manuscript of *The Kingdom of God* is in possession of (H); another was most recently owned by Maitland Dodd, who claims that Thompson presented it to his brother at Palace Court in January 1904. The complete rough draft is at (BC).

29. There exist five notebooks containing opium calculations: Nos. 23, 30, 37, 47, and 47A, all at (BC). They date between 1900 and 1904. In addition, there are four detached notebook covers, (S), which are not possible to date. The lengthiest period covered by these erratic accounts is about three months, though not consecutively. He notes the number of bottles consumed daily as well as the amount in ounces. The bottles were small, containing about 2½ ounces of laudanum each.

30. A receipt preserved at the office of Burns and Oates shows that he

turned in the manuscript of *Health and Holiness* in January 1904. A mention of the Ignatius biography in a letter of February 5, 1905, (S), shows that he had already started the biography by that date.

31. Thompson manuscript fragment, (S).

32. *The Bookman,* April 1927, p. 18. De Quincey also had an unusual and finicky diet; see Eaton's *De Quincey,* p. 325.

33. Monroe, H., *A Poet's Life,* pp. 148–149. She places the incident about 1897, but the Meynell home she describes is the apartment in Granville Place, to which the Meynells moved in 1905.

34. Interviews, April 1964, with Madeline Lucas, Olivia Sowerby, and Francis Meynell.

35. Original letter at (H).

36. Originals of the Thompson letters quoted in this paragraph are at (H); they date to June–July 1905.

37. The original letter, dated August 2, 1905, is at (H).

38. The decline probably began in March 1905. M. Child, the assistant editor of the *Academy,* inquired on April 19, 1905, if he was still interested in reviewing: "We are sorry not to have heard from you about the book we sent you some weeks ago, to be reviewed or returned at your discretion. We were hoping to receive some contribution from you either on that or some other topic, as your work is very much appreciated. I hope before long to send you some other books, but should be glad to hear before doing so whether you are still at liberty to write for us." (S)

39. The quotation in this paragraph is from Thompson to Everard Meynell, August 5, 1905, (H). One concrete indication of the legend that had begun to grow up around his life reached him in 1906, when he was sent a pamphlet written by Father Charles O'Donnell, of the University of Notre Dame. In *Francis Thompson: A Critical Essay,* O'Donnell insisted: "No optimism of intent can overlook the fact of his having fallen, and no euphemism of expression need endeavor to cloak it. Down those few terrible years he let himself go with the winds of fancy, and threw himself on the swelling wave of every passion, desiring only to live to the full . . ." This was only the first of the many mistaken attempts to make Thompson part of the "Yellow Nineties," the aesthetic movement's "art for Art's sake."

Chapter Ten: THE GREEN RECESS

1. Quotations in this paragraph, in order: "I am surprised to hear . . . ," Thompson to Wilfrid Meynell, August 31, 1905 (S; copy in hand of Alice Meynell). "Quack medicines . . . ," Mrs. Blackburn quotes Mrs. Gravely in a letter to Wilfrid Meynell, February 13, 1906, (S). An EM manuscript fragment, (S), notes that a certain Mr. Wrench, a Harrow Road chemist, forwarded laudanum to Crawley.

2. Both quotations in this paragraph are from Thompson to Wilfrid Meynell, March 1906, (S).

3. The typewritten manuscript of the deleted portion is at (S).

4. The letter (S) is undated, but was sent by Mrs. Blackburn to Wilfrid Meynell with a letter of her own dated January 30, 1906; Mrs. Blackburn's letter is quoted in the text immediately following.

5. Both quotations are from Mrs. Blackburn's original letters at (S).

6. Original letter at (BC).

7. Ted Gravely was born on November 3, 1906, at 11 Victoria Road, Crawley; (interview).

8. Unnumbered Thompson notebook (black cover) in possession of Madeline Lucas. Many entries fix the date of the notebook in late 1906.

9. EM, p. 279.

10. Thompson to Wilfrid Meynell, May 9, 1906, (BC).

11. EM, p. 346.

12. The original letter, (H), dates to about June–July 1906.

13. Thompson to Wilfrid Meynell, February 22, 1907, (BC).

14. *Ushaw Magazine,* March 1908. Father Mann does not say his meeting with Thompson took place in April, but he says it was on the eve of Madeline Meynell's wedding, which occurred in that month. He also mentions that Thompson received a letter, during the meeting, from the editor of *The Nation,* conveying thanks for a poem. This was *The Fair Inconstant,* Thompson's last published and perhaps last written verse. It appeared in *The Nation* on April 6, 1907.

15. Blunt noted in his diary under the date of October 16, 1907: "The drug was sent to him by post from London." (*My Diaries,* II, p. 188)

16. Blunt's comments may be found in his *My Diaries,* II, pp. 179–190 *passim.*

17. Connolly, T. L., *In His Paths,* p. 55. Quotes Mrs. Roberts' recollections during an interview in 1938.

18. Unpublished letter of Wilfrid Blunt to Wilfrid Meynell, (S).

19. This entry in Blunt's diaries (II, p. 185) is dated September 12, 1907.

20. EM, p. 349, and VM II, p. 182.

21. Sources for the details in this paragraph: His appearance on entering the hospital, and his attempting to smuggle in drugs, were recalled by Sister Hilary and Mother Clare, who often heard the story from Mother Mary Dearlove, the admissions officer in 1907. The medal round his neck is referred to by Wilfrid Meynell in *The Dublin Review,* April 1910. His weight is mentioned in VM II, p. 182, which quotes a letter of Everard Meynell to his wife. Thompson's admission of the daily laudanum dosage is in a letter from Dr. E. U. Williams to Wilfrid Meynell, November 22, 1907, (S). The record of Thompson's entry into the hospital, with the "morphomania" specification, is No. 315 in the hospital *Register* for 1907.

22. Mrs. Randle to Wilfrid Meynell, November 22, 1907, (S).

23. The will is filed at Somerset House, London. Joseph Arnold Fevre, a twenty-three-year-old clerk, of 15 Eric Road, N.W., had entered the hospital, for hernia, on October 9 and remained to November 15. Facts from the hospital *Register* 1907, entry No. 287.

24. This was reported by Father Vincent McNabb, who visited Thompson a number of times during his last days, in *The Universe,* October 2, 1908.

25. Interview with the author, September 1966.

26. Letter of Dr. E. U. Williams to Wilfrid Meynell, November 22, 1907, (S).

27. The death certificate specifies Ellen T. Fekrenback, head night nurse, as "present at the death."

28. *Harper's Weekly,* December 21, 1907.

Epilogue

1. Original letter is at (S).
2. EM, p. 349.
3. VM II, p. 190.
4. Original letter is at (S).
5. Original letter is at (S).
6. Blunt, W., *My Diaries,* II, p. 189.
7. EM notebook, (S).
8. Interview with the author, April 1964.
9. Letter from Martha Dubay to the author, March 1, 1964.
10. MHW, p. 7.
11. MHW, p. 95.

SELECTED BIBLIOGRAPHY

IN CONTRAST TO THE BIOGRAPHICAL ASPECT, THERE EXISTS A LARGE CRITI-cal literature on Thompson in a wide range of periodicals, though a good portion of it is rather superficial and tends to repetition. A selection of the more important items is given here. Of the twenty or so complete books on the poet and his work (including four in French, four in German, and one in Italian) about a dozen may be deemed to have present value and these are listed, as are a number of other books containing significant discussion. The most extensive bibliography of Thompson commentary available, with well over three hundred entries, is in Danchin, but it is complete only to 1956 and the volume, in French, is not readily found. J. C. Reid and Paul Van K. Thomson also provide lengthy listings.

Alexander, C., *The Catholic Literary Revival*, Milwaukee, 1935.
Allen, H., "The Poet of the Return to God," *Catholic World*, June 1918.
Archer, W., *Poets of the Younger Generation*, London, 1902.
Benét, W., "Greatest Catholic Poet," *Saturday Review of Literature*, April 30, 1932.
Buchen, I., "Francis Thompson and the Aesthetics of the Incarnation," *Victorian Poetry*, Autumn 1965.
Buchen, I., "Source-Hunting versus Tradition: Thompson's 'The Hound of Heaven,'" *Victorian Poetry*, Spring 1964.
Cohen, J., "Francis Thompson," *The Month*, December 1949.
Danchin, P., *Francis Thompson, la Vie et l'oeuvre d'un Poète*, Paris, 1959.
Dingle, R., "Francis Thompson's Centenary," *Dublin Review*, Spring 1960.
Finberg, H., "Francis Thompson," *English Review*, December 1925.
Gardner, E., "The Poetry of Francis Thompson," *The Month*, February 1898.
Gautry, R., *This Tremendous Lover*, London, 1932.
Harrison, A., "The Poetry of Francis Thompson," *English Review*, August 1923.

Kehoe, M., "Francis Thompson: A Poet of Religious Romanticism," *Thought*, March 1940.

Ketrick, P., "Poet of Two Worlds," *Catholic World*, July 1938.

LeBuffe, F., *The Hound of Heaven, an Interpretation*, New York, 1922.

Lewis, C., "The Poetry of Francis Thompson," *Yale Review*, October 1914.

Macklin, M., *An Interpretation of Francis Thompson's Hound of Heaven*, New York, 1930.

Marks, J., *Genius and Disaster*, New York, 1925.

Mégroz, R., *Francis Thompson, the Poet of Earth in Heaven*, London, 1927.

Meynell, A., "Some Memories of Francis Thompson," *Dublin Review*, January 1908.

Meynell, E., *The Life of Francis Thompson*, London, 1913.

Meynell, E., "The Notebooks of Francis Thompson," *Dublin Review*, January 1917.

Meynell, V., *Francis Thompson and Wilfrid Meynell*, London, 1952.

Meynell, W., "Francis Thompson," *Athenaeum*, November 23, 1907.

Moggridge, E., "The Poetry of Francis Thompson," *British Review*, September 1913.

Moore, T., "The Hound of Heaven," *Psychoanalytical Review*, October 1918.

More, P., *Shelbourne Essays, Seventh Series*, New York, 1910.

Nichols, L., "Francis Thompson: Flight and Fall," *Thought*, Spring 1960.

Olivero, F., *Francis Thompson*, Turin, 1938.

O'Rourke, J., "The Christology of Francis Thompson," *Irish Ecclesiastical Record*, February 1930.

Osmond, P., *The Mystical Poets of the Catholic Church*, New York, 1919.

Pope, M., "A Critical Bibliography of Works by and About Francis Thompson," *Bulletin of the New York Public Library*, November 1958, January, March, April 1959.

Reid, J., *Francis Thompson, Man and Poet*, London, 1959.

Shuster, G., *The Catholic Spirit in Modern English Literature*, New York, 1922.

Symons, A., *Dramatis Personae*, London, 1925.

Thomson, P., *Francis Thompson, A Critical Biography*, New York, 1961.

Tolles, F., "The Praetorian Cohorts: a Study of the Language of Francis Thompson's Poetry," *English Studies*, April 1940.

Tynan, K., "Francis Thompson's Place in Poetry," *Fortnightly Review*, February 1910.

Vivante, L., *English Poetry*, London, 1950.

Wilson, G., "His Fruit Not Bread," *Quarterly Review*, April 1941.

INDEX

THE AUTHOR AND HIS BOOK

JOHN WALSH has had a biography of Francis Thompson in mind since his college days, when he was captivated by the poet's unique verse and intrigued by his strange personality. In 1964 he was finally able, under a grant, to devote his full time to its preparation, and twice during the course of his research he visited England in an exhaustive quest for original materials. On the second visit he remained, with his family, for almost a year while consulting a mass of primary documents and visiting the scenes connected with Thompson's life. He has also made a deep study of the extensive Thompson Collection at Boston College.

Mr. Walsh's varied background includes newspaper and magazine writing, and six years as an Associate Editor with a large New York publisher. He spent his military service as a writer-editor with U. S. Army newspapers in Trieste. His other books are *The Shroud* (Random House, 1963), a dramatic presentation of the story of the Holy Shroud of Turin which received much favorable attention, and *Poe the Detective* (Rutgers University Press, 1967), a highly original study of Edgar Allan Poe's tale "The Mystery of Marie Roget." He is now preparing a volume of Francis Thompson's letters, and has begun work on a biography of Emily Dickinson. Mr. Walsh is married, has four children, and lives in northern New Jersey.

STRANGE HARP, STRANGE SYMPHONY was set in type by American Book–Stratford Press, Inc., of New York City. The type face is Fairfield, designed by Rudolph Ruzicka in 1939 for the Mergenthaler Linotype Company.

A HAWTHORN BOOK